Indigenous Knowledge

Indigenous Knowledge

An Alternative for Food Security and Wellness in Africa

Emmanuel O. Oritsejafor

LEXINGTON BOOKS
Lanham • Boulder • New York • London

Published by Lexington Books
An imprint of The Rowman & Littlefield Publishing Group, Inc.
4501 Forbes Boulevard, Suite 200, Lanham, Maryland 20706
www.rowman.com

86-90 Paul Street, London EC2A 4NE

British Library Cataloguing in Publication Information Available

Library of Congress Cataloging-in-Publication Data

Names: Oritsejafor, Emmanuel O., author.
Title: Indigenous knowledge : an alternative for food security and wellness in Africa / Emmanuel O. Oritsejafor.
Description: Lanham : Lexington Books, 2022. | Includes bibliographical references and index.
Identifiers: LCCN 2022017315 (print) | LCCN 2022017316 (ebook) | ISBN 9781793615084 (cloth) | ISBN 9781793615107 (paperback) | ISBN 9781793615091 (epub)
Subjects: LCSH: Food security—Africa. | Traditional farming—Africa. | Ethnoscience—Africa. | Africa—Economic conditions.
Classification: LCC HD9017.A2 O75 2022 (print) | LCC HD9017.A2 (ebook) | DDC 338.196—dc23/eng/20220412
LC record available at https://lccn.loc.gov/2022017315
LC ebook record available at https://lccn.loc.gov/2022017316

This book is dedicated to my mother, Princess Clara Omoyemen Otoki, for her love and commitment to my pursuit of knowledge. Inspiration and strength for this project comes from my ancestors; Oba Ovoramwen, Oba Eweka II, Oba Akenzua, Oba Erediauwa; Prince George Aiwagore Eweka, Papa Joachim "Devode" Branco, Mama Emilia Branco, Mami Clara Novojo Rhodes, Papa Esiedugbone Oritsejafor, and Papa mi John Kakene Oritsejafor.

Contents

Preface

Modernity is premised on the idea that our way is superior to yours. This premise served as an ideological foundation of European colonization of Africa and has also been the driving force behind recent agricultural development strategies such as the Green Revolution and other forms of accelerated approaches for development in Africa.

However, the global challenges of food security and the failure of accelerated growth models to address global hunger and malnutrition in developing economies have simply taken place in an environment in which traditional and indigenous food systems have been neglected, thus contributing to erosion of cheap staple foods and cereal. What has emerged in developing economies globally is massive food insecurity which is not likely to be sustained primarily by technology driven yield improvements nor by an amalgamation of technology and indigenous methods without consideration for the cultural context in which food systems can be further improved.[1] Instead, indigenous agricultural development approaches should be sustained because it is vital to reducing the vulnerability of food-insecure households because indigenous agricultural development approaches are positioned to mitigate in situations where there is high food prices and threats to ecological diversity and biodiversity.

Therefore, this book seeks to elucidate and advocate for the use of Indigenous Knowledge (IK) as an alternative approach for addressing food security and wellness in Africa. In chapter 1, the book provides an overview of food security in Africa. The chapter also highlighted the global nature of IK in regions such as North America, South Asia, and Australia. This chapter suggests that although IK is global in nature its local relevance and adaptation is integral for development and wellness.

In Chapter 2, the book provides an in-depth analysis of the various theories that have been used to explain development in Africa. A close examination of prevailing theories such as Karl Marx's theory of capital accumulation highlights how wealth accumulation processes in Africa has further entrenched poverty and inequalities in Africa. The book reveals that these theories do not go far enough in explaining the social and economic inequalities in developing regions such as Africa without full consideration for the historical, social, and cultural context in which development has emerged in these areas.

Chapter 3 reveals the various development strategies that have been employed by development agencies and other multilaterals at one point or another to advance agricultural development in Africa. The inability of these strategies to address food security through accelerated methods that will increase yields in a sustainable manner has prompted the need for IK as a viable approach that will enhance food security.

Chapter 4 analyzes the concept of *corporate food management regimes.* Corporate food management regimes express the social and ecological contradictions of capitalism and the global-historical processes of accumulation which has contributed to global food insecurity.

In as much as climate induced conditions have had a major impact on food security in sub-Saharan Africa, conflicts such as civil war have equally contributed to food insecurities. Therefore, Chapter 5 provides examples of how civil conflicts in war torn countries such as Liberia and the Democratic Republic of Congo (DRC) have contributed to food insecurity.

The next three chapters review the use of indigenous knowledge (IK) for agricultural development in sub-Saharan Africa as an alternative approach that is germane to the development realities of these states. These chapters explore such questions as "What are the challenges of using IK for development and what are the implications for agricultural development?" Chapter 6 analyzes how the quest for alternative energy through the production of biofuels is likely to impact food stability and consequently heighten food insecurity. However, amidst the recent global pandemic, Chapter 7 analyzes how the coronavirus is likely to contribute to health and food security challenges.

Finally, chapter 8 examines how the growth of liberal market forces have reinforced wealth accumulation through land tenure systems and the subjugation of women as one of the primary productive forces in indigenous agriculture development. Chapter 9 provides a prescriptive analysis on how IK can be used for sustainable agricultural development. This chapter, debunks the assumption employed by development agencies and some policy makers that "our way is superior to yours."

NOTE

1. Cloete, P.C. and Idsardi, E.F. (2013). Consumption of indigenous and traditional food crops: Perceptions and realties from South Africa, *Agroecology and Sustainable Food System*, Vol. 37, p.902–903. Accessed on December 28, 2020, from https://www.tandfonline.com/doi/abs/10.1080/21683565.2013.805179.

Acknowledgments

This book project could not have been accomplished without the support of my family and colleagues in the following global communities: United States, Liberia, Nigeria, Ghana, and Australia.

I am forever indebted to my wife Emma Lydia Oritsejafor who had played an integral role in advancing my academic curiosity into Indigenous Knowledge as a development option for mental health in post war Liberia.

This project also found massive inspiration from Africanists who have a similar desire to address development issues in Africa. I found inspiration from the work of Allan D. Cooper on the Ovambo tribe of Namibia. I am equally indebted to George Klay Keih for his support and inspiration on issues related to development in Africa.

I am grateful to the professional insights of health practitioners in sub-Saharan Africa that were consulted for this project; the support of farming communities in Liberia and Ghana were undoubtedly integral to the outcome of this project. I am also grateful to members of the various indigenous communities that were consulted on this project for their invaluable insights and depth regarding Indigenous Knowledge.

I would like to acknowledge the support of the library staff at North Carolina Central University and other Liberians in the University System of North Carolina who provided support for this project to come to realization. I am forever indebted.

Introduction

The 1996 World Food Summit defined food security as a condition that exists "when all people at all times have access to sufficient, safe, and nutritious food to maintain a healthy and active life."[1] The problem of food security in developing countries is severe, particularly in Sub Saharan Africa (SSA). SSA accounts for more than 950 million people, which is about 13 percent of the global population. This translates into one quarter of the population in Africa. In sub-Saharan Africa (SSA), 30 percent of children under age five are underweight.[2] Factors that have contributed to this problem include general demographic trends in developing nations that are caused by more mouths to feed, public policies that are inconsistent with developmental realities, and lack of non-industrial farming methods.[3]

Undernourishment has been a long-standing development challenge in SSA despite being reduced from 33 percent in 1990–1992 to 23 percent by 2014–2016. In 2014–2016 the percentage of undernourishment in SSA remained the highest among developing regions.[4] However, between 2014–2016, SSA countries have attained slow progress towards food security. Food insecurity has continued to have a profound effect in the region despite the slower increase in demand for food, and the decline in agricultural prices between 2014–2015. Concomitantly, the increased demand for energy, such as biofuels, have brought about the need to further examine food security and its implications for developing regions and SSA.[5]

Despite the continuous efforts of international development agencies and policy makers to address global hunger and poverty using accelerated development strategies, this book suggests that the use of Indigenous Knowledge (IK) is a viable and sustainable approach for agricultural development. IK is a viable agricultural development approach because it is congruent with the developmental realities of indigenous African communities and has been sustained through practice in these communities and other global communities for generations upon generations and is more likely to persevere through the effects of climate change. Thus, the localization of IK shows that there are global parallels that one cannot ignore.

The application of IK in other regions demonstrates the global context for why it is an invaluable development alternative. For instance, Native Indians in the Americas have survived over several generations using IK for agriculture and wellness purposes. In Bangladesh rural farmers have used sophisticated farm forestry practices derived from their indigenous knowledge to conserve soil and induce the regeneration of trees. They have also used IK for pest management generations after generations. In Australia, indigenous knowledge has been used over time to address challenges posed by wild bush fires.

NATIVE AMERICANS AND INDIGENOUS KNOWLEDGE

Native Americans for generations are known to have established IK as a pathway for sustainable development. In fact, similar IK practices used by Native Americans parallel those used in other global regions. For instance, some of the harvesting and horticulture practices of California indigenous cultures were found to be like those used by native peoples in South America, Australia, and Africa. The use of the bark of Dongoyaro tree, which has the same active ingredients of quinine found in Quinoa trees cultivated by Native Indians in South America, is another example of the global nature of IK practices.

There are also parallels in food production systems used by Native American Indians and other cultures in Central America and South America. For example, the Mojave tribe in Southern California and the ancient Incas of South America are known to have sowed and cultivated similar edible seeds of the pigweed. Similarly, several California Indian tribes also cultivate edible oily seeds called chia (*Salvia columbriae*) like indigenous people in Mexico.[6]

However, the food management system of Native Indians, particularly those in the California area, provides the lenses though which one can better understand the cultural context in which IK was used and the importance of IK for the daily survival of the native peoples. The Native Indian's traditional gathering and management systems was shaped by ethnic identities, and it contributed to the wellness of their communities, their economic independence, and the restoration and conservation of endangered plants.[7]

The use of specific plants by each tribe in the America's marks the tribe's distinctive culture which plays a significant role in shaping, defining, and maintaining their cultural identities. For example, the Karuk tribe of Northwestern California gathers and uses the tillers of bear lily for overlay designs in their baskets. In another instance, the western Mono and Miwok tribes gathered rebud (*Ceras orbculata*) shoots for red designs in their baskets.[8]

Health Benefits

Over time, the assimilation of dominant western values has contributed to the loss of land and has contributed negatively to dietary changes among some of the Native Indian tribes of California. In contrast, the traditional wild food cultivated by the tribes offered more variety, fiber minerals and vitamins for the indigenous communities. Examples of the health benefits of the consumptions of foods and other botanic plants in Asia and Africa has shown that indigenous people have been able sustain their wellness by using wild plants and food to improve their quality of life.[9] This is the case with native Indian tribes in North America. These tribes have used botanical plants, food, and roots to improve wellness and other social and economic conditions.

Economic Benefits

Native Indians in the Americas are also known for their self-reliance and economic independence. Their economy was driven by their abilities to cultivate their land, fish, and hunt for other forms of edible foods. This is still the case with the limited number of Northwestern tribes of Karuk and Yurok. In California Native Indians are also known to have used their IK skills to manage the cultivation of plants and crops that have invariably complemented their local artisanship in making baskets.[10]

Conservation and Restoration of Endangered Species

IK in California as in other global regions has served as the modern and sustainable value for managing and conserving locally genetic resources over a millennium. In this instance California Indians have been able to manage the population of plants and other species for food and hunting over an extensive period.[11]

Considering the localized use of indigenous plants and species, and the diversity in the management of plant and endangered regimes among indigenous communities. IK has become globalized although it is recognized to be uniquely tailored to local communities in various forms. However, modernity always seems to shy away from it even though other regions of the developing world such as South Asia has continued to employ IK for development. The use of IK management regimes in Bangladesh presents a profound example on how IK has contributed to food security and sustainable development in agriculture.

BANGLADESH IK AND SUSTAINABILITY

The use of IK technologies in Bangladesh for agricultural development was adopted over several millennia. Its use has also evolved over time against the background and the pressure to adopt modern inputs by various governments and development agencies. Although some farmers had successfully adopted the accelerated growth model using modern inputs, they later returned to the use of IK because they had encountered inadequate profit margins and they found the use of modern technologies far too capital intensive.[12]

However, in Bangladesh, farmers have developed an array of sophisticated farm and forestry practices that have been driven by IK over several generations that has become an integral part of agricultural development. For example, in Bangladesh in the absence of sufficient natural forests, more than 50 percent of timber, 85 percent of fuelwood and 90 percent of bamboo are derived from trees and shrubs that are cultivated from farms around homesteads. Simultaneously, the homesteads are the source of fruits, vegetables and most of the food consumed and resources.[13] The use of IK in Bangladesh has profoundly enhanced agriculture development initiatives because they are sustainable. For example, IK pest management practices in Bangladesh illustrates the invaluable use of IK for regeneration and restoration of food crops through indigenous pest management.[14]

The use of IK practices in improving the wellness of indigenous communities in Bangladesh is equally important in understanding the contours of development in the country and South Asia where many poor rural farmers have limited access to adequate healthcare. Moreover, this book provides similar illustrations through extant literature on the relationship between IK and the wellness of indigenous communities.

The global use of IK is also profound in other regions and areas that have found the technologies and its use are at times important considering the challenges of averting development presented through modern technologies. One such region is Australia which has faced the challenges of bush fires and land management.[15]

The proliferation of bush fire incidents in Australia in 2009 and recently in 2019 has drawn this section of our global illustrations of IK to the indigenous methods and interventions used by the native Australian Aboriginal tribes in managing and burning land to improve soil nutrients. There are substantive examples of how, after several generations, Aboriginal tribes regularly burned their lands in a controlled manner to ensure agriculture and ecological benefits. Although several Australians with Eurocentric views have ignored the use and the utility of IK for land management and the control of bush fires, the essence of IK technologies in Australia has continued to evolve. For instance, the Yanyuwa tribe has found hunting for lizards and goannas sustainable after burning lands because their tracks are visible. Two to three weeks after burning of the land, the fresh greens attract kangaroos, bush turkeys, and other game.[16]

The common features of the examples of IK provided in this book suggests that though the IK technologies are localized, their global dimensions are wide and critical for sustainable development. Though they have been ignored, one of the central questions that I raise in this book is how does one make the traditional new for sustainable agricultural development in Africa? In this regard, this book suggests that the use of IK into development will ensure that food availability will become sustainable in the long term as demonstrated by case studies of how IK is used to enhance food regimes and wellness in Africa.

The following concepts are used in the book to provide better understanding of indigenous practices in Africa:

Sustainable Agriculture

A global framework for the development of agriculture and food system used to increase food availability, utilization, improve human health, create more prosperous rural communities, and mend and rejuvenate the environment.[17]

Sustainable Living

These are the ingenious ways in which Indigenous or folk communities have worked out an efficient and sustainable ways of growing or simply gathering food. The common feature of these practices is that they are inclusive of mechanisms of sustain resources, a feature in which modern machinery and chemicals are not used.[18]

Folk-Indigenous Classification

Folk or indigenous classification refers to how members of a language community, the "folk," name and categorize plants and animals.[19]

Traditional-Indigenous Medicines

Traditional medicines also known as indigenous medicines comprise medical aspects of traditional knowledge developed over generations within various societies before the era of modern medicines. It includes the healing methods, modalities, and its associated practitioners by indigenous groups. These methods are recognized globally by scholars and development agencies. For instance, the United Nations Declaration on the Rights of Indigenous Peoples (UNDRIP) highlights the right of indigenous peoples to their traditional medicines.[20]

Food Management Regimes

Food management regimes involve an important part of agro-diversity systems through which farmers use the natural aspects of the environment for food production, the choice of crops and their management of land and water.[21]

Corporate Food Regimes

Corporate food management regimes are the social and ecological contradictions of capitalism and the global-historical processes in which the deployment of price and credit relations are integral for accumulation through dispossession.[22]

Wellness

Wellness is the process in which healthy habits are practiced daily to attain better physical and mental health outcomes.[23]

This book integrates the theory, practice, and the sustainable use of IK in developing regions and provides a critique of how western development approaches have not necessarily enhanced food security. In this regard, Minnis[24] highlighted how indigenous cultures have used IK to sustain food production by using botanic plants to address various forms of their development processes. He emphasized the importance of plants in language communities and on how the folks name and categorize plants and animals.[25]

"All peoples are dependent on plants. Every morsel of our food, most medicines, much cloth and fiber, many other material needs and for most groups of people in the world even the majority of our fuels are derived from plants."[26]

Similarly, Turner and Deur, in their work on the Indigenous peoples of the Northwest Coast of America echoed the robust and sustainable methods in which the indigenous peoples of this region had "keeping it living"[27] even though they fed themselves with limited plant cultivation.[28] The Northwest region was primarily dependent on diverse plants, fish, shellfish, mammals, and birds which provided sustenance. Salmon, obtained through fishing had remained the staple food of the peoples of this region. Thus, to meet their needs for plant foods Northwest coast peoples often migrate in search of plant foods.[29] Although the Northwest folks were not living in areas in which farming was ubiquitous, indigenes of the Northwest coast used about 300 species traditionally for food and materials and medicines. In addition, they were able to address the environmental challenges and opportunities of the regions by ensuring that fishing, hunting, shellfish gathering, and plant harvesting are miles apart to avoid the ecological compromise.[30]

This book also provides the context in which an indigenous approach to development can be in the forefront of policy makers' approach for addressing food security and wellness. Along these lines, Ferguson[31] suggests a plausible construct for development for the region, which must be contextualized with a construct that departs from the Eurocentric perspective in which Africa is perceived as a failed experience:

> A dark picture, undoubtedly. Suspiciously dark, perhaps, given the apparent continuity here with old western myths of African failure, African savagery, African darkness. Do accounts that cast Africa as a land of failed states, uncontrollable violence, horrific disease, and unending poverty simply recycle old cliches of Western presence and eternal African absence . . .[32]

This book employs qualitative methods such as the Interpretative Phenomenological Analysis (IPA), combined with case study to provide a comprehensive analysis on the significance of IK and how it is used to manage agricultural development in Ghana, Nigeria, Liberia, the Democratic Republic of Congo (DRC), Botswana, South Africa and Zimbabwe.

THE INTERPRETATIVE ANALYSIS

The Interpretative Phenomenological Analysis (IPA) approach was developed as a distinctive method for conducting qualitative research. Though the approach is multidisciplinary, it has origins in the field of psychology and in those fields of inquiry such as Phenomenology and Symbolic Interactionism, which suggest that human beings are not passive perceivers of an objective reality but that they emerge to interpret and understand their world by formulating their own biographical stories into a form that makes sense to them.[33] Smith, Flowers, and Larkin posited that IPA is a qualitative research approach that is "committed to the examination of the process through which people make sense of their major life experiences. IPA is concerned with exploring experience in its own terms."[34]

The aim of IPA is to adopt individuals' subjective reports rather than to formulate objective accounts. It recognizes that the researcher plays a dynamic role in the process; while at the same time, the researcher attempts to gain access into the participants' world. In this regard, Pietkiewicz and Smith suggested that IPA is an epistemological reflexivity. That is, the process of inquiry is preoccupied with questions such as: "How does the research question define and limit what can be found? How does the study design and method analysis affect the data and its analysis? If the research problem is defined differently, how would it impact the understanding of the phenomena being investigated?"[35]

IPA is flexible, expansive, and integrative. For instance, several disciplines such as nursing and psychology and have encouraged the use of this methodology. The IPA is an invaluable approach in the field of psychology because it captures the experiential and the qualitative. The phenomenological approach is a viable research paradigm because it advances the "lived experiences" of the participants into the research, which allows for the experiential and the qualitative to be captured by the researcher.[36]

CASE STUDY ANALYSIS

The case study as a research method is often used in many situations to add to our knowledge of individual, group, organizational, social, political, and related phenomena. The need for a case study is determined by the nature of the complex phenomena that is intended to be studied. Therefore, the case study allows one to focus on a case and retain a holistic and real-world perspective.[37] Such are the examples of how indigenous knowledge can serve as alternative development paradigm for addressing food security in Africa. In this regard, the exploratory nature of the case study used in this book has enhanced a comprehensive approach for better understanding indigenous knowledge (IK) and food security in African countries such as Ghana, Nigeria, Botswana, Liberia, Democratic Republic of Congo (DRC), and South Africa. In addition, related phenomena such as alternative energy, community wellness, COVID-19 pandemic, land tenure, and gender issues are explored.

The book highlights the relationship between indigenous agriculture and the wellness of indigenous communities. It is important to note that this book is, in many ways, a response to the failure of western development which has yet to deliver on any of its promises to end poverty and hunger in Africa. This failure has brought us closer to the need to examine how indigenous communities have address food security and the attendant wellness of their communities.

This book suggests that communities in Africa and in other regions would do well to embrace IK, because it has remained central to their sustainable development. Therefore, the first section of the book focuses on theoretical issues and outlines the various development paradigms that have been used at one point or another to promote and accentuate failed agricultural development projects (ADPs) such as the Green Revolution. The book also explores the nexus of fossil fuels and biofuels as an avenue through which poverty and hunger could be addressed. However, the book also notes that the use of biofuels can also contribute to poverty and hunger as shown by the volatile oil prices in early 2000. Moreover, the demand of biofuels has also contributed to the loss of land for agriculture, which has consequently contributed to hunger in developing regions and sub-Saharan African countries particularly.

Global hunger has also been sparked by war and the crisis of pandemic infections such as SARS, Ebola and recently COVID-19. The book provides a case study of food security in the Democratic Republic of Congo (DRC), one of the largest countries territorially in Africa, and Liberia, one of Africa's oldest Republics. Liberia and DRC have been mired in political and civil crises that have had an adverse effect on food security. In addition, DRC, and Liberia at one point or another have had to face the challenge of widespread Ebola. Along these lines, the book examines the implications of COVID-19 on the surging food prices in sub-Sharan Africa with a comprehensive case analysis of COVID-19 and the attendant social and economic crisis in Nigeria and Ghana.

Western agriculture development approaches have failed to deliver on its promises of accelerated growth and development in Africa. In this regard, a comprehensive analysis of how food regimes have evolved from the pre-1900s until the present provides insights into the nature of capitalist accumulation. The first food regime pre-1914, was driven by capitalist production that promoted exports from white settler colonies to Europe and North America. The second food regime, which commenced from the 1940s until the 1970s encouraged the use of modern capitalist intensive production relations through the industrialization of farming. The third food regime, started in the 1980s until the present can be traced to the oil and food crisis of the early 1970s, and is characterized by the tension between nationalist promoted food programs and economies and transnational capital interests. The evolution of the various food regimes was also contextualized within the nexus of colonial and post-colonial relations. In this regard, the book focuses on the challenges of land tenure in Zimbabwe and Nigeria as examples of how the colonial and post –colonial social relations under settler and indirect rule have had an impact on agricultural development.

Colonialism also created social differentiations that adversely affected women to a larger extent. The book explores the extent to which women, a group that produces over 80 percent of the food that is consumed in sub-Sharan Africa and half of the world's food production, are affected by social differentiations such as land tenure, education, and health in-equalities.[38]

The importance of indigenous knowledge in food production was further underscored in the advancement of this approach with an examination of the relationship between indigenous produced food and their medicinal value. Thus, the book suggests that there is a direct relationship between indigenous produced food and the wellness of indigenous communities. For instance, indigenous vegetables such as bitter leaf is used for treating diabetic patients and Mud Fish is used to treat epilepsy. The book provides instances of the botanical and medicinal value of indigenous food and crops and its application in indigenous communities in Africa.

SUMMARY

Overall, the book captures the technical and non-technical knowledge associated with IK and argues for the integration of this knowledge as a plausible approach to agricultural development in Africa. The book suggest that IK technologies would help Africa to decouple from external tensions that are created through the international division of labor and western development prescriptions. As it stands, if developed economies catch cold, Africa gets pneumonia. Therefore, the use of IK provides an alternative development paradigm for African countries and appears to be a viable development paradigm because it is indigenous to these communities and has been used overtime to address development challenges in these communities over several millennia.

The book uses two qualitative analyses: case study and interpretative method. It offers several case analyses of how IK is used in Africa to address food security and wellness in indigenous communities in Nigeria, Ghana, Liberia, and the Democratic Republic of Congo. In addition, case analysis is also provided on the implications of biofuels development and the COVID-19 global pandemic for food security in sub-Saharan Africa. The interpretative method is also used in this project to buttress the suggestions that IK is a sustainable approach for food security in Africa and for addressing wellness, particularly in the case where there is dearth of social infrastructures such as modern healthcare. Interviews were obtained from a health practitioner in Lagos Nigeria, and a farmer from Liberia and a member of the Royal Court of Benin in Nigeria. The health practitioner in Lagos Nigeria, the farmer from Liberia and the member of the Benin Royal Court were selected purposively because they offer access to a particular perspective on phenomena such as Indigenous Knowledge, Wellness, Food Security, and their implications for indigenous West African communities which may not be applicable to other parts of Africa. Although IPA is an idiographic approach that is concerned with an understanding of a phenomena, we can use a small sample size.[39] In an IPA method, particularly in a case study analysis the sample size depends on the degree of commitment to the case study level of analysis and reporting; it is predicated by the richness of the individual cases and the organizational constraints that the research is operating under.[40]

The knowledge and expertise of the interviewees was also integral in their selection for the interviews. For instance, Mr. S. Z. is a 69-year-old rural farmer from Liberia. He cultivates food crops such as rice, cassava, and eddoes. Dr./Prince is a member of the Benin Royal Court and a trained academic. Dr. CUC has been a medical practitioner for thirty-seven years with specializations in Obstetrics and Neonatology medicine. He has practiced in urban and semi-rural communities of Nigeria.

NOTES

1. World Health Organization Food Security. http://wwww.who.intl/trade/glossary, (accessed June 18, 2008).

2. Wiggins, Steve. "Poor200 Diet," *BBC Focus*, 19, no. 10 (July–September 2008), p. 11.

3. Oritsejafor, Emmanuel O. (2004). Food Security in Africa: The Case of Biotechnology and Environmental Conservation in Nigeria, *Journal of African Policy Studies.* Vol. 10 (2 & 3): 1–22.

4. OECD-FAO, Agricultural Outlook, 2016–2025, p. 60.

5. Ibid., p. 60.

6. Anderson, M. Kat. (2005). Tending in the wild: Native American Knowledge and the Management of California's Natural Resources. University of California Press, p. XVII.

7. Ibid., p. 326.

8. Ibid.

9. Ibid., pp. 326–327.

10. Ibid. pp. 327–328.

11. Cook, M. (2013). Medicine Generations: M. Cook. P., Middletown, DE, 10–138

12. Zaman, H. (2000). Indigenous Knowledge and Sustainability: On the brink of disaster or revolution? In Sillitoe, P. ed; Indigenous Knowledge Development in Bangladesh: Present and Future. London: Intermediate Technology Publications, p. 31.

13. Quddus, M.A. (2000). Use of indigenous knowledge in the sustainable development of Bangladesh farm forestry. Sillitoe, P. ed; Indigenous Knowledge Development in Bangladesh: Present and Future. London: Intermediate Technology Publications, p. 57.

14. Ibid., pp. 59–60.

15. Hendry, J. (2014). Science and Sustainability: Learning from Indigenous Wisdom. New York: Palgrave Macmillan, pp. 21–23.

16. Ibid., p. 23.

17. Sustainable Development Solutions Network (2013). Transformative Changes of Agriculture and Food Systems. Retrieved March 2021, https://sustainabledevelopment.un.org/content/documents/6484106-Transformative%20changes%20of%20agriculture%20and%20food%20systems.pdf, p. 3ff.

18. Hendry, John. (2014). Science and Sustainability: Learning from Indigenous Wisdom. New York: Palgrave Macmillan, p. 40.

19. Brown, Cecil H. (2000). Folk Classification. In Paul Minnis (ed). Ethnobotany: Reader. Norman: University of Oklahoma Press, p. 65.

20. Redvers, Nicole and Blondin, Be'sha. (2020). Traditional Indigenous medicine in North America: A scoping review. *PLOS ONE*, pp. 2–3. Retrieved from https://doi.org/10.1371/journal.pone.0237531.

21. Kranjac-Berisalvlejevic, G. (2004). Managing Agrodiversity the Traditional Way: Lessons from West Africa in Sustainable Use of Biodiversity and Related Natural Resources. New York: United Nations University Press, p. 53.

22. McMichael, Phillip. (2005). Global Development and the Corporate Food Regime. *Rural Sociology and Development*, Vol. 11: 269.

23. https://www.pfizer.com/health-wellness/wellness/what-is-wellness.

24. Minnis, Paul. (2000). Ethnobotany: A Reader. Norman: University of Oklahoma Press, p. 3.

25. Brown, Cecil H. (2000). Ethnobotany: Reader, p. 65.

26. Ibid., p. 3.

27. Deur, Douglas and Turner, J. Nancy (2005). Keeping It Living. Seattle: University of Washington Press.

28. Ibid., p. 3.

29. Ibid., pp. 5–12.

30. Ibid., pp. 11–13.

31. Ferguson, James. (2007). Global Shadows: Africa in The Neoliberal World Order. Durham: Duke University Press, p. 10.

32. Ibid., p. 10.

33. Brocki, J. and Wearden, A.J. (2006). A critical evaluation of the use of Interpretative Phenomenological Analysis (IPA). *Health Psychology*, Vol. 21 (1): 87–108.

34. Smith, J.A. Flowers, P. and Larkin, M. (2012). Interpretative Phenomenological Analysis. Thousand Oaks: California, Sage Publications, p. 2.

35. Pietkrewicz, I. and Smith, J.A. (2012). A practical guide to using interpretative phenomenological analysis in qualitative research. *Psychology Journal*, 182 (2): 361.

36. Alase, A. (2017). The interpretative Phenomenological Analysis: A guide to good qualitative research approach. *International Journal of Education and Literacy Studies*, Vol. 5 (2): 9–19.

37. Yin, K. R. (2014). Case Study Research: Design and Methods. Thousand Oaks, CA: Sage Publisher, p. 4.

38. CPAR report (Winter, 2009). Empowering Female Farmers in Rural Africa, p. 1. Accessed on January 17, 2021, from www.cpar.ca.

39. Smith, A. Jonathan, Flowers, Paul, and Larkin, Michael (2012). Interpretative Phenomenological Analysis: Theory, Method and Research. Thousand Oaks, California, p. 49.

40. Ibid., p. 51.

Chapter 1

Theoretical Issues

The emergence of the nation-state in the 18th century spawned various paradigms that needed to rationalize why some people experience privilege while most do not. Adam Smith conceptualized a system of capitalism that incorporated private property as an engine to produce surplus value. He devoted little focus to the question of how property owners derived their surplus capital in the first place. Karl Marx and Friedrich Engels would later suggest that the accumulation of capital that derives from capitalist economies for their inherent exploitation and alienation of labor is required to produce surplus value. Marx and Engels attributed the accumulation of surplus capital in the pre-capitalist era as resulting primarily from violence and expropriation, but otherwise ignored this phase of capital accumulation as something separate and distinct from capitalism.

As a result of the emergence of the United States as a world power in the mid-20th century, the debates advanced by Smith, Marx and Engels became manifested in the ideologies of modernization and development. It was assumed that capital accumulates in those societies that are most productive, while poverty remains stagnant in communities that are less productive. Nils Gilman[1] offers an exhaustive analysis of how modernization theory partnered with American foreign policy during the early years of the Cold War to persuade African states to embrace capitalism in the aftermath of colonialism. Modernization was reified as an acceptable construct once people accepted what Stanziani calls "the invention of backwardness."[2]

The modernization orientation dominates the contemporary literature of "development studies" to this day. For instance, Moss,[3] like most academics that study development, measures economic status in terms of gross national product (GNP). Utilizing such standards, he can accurately claim about African nations that "South Africa may be a regional giant, but its economy is about the same as the state of Indiana. The other forty-seven economies' total are about the same size as metropolitan Chicago."[4] The problem with this perspective is that it ignores how Africa's wealth is stripped from the continent before calculations of a GNP are ever assembled in the first place. Furthermore, minerals and agricultural crops are extracted from Africa at rates far below market value, and then assembled in places like Indiana and Chicago for final distribution into capitalist markets. In short, because the value of African resources is not gained until they reach their destination, the GDP of Indiana ends up reflecting the surplus value of African resources on the balance sheets of an African state's gross domestic product (GDP).

The scholarly literature on African development also tends to focus on Africa's poverty, and to assign blame for this on any number of factors: weak states (meaning the government has little control over the country outside of the capital), ethnic rivalries and the continuing influence of traditional authorities, bad governance or institutions, excessive regulation by the central state, lack of democratic institutions and values, budget deficits, etc. The problem is that the countries with the highest GNPs such as the United States possess many, if not all, of these characteristics as well, but no one regards the USA as a poor developing state. What contemporary scholars tend to overlook is that in the early days of capitalism, blame for poverty in Europe was also directed at the source of labor as well. Adam Smith avoided any analysis of how Britain subjected the Irish and Scots to slave-like conditions, and he attributed their poverty to their stubbornness to hold on to their traditional ways. Jonathan Swift saw the situation for what it was: "Poor Ireland maketh many rich." Classical political economists characterized Irish civilization as barbaric in recognition of their wretched poverty. Perhaps if Swift observed the world today, he would accept that Africa is the new Ireland.[5]

Scholars of African development note that billions of dollars of aid flow from rich countries to Africa each year, and yet Africans remain in extreme poverty. Generally ignored in such analyses is how such aid is provided with conditions that it goes towards supporting economic activities that are export oriented to facilitate access to Africa's wealth for global consumer markets or is designed as a process for wealth accumulation by national elites for collaborating with major global interests and helping to make millionaires out of these foreign entrepreneurs. Another factor in accounting for African poverty is the manipulation of international trade rules by major economic powers to destroy subsistence farming and community economic initiatives in Africa and elsewhere. For example, local coffee growers in Africa face restrictions on setting the value of their production since global coffee prices are influenced by the terms of the Coffee, Sugar and Cocoa Exchange in New York City, which has been establishing coffee prices since the 1880s. Since 1995, the World Trade Organization has been supporting these global standards with devastating consequences to coffee growers in Ethiopia, Kenya, Burundi, Tanzania, Uganda, and other states.

While modernization theory developed in earnest after World War II, so did dependency theory. The first serious application of dependency theory relevant to Africa came in 1972 with the publication of *How Europe Underdeveloped Africa* by Walter Rodney.[6] Rodney advanced a direct correlation between the enrichment of European economies and the growing poverty of Africa. Immanuel Wallerstein[7] expanded this theory to argue that there is a "world-system" in which periphery nations such as those in Africa contribute to the power of core nations. Each nation plays a specific role in the maintenance of the global economy by providing cheap labor, resources, etc. or by providing finance capital, insurance, consumer markets, etc. Tom Brass aptly notes that Wallerstein was correct to acknowledge that the world economy requires both free and unfree labor, but he overlooked the reality that the combination of free and unfree labor can operate not only in the periphery but also within the capitalist core itself.[8]

This anomaly might also explain why dependency theorists struggled to explain the radical transformation of the economy of India in the early 21st century, or why it was that socialist economies failed to achieve economic growth. Andre Gunder Frank took Rodney's thesis and applied it to Latin America, and he too posited that primitive accumulation was a "companion" to capital accumulation within global capitalism.[9] Capital accumulation depends on primitive accumulation, argued Frank.[10]

PRIMITIVE ACCUMULATION

Adam Smith conceptualized that "the accumulation of stock must, in the nature of things, be previous to the division of labor."[11] As Michael Perelman has pointed out, Marx translated Smith's word "previous" as "ursprunglich" which became translated into English as "primitive." Perelman supports Marx's position that Smith's assertion about primitive accumulation is ahistorical and criticizes the notion that the division of labor has always been present in human societies. Perelman claims that the division of labor is independent of the accumulation of capital.[12] Both Smith and Marx failed to address primitive accumulation; for Smith, it diverted attention away from his central argument that capitalism enhanced the human rights of wage workers and was therefore a major advancement in the development of humanity. For Marx, primitive accumulation diminished the exploitative and violent capacity of capitalism by reducing such economic relations as just one more historical process that oppresses the masses that has included slavery and other forms of forced labor. Marx preferred to see primitive accumulation as something that happened in the transition from feudalism to capitalism, and he reserved most of his critique to the exploitative qualities of capitalism itself.

When Soviet economists analyzed African development during the Cold War, they also acknowledged that African economies had failed to develop due to insufficiencies in primitive accumulation. Polshikov argued that

> An increase in the volume of capital investment is a key factor in accelerating economic growth rates; its stability and dynamics, however, depend not only on the magnitude of the financial resources mobilized but also on the conditions for realizing them productively, because money capital is only the starting point in the process of accumulation and is followed by the stage of its conversion into productive capital. The conditions of transforming surplus value into productive capital is thus decisive for accumulation; it is through this conversion that the self-expansion of capital takes place and the structure of capital investment itself is altered.[13]

Soviet analysts were just as quick to blame Africa's poverty on considerations intrinsic to Africa as were Western scholars. Explains Polshikov, "Because of their great economic backwardness, the complexity of the demographic situation, the predominance of extensive growth factors over intensive ones, the present-day economic development of new African countries is extremely unstable, and scientific and technical advances are employed on a limited scale and in specific forms."[14] At the end of the day, Polshikov argues, "The difficulties being experienced by African countries in increasing accumulation and using it effectively are largely due to the low social productivity of labor."[15] Marxist scholars have been left with two rationales for why socialism has failed to take hold in Africa: the conditions necessary for a socialist transition have yet to be realized, or that for a variety of reasons it is no longer possible to transcend capitalism as a system of production.[16]

The methods used historically to overcome poverty and to generate development begins with "primitive accumulation." In his limited explanation of primitive accumulation, Marx describes it as a pre-capitalist phase of capital accumulation in which laborers are compelled to produce wealth with little or no compensation:

> The discovery of gold and silver in America, the extirpation, enslavement and entombment in mines of the indigenous population of that continent, the beginnings of the conquest and plunder of India, and the conversion of Africa into a preserve for the commercial hunting of black skins, are all things which characterize the dawn of the era of capitalist production. These idyllic proceedings are the chief moments of primitive accumulation.[17]

However, Marx's analysis was premature in failing to examine the social organizations in pre-colonial Africa. In this regard Guyer and Belinga suggests "the lineage mode" and "wealth in people" analysis as a successor to the primitive accumulation of Marx analysis.[18] The lineage mode provides a broader examination of African societies and identified lineages, gender, and generational inequalities. The wealth in people accounts in a descriptive way for interpersonal dependents of all types—wives, children, clients, and slaves that were acquired materially in material terms in pre-colonial Africa.[19]

For this book, there are several concepts contained in this description that shape our contemporary understanding of primitive accumulation and the place Africa serves in the 21st century global economy: extirpation, enslavement, conquest, and plunder. Primitive accumulation, based on Marx's own words, results from removing people and their resources from a territory, subjecting free humans to a state of unfree labor, the theft of land, and the destruction of self-determining communities. Today, we know of these processes by such names as Piracy, Slavery, Organized Crime, Bureaucratic Corruption, Kleptocracy, Eminent Domain and Nationalization/Privatization. Tom Brass[20] offers other examples of primitive accumulation: debt bondage, peonage, sweatshops, convict labor, contract migrant labor, and the gang master system. Each represents activities that fall outside the normal functioning of a capitalist system, for example, where the state engages in violence and domination to secure possession of resources, and where employers and employees fail to respect certain rules of engagement such as the negotiation of wages and labor practices. A mature capitalist system allows the state to enforce rules and procedures that advance the production of surplus capital in ways that reinforce the privileges and influence of the bourgeois class that dominates the respective state. Primitive accumulation tends to operate outside this legal framework. As David Roediger notes, when we speak of primitive accumulation we are addressing "relations of terror."[21]

Perelman provides ample evidence that "primitive accumulation" is not a phase of capital accumulation that precedes capitalism but, rather, is an integral feature of capitalism itself. This perspective is shared by Luxemburg[22]; Miles[23]; Patnaik and Moyo[24]; Bales[25]; Beckert and Rockman[26]; David Ricardo[27] and Sir James Steuart[28] offered much scholarly attention to primitive accumulation in the late 18th century and early 19th century. Since Smith and Marx relegated primitive accumulation to a residual category in their respective theories, we do not have a common language in which to conceptualize the components of primitive accumulation. What we do have is increasing evidence of the role such activities play in creating the surplus value needed to finance industrialization and to subsidize the cost of developing a "middle class" to ensure a level of political stability that would sustain capitalist practices into the future. Surplus profit lies at the heart of capitalism, and it thrives on activities that embrace primitive accumulation. Thus, "development" is not only a development of wealth but a development of poverty.

Leon Trotsky insisted that accumulation occurred both in advanced and in backward societies simultaneously, as part of the same systemic unity.[29]

Antonio Giustozzi counters that primitive accumulation may be a prerequisite to state formation, but not necessarily capitalism. He cites the work of the Arab writer Ibn Khaldun who provides examples where once the power of a ruler is consolidated, others are excluded from possessing property and the leader subsequently appropriates whatever possessions subjects may have for his own use.[30] Giustozzi explains how "Bedouins" conquered various communities and forced them to adopt more hierarchical structures that eventually lead to state formations.[31] This assertion is shortsighted, however, primitive accumulation in the form of colonial and postcolonial and other extraconstitutional activities are still utilized to generate local and regional elites independent of efforts to reify state formation. In either case, the development of capitalist economic structures, and its creation of profit or surplus value, seems to be a product of violent processes.

Regardless of one's ideological orientation, the main question remains: how can African states accumulate the capital necessary to invest in development in the first place? African scholars have struggled to identify the role of the state in creating wealth. Many analysts agree with Mahmood Mamdani that " . . . the nature of political power becomes intelligible when put in the context of concrete accumulation processes and the struggles shaped by these. From this point of view, the starting point of analysis had to be the labor question."[32] The implicit question was whether it is possible to separate the labor question from the state question: that is, can the State service democratic objectives or only capitalist ones? Ellen Meiksins Wood has argued that "capitalism developed in tandem with the process of state formation." She claims that "the economic powers of the feudal lord could never extend beyond the reach of his personal ties or alliances and extra-economic powers, his military force, political rule, or judicial authority." The state offered capitalism a political environment within which to regulate and coerce contracts, and to sustain the conditions of accumulation promised by the system of capitalist property.[33] Robert Miles argues that "the state is not simply a political institution which 'intervenes in' the economy. Rather . . . it is an ensemble of structures and practices which directly constitutes the relations of production. Its very existence is essential to the formation and maintenance of the relations of production that it constitutes, and therefore it is a relation of production in its own right."[34] Miles provides numerous examples of how states enforced policies of primitive accumulation to develop functional capitalist systems, such as helping "settlers" confiscate land from indigenous peoples, creating criminal sanctions for breach of contract by servants, creating migrant labor systems to maximize surplus value of labor, and organizing the violence necessary to suppress resistance by laborers and their families.

The imposition of taxes and tariffs forced many people into wage labor and defined which industries would be targeted for growth and therefore a demand for labor. Analyzing the state separate from the economic system (or vice versa) prevents a full understanding of the structure of power that governs in the modern epoch.[35]

Antonio Gramsci analyzed how the bourgeoisie seizes and retains state power. He examined how the ruling class propagates the ideological values that govern the capitalist system and to ensure the legitimacy of the state itself.[36] Kalyan Sanyal recounts how, in the case of India, neo-Gramscian argument that a general theoretical framework for conceptualizing post-colonial capital and its relation to the state is built on the following claims:

1. The post-colonial bourgeoisie must form alliances with dominant pre-capitalist groups to enter state power.
2. The state, representing the national populace, must legitimize capitalist accumulation on the level of the people-nation.
3. The need for legitimization rules out the process of primitive accumulation.
4. The state therefore must protect, preserve, and promote the pre-capitalist modes of production. The strength of the post-colonial capital thus lies in its ability to use the ideological construct of passive revolution to carry on expanded reproduction in the modern sector and, at the same time ensure reproduction of the pre-capitalist, traditional sectors of the economy.[37]

However, factors that have contributed to food security problems in SSA include political, social, and economic factors such as the food regimes that have historically contributed to the alienation of indigenous farmers from the center of the production system but have contributed to the surge in food prices in most cases, the land tenure system that has marginalized indigenous farmers and women in particularly from their farmlands. Thus, this chapter will examine the political, social, and economic factors that contributed to food security in sub-Saharan Africa as an extension of the predatory system that is intertwined with capital accumulation in sub-Saharan Africa. In this regard, Michael Watts suggests in the case of Nigeria how the predatory nature of capitalism and colonialism had contributed to food security. He suggests as follows:

Colonialism changed the context of environmental variability to the extent that the response systems described for the caliphate, social, and agronomic mechanisms that served to guarantee a margin of subsistence security were gradually eroded. The process of colonial integration in transforming the culture of production also changed the character and genesis of hunger and famine, for the incorporation of northern Nigeria into a global system imposed new stresses on peasant households changed the very organization of agricultural production.[38]

Politically, the extent in which indigenous farmers have been alienated from their farmlands provides the context in which one can better understand the predatory nature of what scholars such as Edelman[39] and McMichael[40] called *food sovereignty.* The concept of food sovereignty began around the early 1980s and was further accentuated in the 1990s by the food sovereignty project with the global trade liberalization policies such as the World Bank Structural Adjustment Program which removed national governments from playing a critical role in the domestic agricultural sectors in the global south but instead advanced the concept of *food sovereignty* as an alternative principle to food security. The perception that food sovereignty could be achieved through the reconfiguration of domestic agricultures to reduce food insecurity through trade rules that benefited transnational agribusinesses rather than national agricultures has exacerbated food insecurity. Moreover, national agricultures are in a dire state because of their inability to self-govern in an environment dictated by rules that are exogenous to their development realities.[41] To underscore the development imbalance created by the World Bank (WB), the World Trade Organization (WTO), and other multi-laterals in developing regions, this book suggest that multilaterals have simply reinforced capital accumulation through the growth model at the expense of *indigenous economics.*[42] Indigenous economics according to Polly Hill is:

> concerned with the basic fabric of existent economic life, with such economic activities as the production of export or other cash crops, subsistence farming cattle raising, fishing . . . internal trading in foodstuffs, transportation, economically motivated migration, indigenous credit granting.[43]

SUMMARY

Africa has been a major focus of academic discussions of poverty and underdevelopment. Most professional audiences embrace a paradigm that there is something endemic to Africa that accounts for the vastness of poverty to be found there. However, this chapter suggests that the problem of development in Africa particularly agriculture development, must be contextualized in the larger framework of capital accumulation.

Therefore, given the increasing inability of the neo-classical model to reconcile its growth needs with the need of African rural farmers to sustain and enrich life, the growth model as advanced by multilaterals for African development is an extension of primitive accumulation. The growth model has undermined the well-being and productivity of African people and their economic viability.[44] Along this line, Okosun in his study of Cocoa farming in Ghana and Cote d'Ivoire suggests as follows:

> Since the end of the European colonization of Africa, (Ghana in 1957, Cote d'Ivoire in 1960), Africa's raw materials have remained indispensable economic staples for Europe and beyond. It is rare that Western corporations ever slash the prices of their own manufactured goods and services to favor African nations. Transactions with Africa are designed to favor foreign capitalists' markets, forcing Africans to pay exorbitant prices for European goods and bank services.[45]

For most of history, workers have been compelled to provide their labor through practices that both Adam Smith and Karl Marx characterized as previous, or primitive accumulation. In recent centuries, "free labor" has been promoted by economic elites, allowing people to sell their labor to the most accommodating bidder. The invitation to engage in "free" labor has not been universally distributed and as a result, a disproportionate percent of black laborers remain trapped in relations characterized as primitive accumulation that typically generates the highest surplus value (profit) within the global economy due to its extreme level of exploitation.[46] It is against this background that this book provides an alternative paradigm through Indigenous Knowledge (IK) which compliments *Indigenous Economics.* Along the same lines, this chapter suggest that primitive accumulation is not inclusive because it concentrates power in the hands of a few elites and creates few constraints on how this power is used.[47]

NOTES

1. Gilman, Nils (2007). Mandarins of the Future: Modernization Theory in Cold War America. Baltimore: John Hopkins University Press.

2. Stanziani, A. (2014). Bondage: Labor and Rights in Eurasia from the Sixteenth to the Early Twentieth Centuries. Oxford: Clarendon.

3. Moss, Todd J. (2011). African Development: Making Sense of the Issues and Actors. Boulder: Lynne Rienner Publishers.

4. Ibid., p. 14.

5. Perelman, Michael (2000). The Invention of Capitalism: Classical Political Economy and Secret History of Primitive Accumulation. Durham: Duke University Press.

6. Rodney, Walter (1974). How Europe Underdeveloped Africa. Washington, DC: Howard University Press.

7. Wallerstein, Immanuel (1974). The Modern World System. New York: Academic Press.

8. Brass, Tom (2013). Labor Regime Change in the Twenty-First Century: Unfreedom, Capitalism and Primitive Accumulation. Chicago: Haymarket Books, p. 145.

9. Frank, Andre Gunder (1977). On So-Called Primitive Accumulation" *Dialectical Anthropology*, Vol. 2(2): 89.

10. Ibid., p. 101.

11. Smith, Adams (1976). An Inquiry into the Nature and Causes of the Wealth of Nations. In R.H. Campbell and A.S. Skinner ed. Vol. 2, New York Oxford Press, p. 277.

12. Perelman, Michael (2000). The Invention of Capitalism: Classical Political Economy and Secret History of Primitive Accumulation. Durham: Duke University Press, p. 25.

13. Polshikov, P. (1981). Capital Accumulation and Economic Growth in Developing Africa. Moscow: Progress Publishers, p. 105.

14. Ibid., p. 200.

15. Ibid., pp. 200–206.

16. Brass, Tom (2013). Labor Regime Change in the Twenty-First Century: Unfreedom, Capitalism and Primitive Accumulation. Chicago: Haymarket Books, p. 138.

17. Marx, Karl (1977). Capital. Vol. 1. New York: Vintage, p. 915.

18. Guyer, Jane and Belinga, Samuel E. (1995). Wealth in People as Wealth in Knowledge Accumulation and Composition in Equatorial Africa. *Journal of African History*, Vol. 36: 91

19. Ibid., pp. 91–92.

20. Brass, Tom (2013). Labor Regime Change in the Twenty-First Century: Unfreedom, Capitalism and Primitive Accumulation. Chicago: Haymarket Books.

21. Roediger, David (2017). Class, Race, and Marxism. London: Verso, p. 27.

22. Luxembourg, Rosa (1951). The Accumulation of Capital. New Haven: Yale University Press.

23. Miles, Robert (1987). Capitalism and Unfree Labor: Anomaly of Necessity? London: Tavistock Publications.

24. Patnaik, Utsa and Moyo, Sam (2111). The Agrarian Question in the Neoliberal Era: Primitive Accumulation and the Peasantry. Cape Town: Pambazuka Press.

25. Bales, Kevin (2012). Disposable People: New Slavery in the Global Economy. Berkeley: University of California Press.

26. Beckert, Sven and Rockman, Seth (2018). Slavery Capitalism: A New History of American Economic Development. Philadelphia: University of Pennsylvania Press.

27. Ricardo, David (2004). The Principles of Political Economy and Taxation. London: Dover Press.

28. Steuart, James (2019). An Inquiry into the Principles of Political Economy: Being an Essay on the Science of Domestic Policy in Free Nations, in which are particularly Considered Population, Agriculture, Trade, Industry, Money. Miami: Hard Press.

29. Brass, Tom (2013). Labor Regime Change in the Twenty-First Century: Unfreedom, Capitalism and Primitive Accumulation. Chicago: Haymarket Books, p. 99.

30. Giustozzi, Antonio (2001). The Art of Coercion: The Primitive Accumulation and Management of Coercive Power. New York: Columbia University Press.

31. Ibid., p. 25

32. Mamdani, Mahmood (2018). Citizen and Subject: Contemporary Africa and the Legacy of Late Colonialism. Princeton, NJ: Princeton University Press, p. 23.

33. Wood, Ellen Meiksins (2017). The Origins of Capitalism: A Longer View. London: Verso Publisher, pp. 169–178.

34. Miles, Robert (1987). Capitalism and Unfree Labour: Anomaly or Necessity? London: Tavistock Publications, p. 181.

35. Ibid., pp. 107–184.

36. Gramsci, Antonio (1973). The Prison Notebooks. London: Lawrence & Wishart.

37. Sanyal, Kalyan (2013). Rethinking Capitalist. Development: Primitive Accumulation Governmentality and Post-Colonial Capitalism. New Delhi: Routledge.

38. Watts, Michael (1983). Silent Violence: Food, Famine and Peasantry in Northern Nigeria. Berkeley: University of California Press, pp. 189–190.

39. Edelman, M. (2013). Food Sovereignty: Forgotten Genealogies and future regulatory challenges of food security: Acritical Dialogue, International Conference, Yale University, September 14–15. Accessed December 6, 2020, from https://academicworks.cuny.edu/gc_pubs/104/.

40. McMichael, P. (2014). Historicizing food sovereignty. *Journal of Peasant Studies*, Vol. 41, No. 6: 933–957. Accessed December 6, 2020, from https://doi.org/10.1080/03066150.2013.876999.

41. Ibid., p. 937.

42. Hill, Polly, (1970). Studies in Rural Capitalism in West Africa. London: Cambridge University Press, pp. 4–5.

43. Ibid., p. 3.

44. Newell, Peter (2012). Globalization and the Environment. Cambridge: Polly Press, pp. 148–149.

45. Okosun, T.Y. (2021). Cocoa in Cote d'Ivoire and Ghana: Chocolate and Neoliberal Capitalism. In Oritsejafor, E & Cooper A. (2021). ed. Africa and the Global System of Capital Accumulation. London: Routledge.

46. Oritsejafor, E. and Cooper, A. (2021). Africa and the Global System of Capital Accumulation. London: Routledge, pp.1–2.

47. Acemoglu, D. and Robinson, J. (2012). Why Nations Fail. New York: Currency Books, p. 81.

Chapter 2

Development Strategies

The challenges of food security in sub-Saharan African countries have under-scored the need for alternative development strategies. These challenges are diverse, and they range from climate-induced food insecurity such as the flood in Mozambique in 2021, to civil unrest in Liberia and the Democratic Republic of Congo (DRC). For instance, since 2015, sub-Saharan African countries have experienced severe climate-induced food insecurity, which are caused by severe drought and flood. The increasing food insecurity that has ensued since 2015 are considered the worst since the turn of the century and have adversely affected the livelihoods of millions of households—par-ticularly, rural small holders.[1] Therefore, a theoretical review of development approaches that have been employed by these agencies and policy makers will provide the context for an alternative agricultural development approach.

DEVELOPMENT ORIENTATIONS

There are four dominant orientations often used by development agen-cies, policy makers, and some social scientists for addressing food security in Africa: Dualism, Agro-Technological, Socio-Anthropological, and the Development orientation. The theoretical works on economic development by the Keynesian school of thought provide some of the dominant orienta-tions to explain the problem of economic decline in developing countries. However, this school of thought appears to have had an enormous influence on contemporary neoclassical theoretical models used for explaining agri-cultural development in developing regions. Examples of such models are the Bohemian notions of static dualism, and the Higginian dynamic dualism.

Dualism

The first neo-classical orientation, dualism, uses the growth model as the point of departure for its own model of economic development. Hayami and Ruttan[2] in their essay on agricultural development, define dualism as: "The attempt to understand the relationship or the lack of a relationship between a lagging traditional sector and a growing modern sector within non-western societies affected by the economic and military institutions of western colonialism.[3]" Within this orientation, dualism can be seen as either static or dynamic, that is, from a sociological and technological perspective. Static dualism is concerned with the description of the two sectors of the economy, showing the static nature of the traditional sector while concurrently recommending that such sectors are best left alone.[4] Boeke[5] in his study of Dutch colonialism in Indonesia suggests that social dualism is the clashing of an imported and external social system with an indigenous system. In most instances the external and imported system is capitalism, and, in some instances, it may be socialism.[6]

However, Boeke provides the following thesis on dualism: the traditional sector, he claimed, could never be transformed by outside resources and materials. Thus, any attempt to transform this sector would only result in the continuance of its inherent problems. The general outcome of this recommendation by Boeke has further encouraged the development of the enclave model of growth within which has emerged the perspective that a high productivity sector producing for export must co-exist with a low productivity sector producing for domestic consumption.[7] Ultimately, the theory suggests that the traditional system of production must be reinforced by organizations of a more western system to create a competitive economic value.[8]

Winger on the other hand, elaborates on "enclave dualism."[9] He views dualism based on technological differences between the modern and the traditional sectors. The modern sector is concentrating on the primary production of commodities in mining and plantation through its importation of technology from outside while the traditional sector is characterized by wide substitution possibilities between capital and labor and the use of labor-intensive production methods.[10]

Arthur Lewis's[11] study on developing countries has likewise made an equal contribution to the understanding of the neo-classical orientation of Dualism. Lewis' analysis is concerned with exploring the relationship between the modern and the traditional sectors. His analysis views developing countries as characterized by an unlimited labor supply in the rural sector, but if this supply is carefully utilized, it can lead to needed economic development in both the traditional and modern sectors.[12] The general premise of Lewis's perspective regarding the problem of development is that people and resources have to be moved out from the traditional sector, agriculture and the rural area into the modern sector, industry and cities.[13]

Gustav Ranis[14] expanded the debate on the relevance Dualism in modern times with a critical review of the theory's implications in the agricultural sector. According to Ranis, Dualism matters and provides an insight when an economy agriculture sector is relatively large and represented substantially by extended family which is at times known as subsistence agriculture in contrast to commercialized or plantation agriculture.[15] According to Ranis the nature of the organizational characteristic of subsistence farming is that at a given technology the man/land ratio does not add much value to productivity, which, if not zero is negative.[16]

However, this model has failed to produce the desired results in most developing countries because policy makers and development agencies have not been able to reconcile the relationship between the traditional and modern sectors of their economies.

Socio-Anthropological

The second neo-classical orientation frequently used in explaining the problem of agricultural productivity in developing economies is the socio-anthropological approach. This approach is concerned with the question of why traditional farmers in developing economies seem to have a negative perception of programs directed at transforming their development. Thus, proponents of this approach suggest that developing agencies cannot become successful in transforming traditional societies until they consider the values and social orientations of these societies because they are conditioned by extended periods of traditionalism. Thus, change in these societies will occur slowly or, in some cases, will never occur.[17]

The assumption that the new has replaced the old made social anthropologists presumptuous. Instead, some scholars suggest that the argument that most social anthropologists have provided in terms of modernity as a precursor for development does not go far enough. The modern as envisaged as a series of states of the world, individualism, markets, liberty, and democratic government in which activities are organized within the framework of a state ruled by an elected government, whose goals were individual self-fulfillment does not provide enough understanding regarding what is considered indigenous perspectives. Instead, modernity as envisaged by most western scholars, is a mythical component of contemporary Europe; thus, it is a charter of social order rather than an aid to its understanding. This argument for modernity is a-missed. The neglect of economic and political context of non-western societies includes their experiences with and their resistance to capitalism. Therefore, modernity is a direct product of Eurocentric perspectives which is inapplicable to the understanding of nonwestern societies.[18] Along these lines Ferguson suggests:

> Africa always seems to come to the question of modernity from without. Generations of Western Scholars have regarded Africa as either beyond the pale of the modern . . . or before it the "primitive," "traditional" place that is always not yet in the time of the up-to-date present.[19]

As a result, the use of the term Modernity has been organized by some anthropologists along the following perspectives:

1. Modernity is very often a mere gloss on the contemporary. For instance, the existence of witchcraft today is an expression of the modernity of witchcraft. The latter is modern because it is part of a process organized within the global capitalist world of today not yesterday. Thus, this notion of what is modern has no specificity and it is only related to a temporary category.
2. Modernity can refer to the leading sector or region of the world, often articulated in hierarchical terms such as the center and the periphery perspective. It includes the center of the "system" the western world and the peripheries are defined in relation to the west-modern world.
3. Modernity is also defined regarding the modern products, or the products of the center. These products are presented globally in the form of images such as CNN and cellphones.[20]

The assumption by Western Social Anthropologists that modernity would drive the problem of agriculture development and in this case food security was also refuted by Logan.[21] She suggests that the measurement of food scarcity by Western scholars using quantitative analysis are not far reaching.[22] Instead, she suggests a reframing of food security approaches along the archaeological perspective of "reasonable past."[23] That is, the challenges and the manifestations of food security can be better addressed when they are examined from their long-term histories. This approach would put into consideration the history of food regimes and security in local communities, the social life of these communities, and the political economy of the state.[24]

Agro-Technological

The third orientation that has been utilized in explaining the reason for rural agricultural decline in Africa is the agro-technological orientation. This orientation has the greatest impact on the development strategies that are designed to help ameliorate productivity problems in the agricultural sector. The most important model within this orientation is the diffusionist model. This model is premised on the belief that new farming methods that have been discovered in developed nations would inevitably lead to higher agricultural productivity when transferred to developing countries.[25]

The challenges of the agro-technological approach for addressing food security in Africa should be approached within the context of the failure of the accelerated approach to development, particularly the failure of the Green Revolution (GR) to accelerate agricultural development in a sustainable manner. For instance, the infusion of agro-technological inputs such as biotechnology have not necessarily enhanced the ecological challenges that farmers face globally, nor has it radically improved the quality of the lives of small holders that have adopted some of these inputs. In this regard, Kumaraswamy, suggests that the use of agro-technological inputs have not necessarily improved the agro-ecological environment. Instead, the use of agro-technological inputs such as biotechnologies have contributed to the non-agricultural sustainability of farming practices.[26]

To mitigate the degradation and environmental implication of agro-technology, Kumaraswamy posits that sustainable agriculture provides a viable option. Sustainable agriculture is the use of natural inputs, cropping patterns, the degree of diversity and cultural practices and methods of plant protection, management of resources and the dependency on local external resources and knowledge. It is in this context that Indigenous Knowledge is argued in this book to be a viable and sustainable option for addressing food security in Africa.[27]

Development Theory

Scholars such as Mouzeli[28] and Brett[29] reject the growth criteria of the neoclassical orientations, where quantitative increases in such indexes as Gross Domestic Product (GDP) and per capita income are yardsticks for measuring development. Instead, they argue that development should be examined through a country's actual economic, political, cultural structure, and its historical development within the context of the world economy.

In this regard, Samir Amin contends that underdeveloped countries have certain characteristics that oblige us to avoid confusing them with the now advanced countries. These characteristics include:

1. The extreme inequality that is typical of the distribution of productivities in the periphery and in the system of prices transmitted to it from the center,
2. The disarticulation due to the adjustment of the orientation of production in the periphery to the needs of the center, which prevents the

transmission of the benefits of economic progress from the poles of development to the economy, and

3. Economic domination by the center, which is expressed in the forms of international specialization and in the dependence of the structures whereby growth in the periphery is financed.[30]

Traditional Methods of Development

Given the challenges of sustainable agriculture development in sub-Saharan Africa, the use of modern agricultural practices, such as biotechnology, has failed to contribute to sustainable agricultural development. Instead, alternative agricultural development approaches, such as the use of traditional farming methods with other forms of modern agricultural practices, must be examined. Often, whether advocated by western scholars and development agencies or by non-western scholars, the most common strategy for rural agricultural development seems to be the replacement of local strategies with western technologies.[31] Consequently, the development orientations often provided seem to suggest that to advance beyond the perennial cycle of food shortages, rural communities must adopt modern technological strategies.[32] Instead, David Iyam suggests:

> Consideration of modern technology is also central to the humanistic perspective of development popular with anthropologists who advocate adapting traditional modes to modern systems. But the results of these approaches have had an unimpressive effect on most Africa's inhabitants because of the divergence between the conceptions of projects and the local conditions.[33]

Traditional Knowledge System

As explained in Chapter One, Traditional or Indigenous Knowledge (IK), is the knowledge that has been acquired over an extensive period and passed on from one generation to another. At times, this knowledge is shared through oral tradition and practices. This knowledge is divided into two categories: technical and non-technical. Technical knowledge refers to the knowledge which integrates skills and which manifests in production systems and socio-cultural systems such as arts and music. Non-technical knowledge are value systems, beliefs customs and rules of behavior.[34]

Traditional technical knowledge research is ethno-technology, and within the scope of science as ethno-science. Ethno-science is defined as the study of a corpus of knowledge, information and expertise handed down from generation to generation.[35] Examples of this knowledge base are the use of ethno-zoology, the study of traditional zoological knowledge, ethno-botany, the study of traditional botanical concepts, and ethno-biodiversity, the study of traditional knowledge in biodiversity conservation and regime management systems.

However, Indigenous Knowledge (IK) and technologies are known as the social capital of the poor. It is their primary asset to invest their struggle for survival, to produce food, to provide shelter and to give them the hope they need to live. The importance of IK is illustrated in the following characteristics:

1. Indigenous knowledge is often localized, and it is rooted to a particular place and set of experiences. It is also generated by people living in those places. Consequently, the transfer of the knowledge to other places runs the risk of dislocating it. We will examine successful globalization of the methods and technologies in subsequent chapters.[36]

2. Indigenous knowledge is often orally transmitted and at times transmitted through imitation and demonstration. Thus, writing it down may change some of its fundamental properties. Paradoxically, writing it down makes it more sustainable over time and allows for limited differentiation in data collection. Thus, it is portable, permanent, and reinforcing.[37]

3. Indigenous Knowledge is also the result of practical engagement in everyday life, and it is often reinforced by experience, and trial and error. Moreover, indigenous knowledge is characteristically the product of many generations of intelligent reasoning; its failure has immediate consequences for the lives of its practitioners and its failure is good measure of Darwinian fitness. The essence of its testing and rigor takes place in in the *laboratory of survival.*[38]

4. The process of observation with the use of IK is empirical and less theoretical. More importantly, the nature of its oral translation inhibits the advancement of true theoretical knowledge.[39]

5. Indigenous Knowledge is accompanied by traditions of repetition which helps maintain sustainability and reinforces ideas and knowledge.[40]

6. The tradition of IK is a fluid and transformative process with no real end when applied to knowledge. Thus, IK is constantly evolving; it is equally a transformative and renewable process that can be reproduced when lost.[41]

7. Indigenous Knowledge, though localized, is characteristically more shared than most forms of knowledge. Thus, it is labeled the *peoples science.* This may very well explain its localized formation with global parallels. In addition, IK is also asymmetrically distributed within a population by gender and age and sustained through distribution in the memories of individuals.[42]

8. The use of IK is at times coherent in rituals; however, it does not exist in its totality in one place or individual. It is devolved in practices and interactions in which people are engaged.[43]
9. Considering the culture-wide and universal wide application, IK is functional and directly applicable.
10. Indigenous Knowledge is also situated within a broader cultural tradition that attempts to separate the technical from the non-technical and the rational from the non-rational.[44]

THE CULTURAL CONTEXT OF INDIGENOUS KNOWLEDGE SYSTEMS

The characteristics of IK must be understood in the context of the interrelationships between knowledge systems since indigenous and local knowledge are not static and must be examined in the context of its dynamism. In this regard, Varghese and Crawford suggest that "there is no single pan-indigenous model of knowledge structure and function globally or even continentally."[45] Instead indigenous knowledge systems are intercultural though they are localized. Along the same lines, this book suggests that knowledge systems such as indigenous knowledge is a sound paradigm that would better advance the development aspirations of developing regions. In this regard, we adopt similar definition of *knowledge systems;* they are as follows:

1. a social network of individuals
2. that exhibits structure and function
3. in the use of specific processes and
4. to understand the conditions and causation of nature.[46]

Knowledge systems allow indigenous communities to use the experiences of community members over a period to build upon the practices and processes of communal development. Thus, an examination of how indigenous knowledge systems enable social and cultural linkages from the individual to the community for human development is a sound framework. The general definition of *knowledge systems* would be better operationalized with an examination of the following social scale of knowledge systems:

Individual Knowledge Systems. The individual's knowledge enables the use of cognitive processes at the personal level for understanding both aggregate and other related properties of the knowledge systems.[47]
Community Knowledge Systems. To better recognize and understand the community knowledge system, there is a need to contextualize this

knowledge with specific knowledge of actors, relationships, boundaries, and identity of the system and their linkages.[48]

Cultural Knowledge Systems. With this perspective, culture is factored in the understanding and the processes of indigenous systems from an indigenous and global perspective as major factors that shape the structure and the function of community knowledge systems. Moreover, it is important to note that every knowledge system is influenced by cultural values. In addition, multiple community knowledge systems can also operate interrelatedly and simultaneously within a particular epoch. In fact, it is the inter-cultural nature of the culture knowledge systems that enables its localization and globalization.[49]

This book suggests that to adopt modern technological strategies for rural agricultural development and address food security, such strategies must consider the environment of adaptability of those cultural institutions in which the agriculture of the rich, the marginal rich or the poor may thrive. As Iyam suggests, though modern technologies are important, they do not provide the end results. Therefore, the social structure of rural communities must be accommodated in the process of instituting development changes.[50] Along the same lines, Joy Hendry posits that indigenous science has made a profound contribution to sustainable development.[51] In the area of agricultural development, Hendry suggests that

> Indigenous peoples around the world have worked out efficient and sustainable ways of growing or simply gathering their food . . . it is interesting to point out first that a common feature of all of them is that they include mechanisms of sustaining the resources, a crucial feature that we "moderns" seem to have forgotten in our enthusiasm for the use of machinery, chemicals, and even the genetic modification we have developed to increase the yield of crops.[52]

The body of literature illustrates that in the absence of the use of machinery and chemicals, consideration for IK as a development strategy augurs well for developing states. For instance, Gana focused on the use of natural plant materials such as agro-chemicals among small-scale farmers in three villages in Niger State, in Northern Nigeria. The study revealed that these farmers were able to reduce and control the population of cowpea pests in the field, and parasitic nematodes found in the soil with the use of botanic chemicals as alternatives to the use of toxic-synthetic agro-chemicals.[53]

In another study, Ajibade and Shokemi found that Indigenous Knowledge (IK) was used effectively by 95 percent of 200 farmers to identify five weather systems such as rainfall, harmattan, thunderstorm, windstorm, and sunshine. The study suggests that if IK is integrated with a western-based weather forecast system, it could prove to be an essential element of the development process for farm communities in Nigeria.[54]

Similarly, IK approaches are used in other regions such as South Asia and Australia. For instance, Bangladesh farmers are noted to have used the store of knowledge they have built over time to enhance food production. For example, in the absence of sufficient natural forests in Bangladesh, more than 50 percent of timber, 85 percent of fuelwood, and 90 percent of bamboo used are derived from trees and shrubs grown by people on their homesteads.[55] In this case, IK is integrated with modern technology to address farm-forestry challenges that were caused by over exploitation of homesteads for food crops and medicinal resources. Farmers in Bangladesh have also developed an array of sophisticated farm-forestry practices that are used to sustain their agricultural needs. For instance, farmers apply soil mulch in bamboo groves in the spring (March and April) to induce regeneration and vigorous growth of young bamboo shoots.[56]

Considering frequent bush fires in Australia, Indigenous Knowledge has been recognized as pivotal for the future of sustainable development of Northern Australia. For example, there is evidence to show that Aboriginal knowledge of the water and traditional ecological knowledge (TEK) are becoming increasingly important for water management in the arid Northern region. The IK of the Miriwoong people has been adopted as a tool for the effective management of water resources in Northern Australia. Similarly, a model of the water management system was developed in the Keep River National Park.[57] The TEK water system model is integral for Australia given recent bush fires in Australia. Bush fires are an important part of the Australian environment. Ecologically, many of Australia's native plants are fire prone and very combustible. At the same time, numerous species in Australia depend on fire to regenerate. Indigenous Australians have long used fire as a land management tool, and it continues to be used to clear land for agricultural purposes and to protect properties from intense, uncontrolled fires.[58] One such indigenous methods to protect private property was noted as follows by Joy Hendry:

> Our guide, Dean, was a generous man, who pointed out that the buildings that now adorn riverbanks at this spot are still used for making a living. . . . He also showed us a small patch of indigenous trees and shrubs that have been planted around the base of a huge skyscraper belonging to a large multi-national company.[59]

The cultivation of such species and shrubs are part of the efforts by the Australian government to avert bush fires and enhance development. Thus, in this book we lay the foundation for the use of IK for sustainable development; particularly using the approach to enhance food security.

SUMMARY

The prevailing challenges of attaining sustainable agricultural development in Africa and in other developing region has drawn policy makers and governments in these regions to dominant paradigms that tend to encourage rapid and accelerated approaches such as the use of modern technologies as the "blueprint" for these regions for development. The dominant nature of western infused development paradigms, for the most part, negated IK as nontechnological.

Contrarily, a close examination of Indigenous Knowledge (IK) suggests that this approach is participatory and involves local communities in a development agenda that is germane to their local cultures. IK not only provides a local relevance for development but is intrinsically technological from the social cultural context of indigenous communities. The technology that accompanies IK are driven by indigenous values and practices.[60] In this regard, the theoretical issues suggest that the accelerated growth models and development orientations such as Dualism and Agrotechnology prescribed by multilaterals such as the International Monetary Fund (IMF) and the World Bank have failed to strengthen development agendas in most African communities because they lack local relevant development formulas.[61] Therefore, a closer examination of IK as a development approach provides a viable option in addressing sustainable agricultural development in Africa.

The characteristics of IK must be understood in the context of the interrelationships between knowledge systems; indigenous and local knowledge are not static and must be examined in the context of its dynamism. Thus, "there is no single pan-indigenous model of knowledge structure and function globally or even continentally."[62] Instead indigenous knowledge systems are global though they maybe localized. Along the same lines, this book suggests that knowledge systems such as indigenous knowledge is a sound paradigm that would better advance the development aspirations of developing regions. In this regard, we adopt similar definition of *knowledge systems;* they are as follows:

1. a social network of individuals
2. that exhibits structure and function
3. in the use of specific processes and
4. to understand the conditions and causation of nature.[63]

Knowledge systems allow indigenous communities to use the experiences of community members over a period to build upon the practices and processes of communal development. Thus, an examination of how an indigenous knowledge system enables social and cultural linkages from the individual to the community for human development appears to be a sound framework.

NOTES

1. Food and Agriculture Organization of the United Nations (2017). Overview of Food Security and Nutrition: The Challenges of Building Resilience to shocks and stresses. Accra.

2. Hayami U. and Ruttan, V.W. (1976). Agricultural Development: An International Perspective. Baltimore: John Hopkins University Press.

3. Hayami U. and Ruttan, V.W. (1976). Agricultural Development: An International Perspective. Baltimore: John Hopkins University Press, p. 19.

4. Ibid.

5. Boeke, J. H. (1953). Economic and Economic Policy of Dual Societies as Exemplified by Indonesia. New York: Institute of Pacific Relations, pp. 3–319.

6. Higgins, B. (1956). The "Dualistic Theory" of underdeveloped areas. *Economic Development and Cultural Change*, Vol. 4(2):100.

7. Boeke, J. H. (1953). Economic and Economic Policy of Dual Societies as Exemplified by Indonesia. New York: Institute of Pacific Relations, pp. 3–319.

8. Purwanto, Bambang (February 2002). Peasant economy and institutional changes in late colonial Indonesia. "International Conference on Economic Growth and Institutional Change in Indonesia in the 19th and 20th Centuries." Amsterdam, February 25–28, p. 1. Retrieved from http://www.cgeh.nl/sites/default/files/economic -growth-and-institutional-change-in-indonesia/ecgrowthpurwanto.pdf.

9. Winger, H.W. (1976). "The distribution of gains between investing and borrowing countries" in Agricultural Development: An International Perspective. Hayami and Ruttan, ed. Baltimore: John Hopkins University Press.

10. Ibid.

11. Lewis, Arthur (1954) "Economic Development with Unlimited Supplies of Labor" Manchester School of Economics and Social Studies, pp. 131–191.

12. Ibid.

13. Acemoglu, Daron and Robinson, James (2012). Why Nations Fail. New York: Currency Books, p. 258.

14. Gustav, Rani (September 2003). Is Dualism worth Revisiting? Yale University Economic Growth Center. Center, Paper No. 870: 4–5.

15. Ibid.

16. Ibid.

17. Foster, G.M. (1967). Tzintunzan: Mexican Peasants in a Changing World. Boston, Massachusetts: Little Brown Publisher, p. 7.

18. Friedman, K.E. and Friedman, J. (2007). Modernities, Class, and the Contradictions of Globalization: The Anthropology of Global Systems. Lanham, MD: Rowman & Littlefield, p. 4.

19. Ibid., p. 176.

20. Ibid., pp. 4–5.

21. Logan, A.L. (2020). The Scarcity Slot: Excavating Histories of Food Security in Africa. Berkeley: University of California Press, p. 21.

22. Ibid.

23. Logan, A.L., Stump, D., Goldstein, S.T., Orjemie, E.A. and Schoeman, M.H. (2019). Critically engaging African food security and usable pasts through archaeology. *African Archaeological Review*, Vol. 36: 419.

24. Ibid., pp. 421–422.

25. Shultz, Theodore (1964). Transforming Traditional Agriculture. New Haven: Yale University Press, p. 145.

26. Kumaraswamy, S. (2012). Sustainability issues in agro-ecology: socio-ecological perspective. *Agricultural Sciences*, Vol. 3(2): 153–154.

27. Ibid., p. 156.

28. Mouzeli, Nicolas (1980). Modernization, underdevelopment, uneven development: prospects for theory of third world formations. *Journal of Peasant Studies*, Vol. 1: 13–15.

29. Brett, E.A. (1973). Colonialism and Underdevelopment in East Africa: The Politics of Economic Change 1919–1939. New York: Nok Publishers, pp. 35–321.

30. Samir, Amin (1976). Unequal Development: An essay on the social formations of peripheral capitalism. New York: Monthly Press Review Press, pp. 9–293.

31. Iyam, David Uru (1995) The Broken Hoe: Cultural Reconfiguration in Biase Southeast Nigeria. Chicago: University of Chicago Press, p. 7.

32. Ibid., p. 7.

33. Ibid.

34. Nkansa Buabeng, Stephen (2004). Traditional methods of resource assessment relative to scientific approach. In Gyasi, E.A.; Berisavljevic, G.K; Blay; E.T. and Oduro, W. Managing Agrodiversity the traditional Way: Lessons from West Africa in Sustainable Use of Biodiversity and Related Natural Resources. New York: United Nations University Press, p. 15.

35. Ibid.

36. Senanayake, S.G.J.N. (2006). Indigenous Knowledge as a key to sustainable development. *Journal of Agricultural Sciences*, Vol. 2(1): 87.

37. Ibid.

38. Ibid., p. 88.

39. Ibid.

40. Ibid.

41. Ibid.

42. Ibid.

43. Ibid.

44. Ibid.

45. Vargeghese, J. and Crawford, S.S. (2021). A cultural framework for indigenous, local, and science knowledge systems in ecology and natural resource management. *Ecological Monographs*, Vol. 9 (1): 2.

46. Ibid., p. 8.

47. Ibid.

48. Ibid.

49. Ibid., p. 9.

50. Ibid., p. 10.

51. Hendry, Joy (2014). Science and Sustainability: Learning from Indigenous Wisdom. New York: Palgrave-Macmillan Publisher.

52. Ibid., p. 10.

53. Gana, F.S. (2003). The usage of indigenous plant materials among small-scale farmers in Niger State agricultural development. *Indilinga: African Journal of Indigenous Knowledge Systems*, Vol 2: 53–64.

54. Ajibade, I.T. and Shokemi, O.O. (2003). Indigenous approach to weather forecasting in ASA Local Government, Kwara State Nigeria. *Indilinga: African Journal of Indigenous Knowledge Systems*, Vol 2: 37-46.

55. Qudus, M.A. (2000). Use of Indigenous Knowledge in Sustainable Development of Bangladesh Farm Forestry. In Paul Sillitoe eds; Indigenous Knowledge Development: Present & Future. London: Intermediate Technology Publications, 2000, p. 59.

56. Ibid.

57. Hendry, Joy (2014). Science and Sustainability: Learning from Indigenous Wisdom, p. 35.

58. What is Bushfire? Australian Government: Applying Geoscience to Australia's Important Challenges. Retrieved March 10, 2020, from https://www.ga.gov.au/scientific-topics/community-safety/bushfire.

59. Hendry, Joy (2014). Science and Sustainability: Learning from Indigenous Wisdom, p. 32.

60. Iyam, David Uru (1995). The Broken Hoe: Cultural Reconfiguration in Biase Southeast Nigeria. Chicago: University of Chicago Press, pp. 8–10.

61. Ibid., p. 11

62. Vargeghese, J. and Crawford, S.S. (2021). A cultural framework for indigenous, local, and science knowledge systems in ecology and natural resource management. *Ecological Monographs*, Vol. 9 (1): 2.

63. Ibid., p. 8.

Chapter 3

Traditional Food Regimes and Food Security in Africa

The concept of *corporate food management regimes* expresses the social and ecological contradictions of capitalism and the global-historical processes in which the deployment of price and credit relations are integral for accumulation through dispossession.[1]

However, there are some historical perceptions that have driven the acceleration for agricultural development in Africa that suggests the use of modern approaches. The central argument of such perceptions in the agricultural sector is driven by the idea that modern agricultural inputs will accelerate agriculture development in developing regions such as Africa.[2] Contrarily, Dibua[3] suggests that the perceived influence of modernization has not necessarily transformed the performance of the agriculture sector in Africa because the development paradigm had as one of its primary focus the production of raw materials for western industries and was not concerned about the establishment of capital or intermediate goods industries.[4] It is along these lines that Polly Hill amplified that that the study of indigenous economics was neglected by colonial authorities and the national governments that ensued in post-colonial Africa in favor of external trade which was predicated on exportation and importation rather on indigenous systems of internal distribution.[5] In this regard, Paul Richards posits that the lack of knowledge about African agricultural practices by the colonialists and development agencies is responsible for the failure of agriculture development in Africa. He suggests:

> . . . agricultural development programmes should put aside evolutionary assumptions when dealing with unfamiliar agricultural practices, seek out the principles upon which these practices are based, and aim to assist further development of their implications.[6]

Therefore, the idea that agriculture development in Africa would not take forth unless it is guided by technology transfer and the importation of appropriate agricultural inputs from other regions is misguided.[7] Michael Watts, along these lines, provides a contextual understanding of how the colonial dispositions of agricultural development played an integral role in the continued peasantization of indigenous communities. He posits that in the case of Nigeria:

> Colonialism pioneered the expansion of the agricultural frontier in the Hausa land and the state was instrumental in encouraging the cultivation of export crops: but in both instances these developments subjected peasant producers to the unfettered clutches of the firms, middlemen, advance system and of course, to the inabilities of the global commodity markets.[8]

Invariably, an examination of the corporate food management regimes provides the lenses in which one can examine the historical and ecological implications of food regimes and the benefits of these foods for indigenous communities. Therefore, the next sections of this chapter will focus on the corporate food regimes and examine the processes in which indigenous communities have continued to use food and plants to enhance community wellness.

THE FIRST CORPORATE FOOD REGIME, 1880–1914

The first food management regime was driven by a global capitalist production relation under colonialism, where agricultural exports from white settler countries in Africa, South America, and Australasia provided unprocessed and semi processed foods and raw materials to the metropolitan states of North America and Western Europe.[9] However, the emergence of refrigerated ships in the 1880s allowed for a broad range of perishables such as butter and meat to be supplied by the colonies to the metropolitan communities in North America and Western Europe.[10]

The first food regime was enhanced by the industrial revolution. Particularly, in the 1880s, the advent of the refrigerated ships advanced the scope of produce that could be supplied by colonies to metropolitan communities. The nature of trade involved the trade of imports such as wheat and meat in exchange for European manufactured goods, labor, and capital. However, the nature of trade between the colonies and the metropole galvanized multi-lateral trade which has been the foundation for the inequity of the international economy. This new trade relation is accentuated by the following relations:

1. Complementary product exchange was replaced by competitive product according to the law of comparative advantage.

2. The settler family farm became a profound avenue in which special-ized commercial agriculture and industrial capital shape the agricultural labor process using chemicals and machineries.
3. The emergence of home markets that were organized along national economic boundaries and into agro-industrial complex.[11]

Though the first food regime was challenged by the global economic recession of the late 1920s and 1930s, however, some aspects of the regime survived. The trade in dairy produce, meat and cereal continued in the Americas and the Australasia. In addition, the production of products such as sugar, tropical crops such as cocoa, coconut, rubber and palm oil has con-tinued at the global scale. Thus, the continuous propagation of monocultural, capital intensive farms that are supervised by expatriates that often work for agri-business corporations.[12]

THE SECOND CORPORATE FOOD REGIME (1947–1970S)

The second food regime also known as the *productivist food regime* was driven by an intense form of capitalist production relations that involved modernization and industrialization of farming. The second regime was gal-vanized by the following distinct processes:

1. The restructuring of the agricultural sectors by agro-food capitals to reach mass markets.
2. The development of durable food and intensive meat commodity complexes.
3. The extension of the state system to former colonies through the process of decolonization.
4. The emergence of the United States as a geo-political power and its dominance as an economic power.
5. The use of state protectionism in the agriculture sector.

The second food regime period was clearly mired by a relationship in which the former colonies were further integrated into the international division of labor. This relationship was advanced by agro-businesses and multinationals such as Coca-Cola, Heinz, Kellogg, Nabisco, Pepsi, and Unilever. These multinationals and agri-businesses continued to source their raw material and other production inputs through global contracts and at times through *backward integration*—a process through which corporate takeovers by multinationals have merged the suppliers with the parent com-pany. Invariably, this process was responsible for the decline in the terms of trade for agricultural commodities from developing countries, thus resulting in the inability of these countries to compete in the global market because the terms of trade are dictated by the metropolitan states and their multinationals. Concomitantly, the nature of the trade relations between the colonies and the metropolitan states during this period also contributed to the decline of the traditional food exports.[13] Invariably, the inequities created by the emergence of the big multinationals in the global agri-food economy contributed to the peasantization of small-scale farmers whereby the latter could not compete in the global market. However, it is important to highlight that the second food regime emerged under two international agreements, the 1945 Bretton Woods Agreement, which established the International Monetary Fund (IMF) and the International Bank of Reconstruction and Development (IBRD) now known as the World Bank. The IMF was primarily preoccupied with monetary stability of exchange rates between national currencies which were pegged to the dollar/gold standard.[14] Then, by 1947 the General Agreement on Trade Treaty (G.A.T.T.) was established, which excluded agriculture from liberal trading practices and alternatively reinforced state protectionism for agriculture exports and imports in favor of major powers.[15]

THE THIRD CORPORATE FOOD
REGIME 1980S–PRESENT

The third food regime emerged out of the capitalist accumulation crisis of the 1970s. This crisis according to Friedmann[16] and Goodman[17] was advanced with the oil and food crisis of the 1970S. However, the surge in grain prices, the increasing costs of national agricultural programs, and the conflict between national regulators and the emerging commercial strength of global corporations led to the eventual demise of the second regime.[18] The following economic crisis according to Atkins further exacerbated the end of the second regime:

1. The E.U. took on the status of an equivalent power bloc to the U.S. which resulted in a decline of the geo-political strength of the United States.
2. Agricultural export competition under subsidies between the U.S. and E.U. was about to result in a trade war.
3. In 1973, traditional pattern of trade with developing countries was disrupted by the U.S.–USSR grain deals, thus removing the American wheat surplus from the international market.
4. The rising commercial power of agricultural corporations also heightened the tension between nationally organized economies and transnational corporations and capital.

5. The contradictions that emerged because of the institutionalized food surpluses, particularly those related with economic cost of farm subsidies in the early 1980s. These contradictions consequently led to the demise of state support for agriculture primarily among developed economies.[19]

Central to the demise of state subsidies for agriculture exports is the expediency and the emergence of a new global regulatory measure and structure that is far more liberal than regulatory guidelines under subsequent regimes. As a result, the liberal policies that emerged brought about competitiveness in the global marketplace which consequently positioned middle economies such as, Mexico, South Korea, Brazil, Taiwan, and India at a disadvantage because liberalization generated a new food system premised by western agricultural development and nutritional schemes that is reinforced by rising income.[20]

The emergence of the third food regime was ushered in by the continued demand for food and the proliferation of big western agri-businesses that employed the use of biotechnology for accelerated food production. The use of biotechnology in food production process entailed the use of genetic engineering methods to address the global demand for foods. Thus, because of the commercial competitiveness of agri-businesses such as Monsanto, Syngenta, and Dupont in neo-liberal global food markets, local food producers in developing economies were further marginalized and continued to receive low prices for their products. At the same time, the big agro-businesses with their economies of scale and control over market prices garnered major profits. For instance, in 2007 major fertilizer companies such as Potash, Mosaic and Yara realized a net income of 139 percent. In the first quarter of 2008, Potash's net income rose 186 percent, and Cargill's, a subsidiary of Mosaic, net income rose more than 1,200 percent. In 2007, the top three grain producers—Cargill, ADM, and Bunge also realized astronomical profits at about 103 percent. Along the same lines, the top three global seed and pesticide companies—Monsanto, Syngenta, and Dupont had about 91 percent profits; while the Asian food giant of Thailand, Charoen, realized 273 percent revenue growth in 2008.[21]

The current trend in the market size of biotechnology companies has shown continued growth and their ability to monopolize food prices because they have economies of scale. Industry trends show that the global food technology market size value in 2018 was approximated at $23 billion and it is projected to rise about 10 percent, or $45 billion, by 2025.[22]

Considering the market share of the biotechnology giants, there remains a massive challenge with food sustainability in developing economies. Moreover, the prescriptions of development agencies such as the World Bank and the Food and Agriculture Organization for accelerated food through various agricultural development schemes, such as the Green Revolution, has not been able to alleviate food security challenges in SSA countries because of the lack of indigenous relevant development approaches.[23] In this regard, an examination of agro-diversity using indigenous methods seems plausible for food sustainability in these countries because the indigenous methods as suggested by Iyami are germane with the development realities of these communities. Thus, the next section of food regimes provides an outlook of agro-diversity and indigenous food management, preservation, and storage systems in sub-Saharan Africa with food management regimes, with Ghana serving as an example of how indigenous approaches are used for agro-diversity and food management. These approaches are not capital intensive, but they are closer to the development realities of these communities where over 55 percent of income are earned from agricultural services by rural farmers.[24]

FOOD MANAGEMENT REGIMES
IN SOUTHERN GHANA

The concept of food management regimes include the techniques and approaches of managing land, water, and the biota for crop and livestock production.[25] Food management regimes involve an important part of agro-diversity systems through which farmers use the natural aspects of the environment for food production, the choice of crops and their management of land and water.[26] However, against the background of factors that have inhibited food sovereignty is the right to produce food and the protection from food dumping and land tenure. This chapter suggests that despite the increased use of technology to advance food productivity, recent global food insecurity, particularly in Africa, has made it imperative that indigenous and traditional food crops should play an integral role in food security.[27] According to Adeleye, sub-Saharan Africa has experienced food insecurity that has led to loss of lives and livelihoods over the past decade.[28] Moreover, African countries collectively were unable to meet the Millennium Development Goal of reducing hunger by half by 2015 and approximately about one-third of its population lives in chronic hunger.[29]

Given the challenges of food security in Africa in general, we examine the nature of food management regimes and suggest that these regimes are by far sustainable because the accelerated approach that was suggested by multilaterals has not been able to reduce the challenges of food security in the continent. Examples of food management regimes in Ghana illustrate the dynamism and sustainability of indigenous food regimes. Farmers in this region often engage various land use and field preparation for management regimes.

INDIGENOUS LAND AND SITE
PREPARATION FOR FARMING

Typically, indigenous farmers often prepare their land and field types to support the sustainability of indigenous farming practices. For instance, in southern Ghana, land for cropping is prepared by slashing and clearing land with cutlass, machete, and by burning the uprooted vegetation. At the same time, trees and vegetation that have medicinal and ecological value are not slashed. Instead, they are nurtured, along with food crops which are interplanted in an indigenous agroforestry method.[30]

The most important implements in this process are the use of indigenous farming implements such as hoes and cutlass for sowing and clearing weeds. The indigenous and natural elements are sustainable and does not contribute to environmental pollution or soil degradation processes that are often associated with modern technologies such as chemical fertilizers. Accordingly, evidence from other developing regions such as Indonesia has shown that uncontrolled application of pesticides can contribute to the damage of soil biomass, and enable microorganisms such as bacteria, fungi, and earthworms.[31] The Indonesia experience showed that productivity by farmers became non-optimal because of factors such as improper cultivation technique, uncontrollable environmental factors, and pest attack.[32]

However, indigenous farming practices in sub-Saharan Africa using indigenous implements such as cutlass, by contrast, has low environmental impact and contributes less to bio-diversity damage. For instance, the use of the *Proka,* a land preparation method that converts vegetation into mulch rather than burning and slashing, has proven to contribute to biodiversity. Thereafter, to prepare the farmland, indigenous farmers apply various forms of management regimes and or practices for the cultivation of food crops, and vegetables for subsistence and commercialization purposes. These regimes vary from one region in Africa to another. However, examples from southern Ghana are common in the West African sub-region. For instance, traditional agro-forestry and the practices of cultivating among trees, tends to conserve trees and regenerates soil fertility through biomass liter.[33] Table 3.1 provides examples of management regimes and their advantages in Ghana.

The use of indigenous agricultural approaches plays an integral role in community wellness for indigenous, national, and regional communities in Africa. Thus, food production, their preservation, and storage must be examined along with their medicinal values to better understand the broad

Table 3.1. Food Management Regimes and Practices in Ghana

Practice Regimes	Agricultural Advantages
Minimal tillage and the controlled use of fire for vegetation clearance.	Minimal disturbance of soil and biota
Proka, a non-burn farming practice that involves mulching by leaving slashed vegetation to decompose in *situ*	Maintain and enhance soil fertility by conserving and stimulating microbes and by human addition of decomposing vegetation; conserves plant propagates including those in the soil.
Bush fallow/land rotation	A process of regenerating soil fertility and conserving plants in the wild to sustain soil productivity
Staggered harvest crops	Ensures food availability over the long haul
Storage of crops, notably yams, in situ in the soil for future harvesting	Enhances food security and secures seed stock
Conservation of forest in the backyard	A process of conserving forest species, source of medicinal plants at short notice, favors agriculture, small farming, and shade-loving crops such as yams.

Source: Edwin A Gyasi (2014). Demonstration sites and expert farmers in conservation of biodiversity. In Gyasi, E.A.; Berisalvljevic, G.K.; Blay, E.T. & Oduro, W. (ed). (2004). Managing Agrodiversity the Traditional Way. New York: United Nations University press, p. 44

implications of food management regimes for sustainable agricultural development.

Indigenous communities are vulnerable to high post-harvest food losses in most African countries. It is estimated that about 50 percent of perishable farm produce that includes fruits, vegetables, roots, and tubers are lost each year. Along the same lines, about 30 percent of food grains, which includes maize and millet, are lost at harvest in West Africa.[34] Food spoilage in most sub–Saharan African countries are caused by several factors such as insects and pests; action of enzymes in food; chemical reaction in food; action of micro-organisms such as bacteria, yeast, and molds; and physical changes in food.[35]

Despite the challenges of food spoilage, indigenous communities have been able to sustain food preservation and storage by employing techniques that are culturally germane to their communities. The following are examples of the indigenous techniques for food storage and preservation:

Pickling, this is the process in which food is soaked in a solution containing salt, acid, or alcohol. The following foods can be pickled: vegetables, meat, seafood, and fruits. The cautionary part of the process is that pickled food cannot be stored at room temperature. However, pickled foods are amalgamated with other methods such as fermenting and canning.[36]

Smoking, it has been historically discovered that certain foods that are exposed to smoke appear to last longer. Examples of such food are meat, fish, and cheese. Smoking has become a sophisticated form of food preservation and storage. The process can be hot and cold; hot smoking is used with fresh or frozen foods and cold smoking is used most often with salted products.[37]

Drying, this is a process through which food is left out in the sun and wind to dry for preservation. Given that most disease-causing organisms tend to thrive in moist environments, drying is a natural and indigenous technique for preventing spoilage.[38]

Curing, is used mostly in the preservation of meats, fish, fruits, and vegetables. The process entails the salting of food for preservation.[39]

Fermentation, this is a process through which naturally occurring chemical reaction in foods are converted into different forms by pathogens. It is a process by which food goes bad and results in the formation of an edible product.[40]

Roasting, this is the process through which foods are preserved. Foods such as peanuts are roasted by stirring in hot sand and in a flat bottom frying pot or wok like pans over hot flame. Meats are also roasted for preservation and to enhance palatability and anti-nutritional factors.[41]

MEDICINAL VALUE OF FOOD IN GHANA

Indigenous approaches to food management regimes, and the preservation of food should be assessed in the continuum of overall wellness of communities. It is with this in mind that one should examine the medicinal value of food and the invaluable contribution of indigenous approaches to community wellness. It is along the foregoing lines that Oritsejafor and Jones suggest that folk and or traditional medicine can become viable means of providing healthcare for all.[42] Thus, indigenous food and vegetation have ecological values that are medicinal and botanical. These values support indigenous life forms regarding their medicinal impact. For instance, trees and herbs used in the Wechiau communities of Northern region of Ghana shows that Ebenaceae trees known as *Gar* are pounded and added to soup and drank for stomach aches. Also, Malvaceae herbs, locally known as *Biri,* are boiled and used to wash eyes with infusion from cobra spits into the eyes. The leaves are also used as vegetables in food and the stem to make ropes.[43] The use of the Anacardiaceae tree also provides food and medicinal values. This tree also known in indigenous communities in Ghana as S*unsugere* or *Manvora* and is eaten raw as a fruit; the stem and branches are used for energy as fuel wood.[44]

These indigenous plants and food crops also have botanic and medicinal values which complement other ecological values. For instance, Moraceae also known as *Konkon* by the indigenous communities in Northwest Ghana is used for curing malaria. The roots are pounded, and the infusion is drunk for malaria. The leaves on the other hand are used to feed goats, sheep, and cows. The Fabaceae tree known by the indigenous communities in Northwest Ghana as *Dowa* is used for multiple reasons that support life forms—the leaves are boiled, and the drink infusion is used to address fever ailment. At times, the leaves are boiled and bathed with to reduce fever. The pulp from the seed is eaten as a fruit or grinded as spice for food.[45]

INDIGENOUS MEDICINE AND WELLNESS IN RURAL COMMUNITIES

The relative importance of traditional medicine within the IK framework used in this book is also critical to understand the application of IK as a framework for development. Traditional medicines are millennia old and have been used as a component of IK. Traditional medicines are different from western medicines which are based on modern scientifically proven evidence which at times evolved from the empirical evidence of traditional medicines in ancient civilizations such as Egypt, Mesopotamia, Greece, India, and China.[46]

The amalgamation of traditional and modern medicine is complimentary in their objective of providing healthcare, but their approach, methods, and philosophies tend to differ. Moreover, the use of traditional medicine is advanced by IK and focuses on the body and the mind for diagnosis, prevention, and treatment. Meanwhile, western medicine is dependent on science and focuses on the suppression of symptoms on targeted parts of the body. The critical challenge between modern and traditional medicine is the limited acceptance of traditional medicine by the modern scientific community.[47] Much of which has gradually begun to change with the endorsement by the World Health Organization (WHO).[48] Developed economies have also found utility in the use of IK in addressing development initiatives in their communities. For instance, IK technologies have been used in addressing health issues such as sinusitis in New Zealand, as well as wildfires and water crisis to sustain the land in Australia.[49]

The next section will focus on the profound nature of indigenous science—it is rigorous, and it is a knowledge collected systematically that can be tried, tested and reproduced for sustainability.[50]

MEDICINAL VALUE OF FOOD IN NIGERIA

In Nigeria, indigenous food plays a pivotal role in indigenous wellness and healthcare. Therefore, the diversity of food grown in Nigeria within the context of their botanical and health value. For instance, it has been suggested by some scholars that mushrooms have medicinal value. In this regard, Oyetayo highlighted that mushrooms that are indigenous to Southeastern and Southwest Nigeria, such as the *Pleutrotus tuber-regium, Lentrimus-Squarulosuss* have medicinal value. *Pleutrotus tuber-regium* for example is used for headache, stomach pain, fever, cold, and constipation.[51]

In Northeastern Nigeria, the study of Lockett, Calvert, and Grivetti suggests that wild fruits such as *Adansonia Digitata* also known as *Kuaka* and *Dererrium Microcarpum,* known as *Taura* among the indigenous peoples of Northeastern Nigeria, have nutritional and medicinal value in the arid Northeastern Nigeria. For instance, barks of edible wild spices such as *Adina Microphecephala* known by the Fulani ethnic group as *Kadanya* is soaked in water for up to a week and then drank for breast milk production. The barks of *Taura* are soaked in water for up to 12 hours and then drank to relieve and control diarrhea.[52]

In Southwestern Nigeria, a survey of the Illaje littoral communities shows how fishes adopted for medical practices had resulted in potent socio-spiritual healing for ages. The Illaje communities known for fishing in the Delta region of Nigeria use fish such as *Ojiji-electric fish* and *Aro-mud catfish* which is mixed with other ingredients to prepare a medicinal concoction to treat various ailments. Ojiji is combined with gun powder (etu) and alligator pepper (itaye) to enhance strong contraction of pregnancy. Aro-Mud fish known scientifically as *Genius Glarias* is used by the Illaje communities for abdominal problems, restoration of womb tranquility, womb attack, and the overheat of the womb.[53] Table 3.2 shows an ethnobotanical study on some pteridophytes of Southern Nigeria, it further illustrates the medicinal value of food in indigenous communities. Examples obtained from 7 plants belonging to 2 families provide evidence of medicinal value of food.

RURAL FARMING AND WELLNESS IN EDO STATE, SOUTH-SOUTH NIGERIA

The range in which indigenous knowledge is used to manage wellness in rural farming communities is profound in Edo State, which is in the south-south geographical zone of Nigeria. Benin, which is the capital of Edo State, seats one of the oldest monarchies in Nigeria that goes as far back as the 900s.[54]

Table 3.2. An Ethnobotanical Studies on Some Pteridophytes of Southern Nigeria

Southern Nigeria Local Plant	Scientific Name	Medicinal Value
Ntutu Umu	Adiantum aethiopicum	Plant is used for gangrenous wounds and bruises.
Ofu isi, Akite, Apa.	Adiantum capillus-veneris	Infusion of leaves drunk against infertility and other women's disease such as vaginal discharge
Ogbogbo, Igba, Doka	Aleuriopteris albomarginata	Decoction of whole plant is taken internally against peptic ulcer.
Abua, Ocha, Abaila	Arthromeris wallichiana	Paste prepared from leaves applied externally as treatment for sprains. It is also used for bone resetting process.
Akukwo, nini	Diplazium esculentum	Leaves are eaten as vegetables with yam. Infusion of fronds used for toothache and used by women for difficult childbirth.
Ami ogwu, Usele	Gleichenia linearis	Extract of whole plant administered internally to children suffering from convulsion after which a cold bath is given to reduce high body temperature. This is sometimes followed by the healer incantations to chase away the evil spirit.
Akwa, nmili, Nze	Nephrolepsis cordifolia	Tubers are cleaned and boiled with salt and water and eaten as food; infusion of fronds is administered to the elderly for treatment of amnesia

Source: Created by the author with data from Nwosu, M.A. (2002). Ethnobotanical studies on some Pteridophytes of Southern Nigeria. *Economic Botany*, Vol. 56, No. 3, p. 256–257.

The Edo speaking people is inclusive of Edo proper commonly the *Bini's*, (Benin), *the Urhobo's*, and the *Esan's* and smaller villages and tribes.[55] The Bini Kingdom was clearly not a subject that was marginalized in the European literature. The Bini Kingdom has been a prominent state in West Africa that attracted commerce and European missionaries from ca. 1485 until the late 19th century.[56]

The language spoken by the Edo ethnic groups are also distinct from that of other smaller groups. However, certain words and the pronunciation of these words are like that of the *Yoruba* in the Southwest of modern-day Nigeria. This is because the Edo people, particularly the *Bini's* share common lineage with the Yoruba's through Oduduwa, the Yoruba divine founder. He was the holder of the title of the Ooni of Ile Ife and the Oba of Bini is the descendant of Oduduwa.[57]

However, to understand the importance of wellness to rural agriculture development, one must underscore the importance and the use of traditional medicine in addressing indigenous wellness. The suggestion is that agricultural development cannot take place in the vacuum of wellness. For instance, the Edo speaking peoples are often engaged in traditional medicine and the worship of deities such as *Ovia*. The Ovia is a cult that is celebrated at the beginning of dry season. The followers of Ovia would often retire to the bush at night and reappear daily for occasional ceremonial purposes. The worship of gods such as *osa* of the *ebo* and of ancestors along with medicine such as *ixumu* are inter-connected with development and the growth of the traditional edo communities.[58]

An examination of how indigenous communities in Benin and the Esan of Edo State have used medicinal herbs to improve wellness underscores the importance of plants for healing and addressing other social and economic development activities such as agriculture.

THE BINI PEOPLE AND COMMUNITY WELLNESS

Traditional medical practitioners are often dynamic in their approach to their practice. That is, at times "They do it all" without specialization. In other instances, there are specialized practices. Accordingly, Dr./Prince asserted:

> What they know depends on their mentors since there is no formal settings for training. They often take secrecy oaths before their mentors. However, there are some who specializes in orthopedic medicine and midwifery. The orthopedic medicine practitioners used to be based at the Ukhegie quarter in Benin City and Oghede village on the outskirts of the village.[59]

Given the rich cultural heritage of the Bini Kingdom and contributions to the wellness of indigenous communities over time and in modern day Nigeria and Edo State, the interview with Dr./Prince of the Bini Kingdom was important and intriguing. He identified the use of plants for wellness through IK in Nigeria, especially in this case, the Bini Kingdom in Edo State. The following are indigenous plants, their local names, botanical names, and how they are used in the Bini Kingdom:

1. Etziza (*Cymbopogon citratus*) is a plant used by traditional practitioners in Bini to ensure *quick* action, it is also used as anti-bacterial and anti-inflammatory medicine.
2. Itoto, a kind of cane root is used as a medicine, and as a preparation for making "one's body smooth and fleshy."

3. Olika niri is a creeper; its roots are used in curing a disease called "black tongue."
4. Ebahanhi (*Piper umbellatum*) is also called the "Cow foot" leaf shrub used for digestive medicine.
5. Ebi-gho-edore (*Ageratum conyzoides*), "billy goat" weed herb for exotic medicine.
6. Ehienedo (*Aframomu melegueta*), alligator pepper, an herb for medicine.
7. Ukpereghodin is a plant with overly sweet fruit used as a cough medicine for children. The leaf is also used for composing charms.
8. Evbe (*Cola acuminate*), *Kola* nut, is used for stimulant.
9. Evbegabari, Evbe-Ibhaja (*Cola nitida*) is used as stimulant.
10. Evbohobitan (*Cola cariciofolia* or *Cola milleni*), monkey cola, wild kola nuts tree used as stimulant.
11. Ovin-edun (*Gracina polyantha* or *Cola millenii*) leaves can be used in combination with other plants as medicine. Leaves are also used for the treatment of ringworm, scabies, gonorrhea, and dysentery.
12. Oriwo (*Veronia amygadalina*), Bitter Leaf, edible vegetables. The mashed leaf juice is also used to control diabetes.
13. Osu (*Hunteria umbellata*) is used to treat diabetic, peptic ulcers, piles, yaws, fevers, and infertility.[60]

The Esan's like the *Bini* people of Edo State have for many generations used plants to improve wellness in rural farming communities. The following are examples of the various plants and their traditional usefulness in the Esan land.[61]

1. *Abrus precatorius*, which is locally known as Empo, is a leaf used to treat cataracts. It is administered with the leaf extract applied on the eyes. It is also used to treat asthma by chewing the leaf.
2. *Acacia sieberiana* is known locally among the Esan people as Alughan. The leaf is used to treat urinary tract disorder. The decoction is taken orally for treatment of urinary tract disorder.
3. *Aframomum melegueta* is also known as Uriema or Usiedo seed and fruit among the Esan people. The seed is used to treat low sperm count and chewed during the breakfast period. The fruit Usiedo is used for women to mitigate against menstrual pain by chewing the combination of the seeds and fruits.
4. *Ageratum conyzoides*, referred to locally by Esan people as Okhekhe leaf, is used for dressing wounds. The decoction is applied to the area of the wound. The combination of the root leaf decoction is taken orally to treat rheumatism skin rashes as well.

5. *Alchomea latiflora*, known locally as Obieyba leaf, is used to stop vomiting. The leaf is grounded with pepper and taken orally.

6. *Allium cepa* is referred to by indigenous communities in Esan land as Alubasa. The bulb leaf of this plant is used for treating asthma and kidney problems. The burnt bulb decoction is taken orally. Similarly for kidney treatment the burnt bulb leaf is taken orally.

7. *Allium sativum*, locally known as Nikhere, are bulb seeds and cloves used to treat asthma and epilepsy. The decoction is taken orally for asthma and the cloves are chewed for epilepsy.

8. *Alstonia booneii*, known locally as Ojegbhukun, is a root bark used for treating epilepsy and for expelling retained placenta. The decoction is taken orally to treat both epilepsy and the retained placenta.[62]

Table 3.3 further illustrates the emphasis of medicinal plants in addressing several types of physical ailments in the Esan rural communities.

The medicinal value of botanical plants used for community wellness among the Edo people accentuates a broader sense of how indigenous knowledge can be employed to address development challenges among indigenous communities. For instance, the use of indigenous botanical plants among the Edo has ecological utility. That is, the use of indigenous botanical plants supports all forms of life. This is the case regarding the use of botanical

Table 3.3. Medicinal Plants used in Esanland of Edo State Nigeria

Species Name	Local Name	Parts Used	Traditional Uses	Preparation and Administration
Amaranthus spinosus	Obiwhne	Roots	For allergy	Roots are mashed, soaked in ethanol, and taken orally
Anacardium occidental	Ikhasu	Bark	For dysentery, for toothache, and for sore gum	Decoction is taken orally, and the bark is chewed
Ananas comosus	Edin-ebo	Fruit	For asthma	Ripe fruit is eaten
Aspilla Africana	Ohawe	Leaf root	To stop vomiting	Decoction is taken orally, and leaf is chewed
Althermanthera Sessalis	Obiewe	Leaves	For eczema	Infusion is applied on affected areas
Azadirachta indica	Dogoyaro	Leaf bark leaf	For Malaria	Decoction is taken orally and used for steam bath.

Source: Okoli, R.I.; Aigbe, J.O., Obodo-Ohaju, J.O., and Mensah, J.K. (2007). Medicinal Herbs used for Managing some Common Ailments among Esan people of Edo State, Nigeria. Pakistan Journal of Nutrition, Vol.6, (5): 492.

plants and food crops by the Edo to enhance ethnoveterinary medicine and live stocks such as goats. The following illustrates how indigenous botanical plants are used to enhance ethnoveterinary medicine for reproduction problems, anorexia and debility, diarrhea, catarrh, and orf, mange, poison, and snake bite for goats.

1. **Reproduction.** The Edo often use the kitchen waste such as yam, and cassava peels, maize gluten meal, and the foliage of Guinea grass cassava to feed goats during part of the prenatal care of goats. While roasted maize grains and medicinal herbs such as *Spondias mombin* (hog plum) are given to the dam after birth. During difficult parturition rural livestock farmers of goat would often apply palm oil to the goat's vagina. To enhance the production of goat milk, farmers feed goats with plenty of maize grains, and water to drink.[63]

2. **Anorexia and Debility.** The appetite of goats that are suffering from anorexia is improved by feeding these live stocks with the leaves of Moringa *oleifera* (horse radish tree). In some instances, farmers feed their live stocks with roasted maize, and dried residues of *Cassava sieviates* plus maize gluten maile. At times, goats' appetites are improved with the fresh leaves of Indian Hemp (*Cannabis sativa*).[64]

3. **Diarrhea, Catarrh, and Orf (mouth blister).** Local farmers used leaves of *Ocimum grattissu* to massage the Angus of live stocks and a liquid extract of the same is dropped in its mouth. At times, the leaves of *Tetracarpidium comophorum* (walnut) with pepper and salt is grinded and the extract is given to the goat orally for the treatment of diarrhea. Along the same lines, the water from the fermentation of cassava or from corn starch (akamu) is dispensed orally to feed goats to curb diarrhea.[65]

   The problem of catarrh with goats is treated by mixing potash (*kaun*) with corn starch and given to eat or at times replaced with corn starch. Along the same lines, hot water is used to press the nose of animals with an application of shea butter to treat *catarrh.*
   Orf, mouth blister is cured by scrubbing the affected area with dried maize cobb and applied alongside hot palm oil.[66]

4. **Poisoning and Snake Bite.** In the event of goat and sheep poisoning, the live stocks are given palm oil orally by drenching the animal with the oil.[67]

SUMMARY

Indigenous Knowledge from the context of agricultural development provides the context in which various agricultural development regimes should be examined. The suggestions provided for indigenous communities must be front and center of their development aspirations.

However, despite recent emphasis by multilaterals on western accelerated agricultural development approaches, the indigenous agricultural approaches have remained technically sound and sustainable. These indigenous communities have continued to contribute to life forms in their communities through food management regimes and through a holistic development approach that have amalgamated ecological and botanical values in the process of food production. The examples of food management regimes in Ghana and Nigeria using botanical plants to support all life forms accentuates the importance of the relationship between indigenous technologies and wellness. These technologies are critical for the development of indigenous communities as demonstrated in the case of Ghana and Nigeria. The essence of these indigenous technologies, as illustrated in the case of Ghana and Nigeria, shows the food management regimes in these countries and the botanical use of plants for wellness. Moreover, it is the suggestions in this chapter that agricultural development would be inconsequential without examining the relationship between plants, their medicinal use, and their ecological importance as demonstrated in the case of the Edo in South-South region of Nigeria.

The use of IK in the South-South among the Esan and Bini provides a sound argument that IK is integral for social and economic development of indigenous communities. The interview of Dr./Prince of Benin buttresses the importance of IK for development. Moreover, in our comparative analysis of the use of IK among the Bini and the Esan we found several areas of commonalities in the strategic use of IK for food management and wellness.

NOTES

1. McMichael, Phillip (2005). Global Development and the Corporate Food Regime. *Rural Sociology and Development,* Vol. (11): 269.

2. Hayami U. and Ruttan, V.W. (1976). Agricultural Development: An International Perspective. Baltimore: John Hopkins University Press.

3. Dibua, Jeremiah (2005). Modernization and the Crisis of Development in Africa: The Nigerian Experience. Hampshire: Ashgate Publishing Company, p. 177.

4. Ibid., p. 30.

5. Hill, Polly (1970). Studies in Rural Capitalism in West Africa. London: Cambridge University Press, p. 4.

6. Richards, Paul (1985). Indigenous Agricultural Revolution: Ecology and Food Production in West Africa. Boulder: Westview Publishing, p. 43.

7. Ibid.

8. Watts, Michael (1983). Silent Violence: Food, Famine and Peasantry in Northern Nigeria. Berkeley: University of California Press, p. 189.

9. Atkins, Peter J. (2015). Food regimes as an organizing concept, p. 3. Retrieved on June 29, 2019, from https://www.researchgate.net/publications/271327020.

10. Ibid., p. 3.

11. Ibid., p. 4.

12. Ibid., p. 4.

13. Ibid., p. 5.

14. Ibid., p. 6.

15. Ibid.

16. Friedmann, H. (1994). The International relations of food: The unfolding crisis of national regulation. In Harris-White, B. and Hoffenberg, R. (eds). Food Multidisciplinary Perspectives. Oxford: Blackwell, pp. 174–204.

17. Goodman, D. (1991). Some recent tendencies in the industrial organization of agri-food system. In Friedland, W. Busch, L., Buttel, F. and Rudy, A. (eds). Towards a New Political Economy of Agriculture. Boulder: Westview, pp. 37–64.

18. Atkins, Peter J. (2015). Food regimes as an organizing concept. p.3. Retrieved on June 29, 2019, from https://www.researchgate.net/publications/271327020, p, 6.

19. Ibid., p. 7.

20. McMichael, P. (1992). Tensions between National and International Control of the World Food Order: Contours of a New Food Regime. *Sociological Perspectives*, Vol. 35(2):359.

21. McMichael, P. (2009). A food regime analysis of the world food crisis. *Agriculture Human Values*, Vol. 26:290 DOI 10.1007/S10460-009-92185.

22. Global Food Biotechnology Market Size by Type. Industry Analysis and Report, Regional Outlook Growth Potential, Price Trends, Competitive Market Share and Forecast, 2019–2025, https://www.gminsights.com/industry-analysis/food-biotechnology-market?utm_source=globenewswire.com&utm_medium=referral&utm_campaign=Paid_globenewswire.

23. Iyam, David Uru (1995). The Broken Hoe: Cultural Reconfiguration in Biase Southeast Nigeria. Chicago: University of Chicago Press, p. 11.

24. Davis, Benjamin, Di Giuseppe, Stefania and Zezza, Alberto (2017). Are African households (not) leaving agriculture? Patterns of households' income sources in rural sub-Saharan Africa. *Food Policy*, Vol. 67: 157.

25. Edwin A. Gyasi (2004). Management Regimes in Southern Ghana. in Gyasi, Edwin A. & Kranjac-Berisalvlejevic, G. (2004). Managing Agrodiversity the Traditional Way: Lessons from West Africa in Sustainable Use of Biodiversity and Related Natural Resources. New York: United Nations University Press, p. 53.

26. Ibid.

27. Cloete, P.C. and Idsardi, E.F. (2013). Consumption of Indigenous and Traditional Food Crops: Perceptions and Realities from South Africa. *Agroecology and Sustainable Food Systems*. Vol. 37: 902–903.

28. Adeyeye, Samuel Ayofemi Olalekan (2017). The role of food processing and appropriate storage technologies in ensuring food security and food availability in Africa. *Nutrition and Food Sciences*, Vol. 47(1): 122.

29. Ibid., p. 123.

30. Gyasi, Edwin A. (2004). Management Regimes in Southern Ghana. In Gyasi Edwin A. & Kranjac-Berisalvlejevic, G. (2004). Managing Agro-diversity the Traditional Way: Lessons from West Africa in Sustainable of Biodiversity and Related Natural Resources. New York: United Nations University Press, p. 54.

31. Joko, T., Angorro, S., Sunsko, H. R. amd Rachmawati, S. (2017). Pesticide's usage in the soil quality degradation potential in Wanasari subdistrict Berbes Indonesia. *Applied and Environmental Soil Sciences*, Vol. 2017: 1–2. https://doi.org/10.1155/2017/5896191.

32. Ibid., pp. 1–2.

33. Gyasi, Edwin A. (2004). Management Regimes in Southern Ghana. in Gyasi, Edwin A. & Kranjac-Berisalvlejevic, G. (2004). Managing Agro-diversity the Traditional Way: Lessons from West Africa in Sustainable of Biodiversity and Related Natural Resources. New York: United Nations University Press, p. 58.

34. Adeyeye, Samuel Ayofemi Olalekan (2017). The role of food processing and appropriate storage technologies in ensuring food security and food availability in Africa. *Nutrition and Food Sciences,* Vol. 47(1): 127.

35. Ibid.

36. Ibid. p. 128.

37. Ibid.

38. Ibid., p. 129.

39. Ibid.

40. Ibid.

41. Ibid., p. 130.

42. Oritsejafor, E. and Jones, E. (2004). Folk and Modern Medicine in Africa: A case study of mental health care in Liberia. Vol. XXIX (2):1.

43. Asase, A. and Yeboah, A.A.O. (2012). Plants used in Wechiau community Hippopotamus sanctuary in Northwest Ghana. *Ethnobotany Journal and Applications*, Vol. 10(1): p.610. Accessed on December 3, 2020, from http://www.ethnobotanyjournal.org/index.php/era.

44. Ibid.

45. Ibid., p. 611.

46. Lemonnier, N., et al. (2017). Traditional Knowledge-based medicine: A Review of history, principles, and relevance in the present context of p4 systems medicine. Progress in Preventive Medicine. Vol. 2(7): 1–14. Retrieved September 15 from https://journals.lww.com/progprevmed/Fulltext/2017/12000/Traditional_Knowledge_based_Medicine__A_Review_of.1.aspx?context=FeaturedArticles&collectionId=1.

47. Ibid.

48. Oritsejafor, E. and Jones, E. (2004). Folk and Modern Medicine in Africa. *Liberian Studies Journal*, Vol. XXIX (2): 1.

49. Hendry, Joy (2014). Science and Sustainability: Learning from Indigenous Wisdom. New York: Palgrave Macmillan, pp. 21–37.

50. Ibid., p. 1.

51. Oyetayo, V.O. (2011). Medicinal uses of mushrooms in Nigeria: Towards full and sustainable exploitation. *African Journal of Traditional Complement Alternative Medicine*, Vol.8(3): 268.

52. Lockett, C.T., Calvert, C. C. and Grivett, L. E. (2000). Energy and micronutrient composition of dietary and medicinal wild plants consumed during drought. Study of rural, Northeastern Nigeria. *International Journal of Food Sciences and Nutrition,* Vol. 51: 199.

53. Ehinmore, O.M. and Ogunode, S.A. (2013). Fish in indigenous healing practices among the ilaje of coastal Yoruba land of Nigeria: A historical perspective. *European Scientific Journal*, Vol. 9(14):200. Retrieved September 12, 2021, from https://citeseerx.ist.psu.edu/viewdoc/download?doi=10.1.1.839.7794&rep=rep1&type=pdf.

54. The Kingdom of Benin. Accessed February 9, 2021, from https://www.bbc.co.uk/bitesize/topics/zpvckqt/articles/z3n7mp3#:~:text=The%20kingdom%20of%20Benin%20began,and%20built%20up%20an%20empire.

55. Thomas, N.W. (1910). The Edo-Speaking People of Nigeria. *Journal of the Royal Africa Society*, Vol. 10(37): 1–2.

56. Osadolor, Osarheme Benson and Otodie, Enahoro Leo (2008). The Benin Kingdom in British imperial histography. *History in Africa*, Vol. 35: 405.

57. Bondarenko, D.M. and Roese, P.M. (1999). Benin prehistory: The origin and settling down of the Edo. *Anthropos*, Vol. 4 (6):542–552

58. Thomas, N.W. (1910). The Edo-speaking people of Nigeria. *Journal of the Royal Africa Society*, Vol. 10(37): 1–2.

59. Interview with Dr./Prince of the Bini Kingdom (February 13, 2021). Plants and Uses in Traditional Medicine in Edo/Benin. The interview focused on the use of botanical plants for wellness in Edo State Nigeria.

60. Ibid.

61. Okoli, R.I., Aigbe, J.O., Obodo-Ohaju, J.O. and Mensah, J.K. (2007). Medicinal herbs used for managing some common ailments among Esan people of Edo State, Nigeria. *Pakistan Journal of Nutrition*, Vol. 6 (5): 492.

62. Ibid.

63. Bamikole, M.A. and Ikhatua, U.J. (2009). Compilation and adoption of ethno-veterinary medicine, traditional and other management practices by small ruminant farmers in Edo State. Nigeria. *Tropical Animal Health Production*, Vol, 41: 1552, DO1 10. 1007/s11250-009–9346–3.

64. Ibid.

65. Ibid.

66. Ibid.

67. Ibid.

Chapter 4

Food Security in War Torn Countries

THE CASE OF LIBERIA AND DEMOCRATIC REPUBLIC OF CONGO (DRC)

In as much as climate induced conditions have had a major impact on food security in sub-Saharan Africa, conflicts such as civil war have equally contributed to food insecurities. For instance, since 2000, 48 percent of civil conflict communities are in rural communities where access to rural lands is integral to the livelihoods of many in these communities. As a result of conflict, rural communities have also continued to encounter acute food and nutrition shortages. This is the case in Sudan, Democratic Republic of Congo, and Somalia where 2.8 million people have encountered acute food shortage and nutrition insecurity.[1]

This chapter examines the binary effects of an endemic crisis—Ebola, and conflict induced food security with a case study of food security challenges in conflict communities of Liberia. The chapter also illustrates how the use of IK could serve as an alternative strategy for agricultural development in these communities.

THE CASE OF LIBERIA

Liberia is Africa's oldest independent republic founded by formerly enslaved persons who returned from the United States in 1822. Liberia declared its independence in 1847 and in the years that followed independence, the settler group of Americo-Liberians became a dominant political and economic force in Liberia at the expense of the various indigenous groups. Over time, political tensions developed between the Americo-Liberians and the indigenous groups in Liberia. Most of these tensions evolved out of the political and economic subjugations of the indigenous groups.

By 1980 the Americo-Liberian led administration of President Tolbert was overthrown through a military led coup by Sargent Samuel Doe.[2] The military came to power with the promise to address corruption by the political and economic elites that were mostly Americo-Liberians. However, in response to the violation of human rights and brutality by the Doe administration, Charles Taylor, an Americo-Liberian, led an insurgency with the support of his revolutionary group—the National Patriotic Front of Liberia (NPFL) to topple the Doe government by 1990. The Taylor administration did not radically depart from some of the brutality and human rights violations that accompanied the former regime. As a result, the country was thrown into a brutal 14 years' war that ended after peace negotiations in August 2003.[3] The Liberian civil war had an adverse impact on the political economy of the country particularly the agriculture sector which had been the mainstay of the economy. The Liberian civil war affected the economy and its Gross Domestic Product (GDP) growth, with negative growth rates recorded between 51.0 percent and 106.3 percent.[4]

After the civil war, and the development of several agricultural rehabilitation programs such as the Agriculture Production and Productivity Enhancement Project, Liberia was ranked as the thirteenth lowest country in terms of human development by the United Nations Development Program (UNDP). Sixty percent of Liberians still face poverty and 40% are vulnerable to food insecurity.[5] Therefore, an examination of the nature of food insecurity in Liberia will provide an understanding of the breadth and depth of the development challenges that has ensued in Liberia's agricultural sector thus paving the way for an alternative policy direction.

The next section provides a review of the literature followed by a conceptual framework. The conceptual framework provides the context through which an alternative approach for sustainable agricultural development could be advanced in the case of Liberia.

The emerging literature on food security in Liberia has suggested that food security is a major impediment for attaining sustainable agricultural development. According to Johnson, "Liberia is food insecure . . . and at least four in every 10 Liberians are unable to access the adequate amount of food to meet their nutritional requirements."[6]

The conditions of the post war environment between 2003 and 2013 also increased food insecurity in Liberia as in other African countries that were mired by conflict such as the Democratic Republic of Congo (DRC). These countries were further impaired by surging food prices and declining household income. Consequently, these conditions quickened the inability of these communities to attain food security. Therefore, civil conflicts affect the food security in developing countries such as Liberia and DRC in a significant way.[7]

The adverse political economy environment of Liberia draws one attention to the chronic food insecurity in Liberia. Along these lines, in 2017 an assessment of chronic food insecurity in Liberia facilitated by the United States Agency for International Development (USAID) shows that 32 percent of Liberia's 4.2 million people were classified as moderate or severely Chronic Food Insecure (CFI).[8] CFI was highest in the Southeastern regions, Grand Gedeh, Rivercess, Sinoe, Grand Kru, Maryland, and River Gee, where it ranged between 40 and 45 percent; this compares to other rural areas of Liberia has been 30 to 35 percent.[9]

The agriculture sector provides sustenance for 70 percent of Liberia's population that are engaged in the farming of rubber, rice, oil palm, and cocoa. However, low agricultural productivity has contributed to Liberia importing more than 80 percent of its staple foods, thus exposing the country to the global market price volatility.[10] It is projected that Liberia spends about $20 million on food imports every year, which is about 15 percent of national Gross Domestic Product (GDP) and loses about $5 million every year to post harvest wastage.[11]

Liberia is also a country that is dependent on food imports which suggests that Liberia is challenged by food security. Therefore, to address this development in-balance alternative frameworks must be explored. One such framework prescribed by an agriculturally based organization for Liberia, Africa Rice, is the use of modern technologies that is not labor intensive.[12] Similarly, Lovendall suggested that mechanized farming has its strengths regarding agricultural development in Liberia. However, he recognized the cost related weaknesses for rural farmers.[13] That is, the capital-intensive nature of mechanized farming is not likely to be plausible for Liberian farmers who are, for the most part, smallholders.

However, Djebou, Price, Kibriya, and Ahn found in their comparative study of agricultural assets and food security of rural households in Ghana, Senegal, and Liberia that even when modern technologies are accounted for as inputs, the usage of technologies such as tractors were not statistically significant in the case of Liberia. The study found that 54 percent of households in Ghana were food secured; 37 percent and 12 percent in Senegal and Liberia respectively were food secured. Thus, it was suggested that there was a correlation between income and food security status of households.[14]

In contrast to the use of mechanized or commercial farming in Liberia, this book suggests that an indigenous agricultural approach using *Traditional Food Regimes* is sustainable and less capital intensive. At the same time, a *Traditional Food Regime* would abate the dependency on imported food and enable sustainable yields through local production. Accordingly, Thomasson, suggests that post-war Liberia is in a better position to face the challenges of development-agriculture and providing health care with the adoption of Indigenous Knowledge (IK). He further propounded that IK systems can contribute to recovery, and maintain and enhance the lives of rural Liberians. For instance, the use of traditional seed and traditional metallurgy can be pivotal in rebuilding the agricultural sector.[15]

POLITICAL ECONOMY OF FOOD SECURITY IN LIBERIA

Agriculture is a major contributor to Liberia's economy and a primary source of livelihood and employment to about 70 percent of the population.[16] However, 20 years after the civil war, Liberia is ranked as one of the lowest countries in terms of human development. Sixty percent of Liberians face poverty and 40 percent are vulnerable to food insecurity. It is noteworthy that the country's economy rebounded strongly after the 2008–2009 global economic crisis and grew at about 8.1 percent because of foreign direct investment (FDI) inflows and increased production in iron ore.[17] But in 2014, Liberia experienced an economic downturn because of several factors that are not limited to mal-administration and other forms of public corruption. For instance, the outbreak of the Ebola Virus Disease (EVD) has been a significant impediment for economic growth as illustrated in Table 4.1.

Table 4.1 shows the economic impact of EDV on food security in Liberia, Guinea, and Sierra Leone. It is important to note in the case of Liberia that the Gross National Product declined close to 4 percent and the need to import cereal surged because of an 8 percent decline in the production of the same commodity. Along the same lines, 63 percent of Liberians became food insecure because of EDV and the share of the rural food insecure people rose to about 76 percent because of EDV.[18]

Thus, food insecurity in Liberia is profound with about every fifth household considered food insecure. The effect is far reaching, particularly among rural communities. To underscore the severity of food insecurity in Liberia this study will employ the food insecurity description in Table 4.2 for assessment. Table 4.2 is employed to classify the extent to which Chronic Food Insecurity (CFI) is prevalent among the various counties. This assessment is representative of the national CFI crises and the concomitant human development challenges that Liberia has continued to confront in the post-war period.

Table 4.3 shows that 32 percent of Liberia's 4.2 million people were classified as moderate or severe CFI. The estimated CFI prevalence of moderate and severe CFI was profound in Southeastern regions of Grand Gedeh,

Table 4.1. The Economic Impact of Ebola

Economic Impact of Ebola	Liberia	Sierra Leone	Guinea
Estimated GNP loss by Ebola (mil. USD)	180	920	540
Estimated reduction of GNP growth rate by Ebola (with remaining growth rate for 2015)	3.8% (3%)	6.9% (2%)	4.1% (0.2%)
Reduction of cereal production 2014 in relation to 2013	8% (From 323,00 t)	5-8% (From 2.8 mil t)	3-8.5% (From 3.04 mil t)
Need to import additional cereal because of Ebola	65,000 t	55,000 t	44,000 t
Additional food insecure people because of Ebola (March 2015)	290,000 (63% increase)	280,000 (62% increase)	470,000 (48% increase)
Share of rural food insecure people because of Ebola	76%	76%	90%
National self-sufficiency rate in food	20%	85%	85%
Cereal import requirements 2015	445,000 (24% more)	300, 000	440, 000
Need for food assistance from out-side 2015 (in tonnage of cereals)	90,000	55,000	44,000
Number of documented Ebola cases (April 2105)	10,042	12,201	3,548
Number of Ebola deaths (April 2015)	4,486	3,857	2,346

Source: Buntzel, R. (February 2015). Impact of Ebola on Food Security in West Africa. Rural 21-International Journal for Rural Development, p.43. Retrieved on March 18, 2019, from https://www.rural21.com/english/search/detail/article/the-impact-of-ebola-on-food-security-in-west-africa.html.

Rivercess, Sinoe, Grand Kru, Maryland and River Gee. The range of moderate to severe CFI is between 40 to 45 percent in the foregoing areas when compared to a range of 30 to 35 percent in other rural areas. The classification shows that a prevalence of moderate and severe CFI was lowest in greater Monrovia.[19]

The prevalence of CFI in rural communities is attributive to income inequalities in these communities when compared to urban communities such as Monrovia and Montserrado. This assumption is supported by Djebou, Price, Kibriya, and Ahn, in their comparative analysis of agricultural assets between Ghana, Senegal and Liberia where they suggested that 326 households surveyed in each of these counties showed that in Ghana, income distribution was estimated at 1735 United States Dollars (USD); 1344 USD for Senegal and 926 USD for Liberia.[20] Given the challenges of CFI in Liberia, the next section suggests that IK such as *Traditional Management Regimes* are alternative development options that should be considered to address CFI.

Table 4.2. Liberia-IPC Chronic Food Insecurity Level Descriptions

Level of Chronic Food Insecurity	Descriptions
Level1–No CFI	In a common year, households (HH) are continuously able to access and consume a diet of acceptable quantity and quality for an active and healthy life. HH livelihoods are sustainable and resilient to shocks. HHs are not likely to have stunted children.
Level 2—Mild CFI	In a common year, HHs can access a diet of adequate quantity, but do not always consume a diet of adequate quality. HH livelihoods are borderline sustainable, though resilience to shocks is limited. HHs are not likely to have moderately or severely stunted children.
Level 3—Moderate CFI	In a common year, HHs have ongoing mild deficits in food quantity and/or seasonal food quantity deficits for 2 to 4 months of the year and consistently do not consume a diet of adequate quality. HH livelihoods are marginally sustainable and resilience to shocks is extremely limited. HHs are likely to have moderately stunted children.
Level 4 - Severe CFI	In a common year, HHs have seasonal deficits in quantity of food for more than 4 months of the year and consistently do not consume a diet of adequate quality. HH livelihoods are very marginal and are not resilient. HHs are likely to have severely stunted children.

Source: United States Agency for International Development, Famine Early Warning Systems Network (FEWS NET) Assessment of Chronic Food Insecurity in Liberia, June 2017. Retrieved from https://reliefweb.int/report/liberia/assessment-chronic-food-insecurity-liberia-june-2017.

TRADITIONAL FOOD MANAGEMENT REGIMES IN LIBERIA

Given the challenge of food security in sub-Saharan Africa, and Liberia in this case, it is instructive that policy makers and development agencies should continue to embrace and encourage agro-diversity and traditional farming practices. The use of indigenous methods for managing the land, water, and biota for crop and livestock production is not only a practical approach for addressing food security, but also preferable since it is not capital intensive, and therefore, sustainable.

Traditional food management regimes have been successfully adopted in other developing regions such as south-west Asia. For example, Bangladesh has developed an array of sophisticated farm practices to sustain their agricultural needs including the use of dried Neem leaves to protect stored grains from insect infestation.[21]

Table 4.3. Classification of Chronic Food Insecurity in Liberia

Regions	Counties	Pop	Level 1	%	Level 2	%	Level 3	%	Level 4	%	%≥ L2	%≥ L3
North Central	Bong	402,624	121,000	30	141,000	35	101,000	25	40,000	10	70	35
	Lofa	334,267	100,000	30	117,000	35	100,000	30	17,00	5	70	35
	Nimba	557,820	167,000	30	195,00	35	139,000	25	56,00	10	70	35
Northwestern	Bomi	101,560	30,000	30	36,000	35	25,000	25	10,000	10	70	35
	Gbarpolu	100,677	40,000	40	30,000	30	25,000	25	5,000	5	60	30
	Grand Cape	153,423	38,000	25	69,000	45	38,000	25	8,000	5	75	30
South Central	Grand Bassa	267,658	120,000	45	54,000	20	67,000	25	27,000	10	55	35
	Margibi	253,448	89,000	35	89,000	35	63,000	25	13,000	5	65	30
	Monrovia	1,169,602	409,000	35	468,000	45	175,000	15	58,000	5	65	20
	Montesarado		54,000	30	72,000	40	36,000	20	18,000	10	65	30
Southeastern A	Grand Gedeh	147,914	44,000	30	52,000	35	37,000	25	15,000	10	70	35
	Rivercess	86,335	26,000	30	22,000	25	26,000	30	13,000	15	70	45
	Sinoe	123,620	49,000	40	19,000	15	37,000	30	19,000	15	70	45
Southeastern B	Grand Kru	69,920	21,000	30	21,000	30	17,000	25	10,000	15	70	40
	Maryland	164,123	41,000	25	57,000	35	41,000	25	25,000	15	75	40
	River Gee	80,637	28,000	35	20,000	25	20,000	25	12,000	15	65	40
Grand Total		4,194,00	1,377,000	34	1,434,00	35	947,000	23	374,000	9	68	32

Source: United States Agency for International Development Famine Early Warning Systems Network (FEWS NET) Assessment of Chronic Food Insecurity in Liberia, June 2017. Retrieved from https://reliefweb.int/report/liberia/assessment-chronic-food-insecurity-liberia-june-2017.

The utility of the traditional food management regimes for addressing CFI in Liberia was also advanced by Thomasson, when he suggested that the key to reconstructing post-war Liberia is in rebuilding the country's traditional agriculture sector. He suggested that the problem of CFI is further accentuated by nature of a land tenure system implemented by the Liberian elite in collaboration with western capitalist interests:

> In the 1920s, the United States and Firestone Rubber coerced and enticed the Liberian elite into leasing land for the huge Harbel rubber-plantation proclaimed as the world's largest. Before this land was commandeered, the rural sector in Liberia had been self-sufficient in rice production. Later, the ruling elite diverted more land to meet personal and international lenders' demands for an export economy and cash crop.[22]

INTERVIEW WITH SMALL FARM HOLDER FROM LIBERIA

To further advance the importance and the continuous relevance of the traditional food management regimes and the use of Indigenous Knowledge in agriculture in Africa, I interviewed a small farm holder from Liberia, Mr. Z. S. is a 69-year-old farmer with three children.[23]

The interview with Mr. Z. S. was facilitated at Montserrado County in Monrovia at Mamba point on May 24, 2018.[24] The interview model used was an Interpretative Phenomenology Approach (IPA). The IPA is a qualitative research approach that is "committed to the examination of the process through which people make sense of their major life experiences. IPA is concerned with exploring experience in its own terms.[25]

Mr. Z. S. has been a farmer all his life and has about a fifth-grade education.[26] He grows a varieties of food crops such as rice, cassava, pineapple, plantain, eddoes, and pumpkin on a sixteen (16) acre community land using IK. Table 4.4 provides a description of *Traditional Food Management Regimes* used by Mr. Z. S.

Mr. Z. S. gave an account of how IK is used for rice storage after harvest. Firstly, he gave an account of the IK model used for growing food crops such as rice. 2 tin of rice seed is spread on 1 acre of land. Since Mr. Z. S. is involved in mixed farming on 16 acres of land, 20 rice tins are used on 10 acres of land for rice farming and about 6 acres of land is used to plant eddoes, peppers, plantain, and pumpkins.

After the rice is harvested, the rice is stored in a hut kitchen and covered with Arista, sand, and rocks. The harvested rice is grilled under intense heat and dried for the next farming year, and sometimes beyond the farming

Table 4.4. Traditional Food Management Regimes: The Case of Liberia

Practices/Regimes	Major Food Development Advantages
Rice Storage: harvested rice is kept in the grilling storage arista made from rock and sand. Fire is kept under the arista to keep rice dry for the next season. Sometimes the dried rice is kept beyond the next season	The storage system provides preservation and sustainability even with limited technologies. From the 16 acres of farmland, mixed farming methods are used. Whereby 10 acres is used to plant rice and 6 acres is used to plant vegetables and other food crops. The mixed farming helps sustain soil nutrients which enhances farm harvests.
Yam and eddo's storage: cover with leaves and dirt	Protect from pest and bugs
Maize storage and preservation: Maize is hung in the farm hut-burnt with fire to dry for the next farming season	Protect from pest and bugs.

Source: Interview with Mr. Z. S. May 24, 2018, 5:30pm Monrovia-Liberia Interpreter. Mr. Thomas Tweh.

year. Thereafter the rice is dried, beaten and cleaned in the farm Moffat and approximately 2 tin (1 acres) of rice is sold in the local market. Quite often the local production such as rice are sold to purchase other items such as salt and other items not produced locally.

Mr. Z. S. spoke of the challenges he has encountered as a local farmer. He was concerned that local farmers are given little support by the government. Although he is engaged in mixed farming, he has found it challenging to engage in mixed farming to support his family and children's education. As a result, he has become dependent on non-farming income from fishing and hunting to support his family. "I catch fish or set trap to catch ground hog to take care of family." However, he noted that his reliance on planting two crops made it financially viable to support his family. He asserts "two crops are planted to support the children education."

The traditional food management regimes used by Mr. Z. S. as illustrated in Table 4.4 are management regimes that are also used by the rice farming community in Gbarpolu County in Liberia over several generations. These regimes have proven viable for community wellness and the sustainability of food crops among the farming communities. In this regard, Mr. Z. S. discussed how farming has been integral to the social and economic conditions of his community.

FOOD SECURITY IN THE DEMOCRATIC
REPUBLIC OF CONGO (DRC)

The Democratic Republic of Congo (DRC) is the largest and one of the least developed countries in sub-Sahara Africa that has been mired by civil unrest for over twenty-five years. In addition, the country has also faced several epidemic episodes of Ebola.[27] The advent of the civil war has contributed acutely to poverty in DRC—especially in the rural areas. In 2018, it was reported that 72 percent of the population, particularly in the Northwest and the Kasai regions, are living in extreme poverty on about less than $1.90 per day.[28]

Despite the perennial political conflicts in the DRC, the country is still recovering from these conflicts that began in the 1990s. However, the county recently went through political transition after several postponements of the presidential elections, Felix Antoine Tshisekedi Tshilombo, the son of Etienne Tshisekedi the country's former opposition leader won the election in 2108 and took over from Joseph Kabila who had governed for 18 years.[29]

POLITICAL ECONOMY OF DRC

Democratic Republic of the Congo (DRC) is ranked 179th of 189 countries on the 2019 Human Development Index and possesses the second largest hunger crisis in the world after Yemen. The country has also faced some economic challenges that are related to the global fiscal crisis of 2009–2011 which has exacerbated human security challenges in the country. For instance, in the Eastern region, access to education, healthcare, employment and other basic human needs had almost become elusive.[30]

However, hunger and conflict fuel one another, with armed conflict and widespread displacement prevailing for the past twenty-five years. The number of severely food-insecure people in DRC is 15.6 million. An estimated 3.4 million children are acutely malnourished. Thus, access to food is a major challenge for a significant part of the DRC population.[31] According to the United States Agency for International Development (USAID), armed conflict and floods have continued to contribute to food security challenges in many parts of central and eastern DRC in 2019 and 2020. These factors contributed to below average harvests through central and eastern DRC and led to food shortages in areas such as Huri, North Kivu and South Kivu provinces.[32] Based on the acute food insecurity classification for DRC: Phase 1: minimal, Phase 2: stressed, Phase 3: crisis, Phase 4: emergency and Phase 5: famine; between July and December 20, apart from the 15.6 million people in phase 3, 11.7 million people were also in phase 3 crisis mode and 3.9 million were in the phase 4: emergency mode. 13.6 million people are projected to be in severe acute food insecurity out of which 3.6 million people are expected to be in phase 4-emergency.[33]

The acute food insecurity in the DCR is also advanced by the outbreaks of periodic episodes of the Ebola Virus Disease (EVD). DRC had about ten EVD outbreaks between September–October 1976 and August 2018. This is the third outbreak in two (2017–2018) years and the second in 2018.[34] Figure 4.1 provides geographical information on the outbreak of Ebola in 2019.

EVD in the DRC has claimed thousands of lives in North Kivu and Ituri provinces. The EVD outbreak in 2019 and 2020 is the worst outbreak in the country's history and the second largest and deadliest EVD outbreak globally.[35]

Invariably, the outbreak of EVD has contributed to food insecurity, and an attendant refugee crisis. DRC's 80 million hectares of arable land has the potential to feed 2 billion people. However, only 10 percent of its arable land is cultivated. Although subsistence farming is prevalent in DRC, small holders produce 42 percent of the food they consume. This means that with the advent of EVD these small holders are unable to meet the demand for

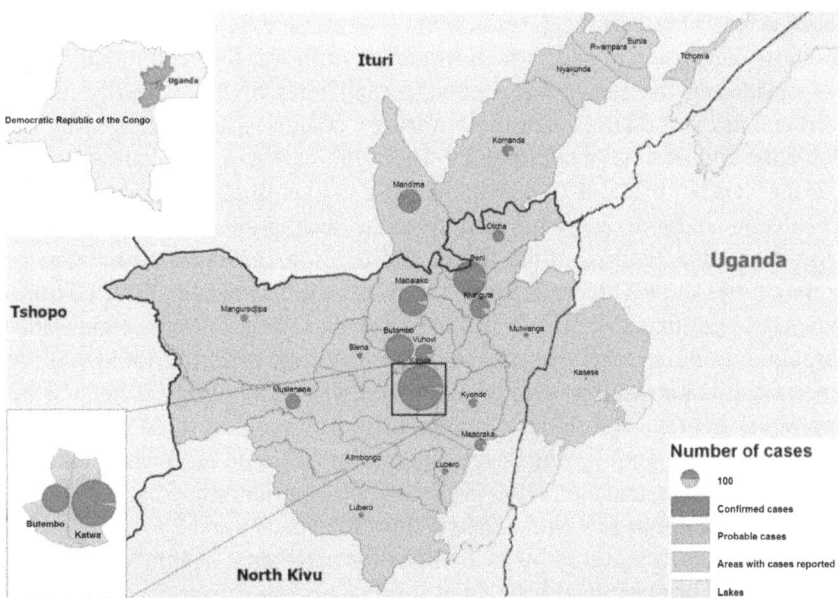

Figure 4.1. Distribution of Ebola in the DRC in 2019. *Source:* European Center for Disease Prevention and Control (February 15, 2021). "Outbreak of Ebola Virus disease in North Kivu Democratic Republic of the Congo-2021." Accessed from https://www.ecdc.europa.eu/en/news-events/outbreak-ebola-virus-disease-north-kivu-democratic-republic-congo-2021. Material under CC BY 4.0 license.

food in a war-torn environment.[36] At the same time, increasing conflict among various ethnic groups have further propounded the food security problems. For instance, about 900,000 Congolese nationals are refugees in neighboring countries while DRC, already struggling with internal conflict, is also the host of more than a half-million people, notably refugees from Burundi, Central African Republic, and South Sudan.[37]

The food security problems in DRC have further created social and economic challenges that are unprecedented because of the direct link between civil conflict and hunger. As a result, DRC has witnessed an unimaginable deficiency in infrastructure. Educational, healthcare and transportation infrastructures have all been depleted by war.[38] Concomitantly, the institutional impact of conflict has immensely contributed to food insecurity in most regions in the DRC. Along these lines, Vlaseenroot and Raeymaekers assert that:

> Chronic violence and conflict tend to reshape existing mechanisms of food production and food access, distort the available assets and choices of households, and force households into changing their livelihood systems.[39]

However, it should be noted that in some instances armed combatants and rebel actors also use local agricultural resources for sustenance and thus promote cooptation to access food resources from war torn communities.[40]

Considering the social and economic challenges of food security in war torn countries, the DRC, like most war-torn countries, is challenged by the depletion and decline in biodiversity. The significant harm to biodiversity for instance has led to about 33 percent increase in overall rate of deforestation.[41] The decline in biodiversity has also led to the decimation of the population of large mammals, the loss of the forests and farming lands that the indigenous communities in DRC have depended on over time.[42] However, these communities have continued to sustain wellness and the vitality of their communities through traditional food management regimes as illustrated in Table 4.5. For instance, it is known that wild edible plant (WEP) knowledge is integral for the wellness of several African communities and many of these plants are a genetic resource pool for the development of novel food products.[43] Thus, in Turumbu, Mbole, and Bali DRC in the Tshopo Districts study by Termote et. al. shows that about 166 wild edible plants (165 species and 2 varieties) were documented as being used by 71 families for nutritional health.[44] The use of these WEPs for nutritional health and survival underscores the importance of indigenous knowledge in wellness among indigenous communities in DRC and other regions as suggested in this book.

The food regimes management adopted in war torn countries such as the DRC and Libera are critical for sustainability and wellness. In the case

Table 4.5. Traditional Food Regimes in the Democratic Republic of Congo

Food Crops	Management Regimes
Cassava	Dried and processed into flour or granular product[a]
Bush meat[b]	Smoked or Dried
Sugar Cane	Consumed directly or juiced[c]

Sources:

[a] Burns, A., Gleadow, R., et. al. (2010). Cassava: The Drought, War and Famine Crop in a Changing War. Sustainability, 2, p. 3576.

[b] Currie, J.T. and Meeuwig, J. (2003). Bushmeat and food security in the Congo Basin: Linkages between wildlife and the people's future, p.71.

[c] World Data Atlas Democratic Republic of Congo, Agriculture Production Quantity (Tons). Retrieved from: https://knoema.com/atlas/Democratic-Republic-of-the-Congo/topics/Agriculture/Crops-Production -Quantity-tonnes/Sugar-cane-production.

of DRC, the production of Cassava which is considered as a war crop is important for sustaining the food security of most indigenous communities. They are processed into flour and/or granular products for sustaining daily nutrition.[45] Therefore, in the times of civil conflicts and wars, indigenous food crops are important to meet the urgent needs of various indigenous communities.

SUMMARY

Overall, food insecurity has remained one of the most profound development challenges facing Liberia and DRC. The social and economic implications of food security is exacerbated by social crises such as EVD and continued income inequality among rural small holders. Therefore, policy makers and development agencies must continue to provide social and economic safety nets such as nutritional programs, credit facilities, and universal free education for farming communities to better address the adverse effects of high food insecurity.

This study also suggests that the prevailing view by development agencies that accelerated agricultural development programs are best suited for addressing food insecurity in developing economies such as Liberia and the DRC has not yielded sustainable results because they are exogenous to the development realities of indigenous communities. Instead, it was demonstrated that Traditional Food Management Regimes are far more sustainable because it is congruent with the development realties of rural communities. In addition, the national governments of Liberia and DRC must take steps to continue to support and address some of the underlying public health challenges in their communities through conscious efforts to educate rural and urban communities. In addition, collaboration between local and international communities has also proven to be vital in suppressing and eradicating the increasing threat of EVD and food insecurity. For instance, the World Health Organization partnership with local communities in West Africa, (Liberia, Sierra Leone, and Guinea) has been pivotal in providing messaging and support for areas of intense transmission of EVD in Liberia and the DRC.[46] The partnerships to address development crises such as food insecurity and related challenges such as EVD must be implemented with consideration that such partnerships would not promote the alienation and the stigmatization of local communities that are adversely affected by Ebola and Food Insecurity.[47] The need for such partnership is important given the social and economic implications of Food Insecurity in both DRC and Liberia. For instance, 13.6 million people in DRC were expected to face food crisis (IPC3) or worse levels of acute food insecurity and required emergency food assistance. Moreover, the conflict environment in both Liberia and DRC not only made food insecurity prevalent, but it was also accompanied with social problems such as internal displacements (IDPs), political violence, and rape as an instrument of war.[48]

In this regard, Oritsejafor suggests that use of the *Social Learning Theory (SLT)*-framework as developed by Bangura provides a context in which development programs that are germane to local realities can be implemented to address health crisis such as Ebola and other attendant challenges such as food insecurity.[49] Oritsejafor and Jones posit that the use of SLT can reduce risk taking health behavior among community members who can learn appropriate ones from observing others. Therefore, safe health practices can be learnt visually from observing community members that are respected health care providers and practitioners.[50] Along these lines, the amalgamation of indigenous knowledge, if used appropriately with sustainable technologies as suggested by Iyam could address food security in developing communities.[51]

The challenges of social and political crisis such as the civil war in Liberia and the Democratic Republic of Congo (DRC) portends that being mired by civil conflicts and simultaneously health crises such as the EBOLA are likely to exacerbate severe food insecurity challenges. As a result, these countries had to revert to coping mechanisms that were passed on over several generations. Thus, the interview of farmer Z. S. from Gbaporlu illustrates the coping mechanism of rural communities to produce food using various traditional food management regimes. These regimes have remained the most sustainable national food management system even in the periods of national crisis such as civil war and health crises such as EBOLA.

The next chapter will examine the use of Indigenous Knowledge (IK) as an alternative approach for Agricultural Development in sub-Saharan Africa.

NOTES

1. Food and Agriculture Organization of the United Nations. Peace and Food Security: Investing in resilience to sustain rural livelihood and amid conflict. Retrieved on March 11, 2020, from http://www.fao.org/resilience/resources/resources-detail/en/c /405395/.

2. Liberia Ministry of Agriculture (2017). Comprehensive Assessment of Agriculture Sector: The Synthesis Report. Vol. 1: 8

3. Ibid.

4. Cassell, D.L., Jr. (2013). Agricultural Policy in Liberia: A vision for the future. Liberian Studies Journal, Vol. 38(1): 72.

5. Liberia Ministry of Agriculture (November 14, 2015). World Food Day. Theme: Social Protection and Agriculture: Breaking the Cycle of Rural Poverty. Retrieved March 17, 2019, from http://moa.gov.lr/doc/MOA%20_%20WFD%20SPECIAL %20EDITION.pdf.

6. Johnson, W. S., Jr. (2010). Post-conflict food security and peace building. *Liberian Studies Journal,* Vol. 35 (2): 28–54.

7. Ibid., pp. 30–33.

8. United States Agency for International Development (2017). Assessment of Chronic Food Insecurity in Liberia. Retrieved March 16, 2018, from https://reliefweb .int/sites/reliefweb.int/files/resources/Liberia%20Chronic%20Food%20Insecurity %20Report.pdf.

9. Ibid.

10. Liberia Ministry of Agriculture (November 14, 2015). World Food Day. Theme: Social Protection and Agriculture: Breaking the Cycle of Rural Poverty. Retrieved March 17, 2019, from http://moa.gov.lr/doc/MOA%20_%20WFD%20SPECIAL %20EDITION.pdf.

11. Worzie, P.T. (2016). Reducing rice importation in Liberia. *NEPAD Transforming Africa-Policy Brief,* 1–2.

12. Tamba, G.T. (2018). New farm technologies will make Liberia food-secure. *Liberian Observer.* Retrieved March 17, 2019, from https://www.liberianobserver .com/news/new-farming-technologies-will-make-liberia-food-secure/.

13. Lovendall, T. (2007). Mechanization and Post-Harvest Study. (ed) Institutional Capacities and Renewal Strategies for Rural Development in Liberia. *International Food Policy and Research institute (IFPRI)* Consultancy White Paper.

14. Djebou, Dagbegnon C.S., Price, E., Kibriya, S. and Ahn, J. (2017). Comparative Analysis of Agricultural Assets, Incomes, and food Security of Rural Households in Ghana, Senegal, and Liberia. *Agriculture* Vol. 7(38): 1–13. Doi:10.3390/ agriculture7050038.

15. Thomasson, G.L. (1991). Liberia's seeds of knowledge. *Cultural Survival Quarterly Magazine.* Retrieved March 15, 2019, from https://www.liberianobserver .com/news/new-farming-technologies-will-make-liberia-food-secure/.

16. Liberia Ministry of Agriculture (November 14, 2015). World Food Day. Theme: Social Protection and Agriculture: Breaking the Cycle of Rural Poverty. Retrieved

March 17, 2019, from http://moa.gov.lr/doc/MOA%20_%20WFD%20SPECIAL %20EDITION.pdf.

17. United States Agency for International Development (2017). Assessment of Chronic Food Insecurity in Liberia. Retrieved March 16, 2018, from https://reliefweb .int/sites/reliefweb.int/files/resources/Liberia%20Chronic%20Food%20Insecurity %20Report.pdf.

18. Buntze, I.R. (February 2015). Impact of Ebola on Food Security in West Africa. Rural 21-International Journal of for Rural Development, p.43. Retrieved on March 18, 2019, from https://info.brot-fuer-die-welt.de/sites/default/files/blog-downloads/ rural2015_ebola_impact.pdf.

19. United States Agency for International Development (2017). Assessment of Chronic Food Insecurity in Liberia. Retrieved March 16, 2018, from https://reliefweb .int/sites/reliefweb.int/files/resources/Liberia%20Chronic%20Food%20Insecurity %20Report.pdf.

20. Djebou, Dagbegnon C.S., Price, E., Kibriya, S. and Ahn, J. (2017). Comparative Analysis of Agricultural Assets, Incomes, and food Security of Rural Households in Ghana, Senegal, and Liberia. *Agriculture* Vol. 7(38): 1–13. Doi:10.3390/ agriculture7050038.

21. Qudus, M. Stillitoe P., ed. (2000). *Use of Indigenous Knowledge in the Sustainable Development of Bangladesh Farm Forestry in Indigenous Knowledge Development in Bangladesh: Present and Future*. London: Intermediate Technology Publications.

22. Thomasson, G.L. (1991). Liberia's Seeds of Knowledge. Cultural Survival Quarterly Magazine. Retrieved March 15, 2019, from https://www.liberianobserver .com/news/new-farming-technologies-will-make-liberia-food-secure/.

23. Interview with Mr. Z.S. (May 24, 2018: 530pm). Traditional Food Management Regimes. Interpreter. Mr. Thomas Tweh. Monrovia, Liberia.

24. Ibid.

25. Pietkrewicz, I. and Smith J.A. (2012). A practical guide to using interpretative phenomenological analysis in qualitative research. *Psychology Journal*, 182 (2): 361.

26. Interview with Mr. Z. S., (May 24, 2018: 5:30pm). Traditional Food Management Regimes. Interpreter. Mr. Thomas Tweh. Monrovia, Liberia.

27. World Food Program: The Democratic Republic of Congo. https://www.wfp .org/countries/democratic-republic-congo.

28. The World Bank in DRC, p. 1 Accessed on February 2, 2021, from https://www .worldbank.org/en/country/drc/overview.

29. Ibid.

30. Abegunrin, Olayiwola (2014). Africa in the New World Order: Peace and Security Challenges in the Twenty-First Century. Lanham: Lexington Books, pp. 101–102.

31. Ibid.

32. https://www.usaid.gov/democratic-republic-congo/food-assistance.

33. http://www.ipcinfo.org/ipc-country-analysis/details-map/en/c/1152131/.

34. https://www.wfp.org/countries/democratic-republic-congo.

35. Ibid.

36. Ibid.

37. Ibid.

38. Lecoutere, E., Vlassenroot, K. and Raeymaekers, T. (2009). Conflict, Institutional changes, and food insecurity in eastern D. R. Congo. *Africa Focus,* Vol. 22(2): 42.

39. Ibid., pp. 43–44.

40. Koren, Ore and Begozzi, Benjamin E. (2017). Living of the land: The connection between cropland, food security and violence against civilians. *Journal of Peace Research*, Vol. 45(3): 351–352.

41. Milburn, Richard (2014). The roots to peace in the Democratic Republic of Congo: conservation as a platform for green development. *Royal Institute of International Affairs*, Vol. 90(40): 874.

42. Ibid., p. 872.

43. Termote, Celine, Van Damme, Patrick and Djailo, Benoit Dheda'a (2011). Eating from the wild: Turumbu, Mbole, and Bali traditional knowledge on no-cultivated edible plants, District Tshopo, DRC Congo. *Genetic Resource Crop*, Vol. Vol 58: 585. DOI 10.1007/s10722-010-9602-4.

44. Ibid.

45. Burns, A., Gleadow, R., et. al. (2010). Cassava: The Drought, War and Famine Crop in a Changing War. *Sustainability*, Vol. 2: 3576.

46. Risk Communication and Community Engagement Preparedness and Readiness Framework: Ebola Response in the Democratic Republic of Congo in North Kivu https://apps.who.int/iris/bitstream/handle/10665/275389/9789241514828-eng .pdf?ua=1

47. Ibid.

48. Food Assistance Fact Sheet—Democratic Republic of The Congo (May 6, 2020). Accessed on February 2, 2021, from https://www.usaid.gov/democratic -republic-congo/food-assistance

49. Oritsejafor, E. and Jones, E. (2004). Folk and Modern Medicine in Africa. *Liberian Studies Journal,* Vol. XXIX (2): 9

50. Ibid.

51. David Uru Iyam, (1995). The Broken Hoe: Cultural Reconfiguration in Biase Southeast Nigeria. Chicago: University of Chicago Press, p. 7–8

Chapter 5

Indigenous Knowledge (IK) and Agro-Eco-systems

THE CASE OF NIGERIA AND GHANA

This chapter will examine the use of indigenous knowledge (IK) for agricultural development in sub-Saharan Africa as an alternative approach that is germane to the development realities of these states. What are the challenges of using IK for development and what are the implications for agricultural development?

The policy initiatives that have been used to address chronic food insecurity in sub-Saharan Africa has typically been predicated by development models that are often exogenous to the development realities of these developing countries. Programs such as the *Green Revolution (GR)* in the 1970s was advanced by development agencies such as the United Nations Food and Agriculture Organization with the idea that sustainable agricultural development could be attained by sub-Saharan African countries with the use of agricultural inputs that will yield rapid and accelerated food production. This position was further supported by the Agro-Technological orientation which suggests that new farming methods that have been discovered in developed economies would invariably lead to high agricultural productivity when transferred to developing economies.[1]

While there are various forms of modern strategies that have been used to address accelerated food production, however, the use of biotechnology and the production of Genetic Modified Crops (GMCs) has been in the forefront of strategies that have been suggested to accelerate food production.[2] Biotechnology, including the GMCs, are the manipulations of biological organisms to make products that are supposed to benefit human beings. Biotechnology is used in diverse areas such as food production, waste disposal, mining, and pharmaceuticals. The first achievement in biotechnology occurred in food production around 500 BC when diverse strains of plants and animals were hybridized (crossed) to produce greater genetic variety.[3]

The benefits of biotechnology for agricultural development in Africa was propagated by scholars such as Keese, Omitogun and Sonaiya, when they argued that molecular biotechnology is one approach that could vastly address food security challenges in Africa if development measures that are related to extensive bio-safety measures and strong indigenous bio-technology community are established.[4] However, these recommendations do not go far enough in addressing the social, economic and environmental implications for adopting biotechnology. For instance, rice farmers in Africa and Asia that moved from growing their traditional varieties, and instead, adopted one or two varieties lost most of their crops within three to five years.[5] Similarly, in Bangladesh, after the adoption of genetic modified rice seeds (Golden Rice), upon the recommendation of the World Bank and the International Rice Institute, the country faced nutrient deficiency because high-yielding crop varieties like *Golden Rice* tend to destroy crop diversity.[6]

However, recent development strategies, such as the position provided by the 2001 United Nations Human Development (UNDP) Report, provide the context for further discussion regarding the question on whether technological inputs such as GMCs could address food security problems in Africa. The report recognized disparities in the generation and diffusion of technologies between developed and developing economies in the area of agriculture.[7] The UNDP report provides concerns in regard to the bio-safety on the use biotechnology for agricultural development in developing economies.[8] Thus, against the background of recent outbreak of *mad cow disease* in Europe and North America, and the deepening food crisis in Africa, there are growing concerns on how the use of modern technological inputs such as fertilizers and GMCs may further complicate global food security. This fear is heightened by the fact that extraordinarily little is known about GMCs and how their potential negative consequences could lead to far reaching domino outcomes that will affect food production.[9]

Harwood suggests that the evidence that yields, food production food calories per capita, and declining levels of malnutrition would be addressed by the promotion of Green Revolution (GR) for agricultural development in developing economies is not accurate. Instead, what has been observed as in the case of India is that Green Revolution tends to boost yields and profitability in small numbers of targeted areas.[10] Similarly, Pielke posits that GR is a political myth of "averted famine." The suggestions that the use of modern technological input in agricultural development will lead to increase yields was not an achievable option. Instead, developing economies have had to adjust to growing global population that has contributed to famine and challenges to the global food supply.[11]

Albeit the 2001 Human Development Report provided cautionary words regarding the use of GMCs in developing countries, especially, the environmental risks it poses. However, it does not seem to go far enough in addressing the social and economic implications of such inputs for farmers in developing economies. Some of the problems associated with GMCs and other modern technologies are reduction of crop diversity, degradation of the ecosystem through accidental release of pest resistant organisms into the environment, lack of proper screening for toxins and allergens that could be introduced into diets and increasing farmers dependence on transnational agri-business.[12]

The critical challenge for policy makers and agriculturalists is to examine the extent to which modern technologies such as biotechnology can ameliorate the problems of food security in sub-Saharan Africa and other developing areas. Recent studies have suggested that large farms that are beneficiaries of biotechnology tend to experience the negative impact of biotechnology in their environment. Accordingly, Rickard and Gorelick suggest that large holders systematically erode their own foundation because of the reliance on the utilization of heavy machinery and chemicals which extracts about twenty (20) pounds of topsoil for every pound of grain that is harvested.[13] Furthermore, the consistent use of identical crop strains by large farmers has also contributed to the displacement of several local varieties of crops. Consequently, 75 percent of the world's agricultural diversity has disappeared in the last 100 years.[14]

Given the challenges related to the application of modern technologies as a solution in addressing food security in Africa, the search for an alternative development approach that is sustainable and environmentally friendly has become more profound. For this reason, any attempt to address food security problems in African countries can only be better addressed if the country's resource base is properly maintained.

Therefore, the efficient management of environmentally derived resources is critical to attain the objectives of sustainable agricultural development in Africa. These objectives are as follows:

1. Assessment of the importance and effects of resources on agricultural and rural development.
2. Assessment of the consequences of the misuse of the environment
3. Implementation of policies and strategies that will enhance a proper management of the environment objectives.[15]

The forms of agriculture related environmental degradation most often observed in most sub-Saharan African countries are deforestation and soil erosion. In some instances, deforestation has been caused by the demand for new land for farming, building needs, and timber harvesting. Soil erosion on the other hand is caused by inappropriate farming systems adopted by local farmers, and road construction and land maintenance methods associated with large farming systems. The effect of such environmental degradation has led to the loss of flora, and fauna, and the decline of surface and underground water supply.[16] Therefore, large scale farming that encourages the use of biotechnology and other conventional efficiency analysis tends to disregard the social and environmental costs of large industrial scale farming. It also ignores the human health costs of consuming foods that are contaminated by pesticide hormones and other poisons from farms with topsoil loss, water and air pollution, and the loss of biodiversity.[17]

Therefore, before meaningful agriculture activities can take-off, proper management of the environment and natural resources must be part of the development priorities. In this regard, the use of IK as a development approach has become more profound in the 21st century for sub-Saharan African countries and other developing regions as they attempt to address specific development challenges such as hunger and poverty in these regions. Along these lines, Powell, Thilsted, Ickowitz, Termote, Sunderland and Herforth, suggests that traditional knowledge is integral for maintaining diversity in a complex, socio-ecological agricultural systems as well creating an environment for continued learning and experimentation for gaining new and adaptive plant varieties.[18] Thilsted, et. al. further suggests that traditional values and preferences are likely to help maintain and foster the linkages between diet, nutrition, biodiversity, and sustainability.[19]

INDIGENOUS KNOWLEDGE (IK) AS A FRAMEWORK FOR AGRO-ECO-SYSTEMS

Indigenous knowledge (IK), as suggested in previous chapters is a framework that is referred to as local knowledge, and at times, as traditional knowledge that is passed on from generation to generation. It exists within and develops around the specific environment of people indigenous to a particular geographic area. Nonetheless, IK is dynamic, and compelling to development challenges through local adaptations, experimentation, and innovation under diverse and heterogenous conditions.[20] The next section illustrates the relationship between indigenous knowledge and agro-eco systems in Nigeria and Ghana to provide a better understanding on how IK enhances food security in sub-Saharan Africa and other developing areas. The next section also accentuates the immense contribution of IK to agricultural development initiatives in sub-Saharan Africa.

INDIGENOUS KNOWLEDGE AND AGRO-ECO SYSTEMS IN NIGERIA.

The Nigeria agriculture sector plays an integral role in Nigeria's economic development. The sector contributes 37 percent of the Gross Domestic Product (GDP) and employs about 65 percent of the labor force.[21] Nigeria's agricultural output is driven by mostly small-scale holders. That is, about 90 percent of Nigeria's agriculture output is dependent on small-scale farmers that cultivate on an average of 5 hectares of land.[22] However, Nigeria has continued to encounter the challenges of food security. The country is faced with acute malnutrition, slow progress in abating hunger and emerging socio-economic conditions such as income inequalities; and Nigeria by all recent estimates' accounts for about 14 percent of all annual maternal deaths globally and 13 percent of all global deaths of children under age five.[23] This suggests that there is a linkage between food, nutrition, and infant mortality. Nigeria is reported to rank first in Africa and third globally regarding the prevalence of malnutrition; thirteen million Nigerians out of a population close to 165 million are facing hunger and acute social and economic disparities in both rural and national urban centers.[24] In this vein, it is critical to identify a development approach that can better serve the needs of the Nigeria communities particularly at a time in which Nigeria is also encountering social, economic and political crises. Given the need to address food insecurity and the overall wellness of Nigerians, IK provides a sustainable option for development.

Nigerian farmers for centuries have sustained the national food supply chain using IK.[25] In this regard, this section illustrates how the use of IK should remain at the forefront of food security because they have proven sustainable. An examination of agro-eco systems in Nigeria with a specific focus on indigenous *land use systems*, *soil fertility management practices*, and *pest management practices* reinforces how the use of IK has enhanced food security.

Land Use Systems. Indigenous land use systems in most developing countries such as Nigeria are predicated by indigenous systems of forest gardening—silvi horticulture. Rural land that is used for silvi horticulture cultivation represents about 15–50 percent of the land used. The land is used to cultivate a variety of products such as fruits and vegetables, and non-food products such as firewood, timber and herbal medicines.[26] Similar methods of conservation and biodiversity were used in other developing countries such as Bangladesh in the absence of sufficient natural forests; over 50 percent of timber, 85 percent of fuelwood and 90 percent of bamboo used in Bangladesh emanates from trees and shrubs by people on their farmlands.[27] In Bangladesh, farmers have developed an array of sophisticated farm forestry practices that are used to sustain their agricultural needs. For example, farmers apply soil mulch in bamboo groves in the spring to induce regeneration and vigorous growth of young bamboo shoots.[28]

Soil Fertility Management Practices. Indigenous farmers in Nigeria and other developing countries have employed useful techniques overtime to maintain and improve soil fertility. The knowledge of these farmers has proven pivotal in the quests for sustainable agricultural development. This was the case in a soil survey that was conducted in Kaduna State-Nigeria where indigenous knowledge in soil fertility was amalgamated with modern soil science. It was proven that indigenous classification of soil was integral in grouping soils into classes that could be used for soil management practices.[29] However, the importance of IK in soil fertility management practices are dynamic and common in all parts of Nigeria. In the Southern part of Nigeria, six common practices that were often employed by rural farmers in Ekiti State are: 1. mulching, 2. organic manure application, 3. shifting cultivation, 4. crop rotation, 5. trash burning and 6. fallow.[30]

Pest Management Practices. Pests are any organism that feeds on and damages cultivated plants. These organisms at times attach plant products in the field or in storage and at times during the transportation of harvests. Therefore, pest management practices are important to sustain food security. Pests include insects, fungi, viruses, nematodes, weeds, rodents, and at times birds.[31]

In Nigeria, to increase food production and sustain food security, indigenous farmers have developed the efficient use of various traditional methods in addressing food production:

Cultural Control. This is the use of cultural content in pest management where changes in cultural practices are used for crop production in a way that adverts pest population with the creation of unfavorable conditions.[32]

Water Management. The severity in which foot and root rot diseases of irrigated wheat are reduced by controlled irrigation. Aphid infestation on a variety of crops increases during periods of water stress.[33]

Reducing Vulnerability to Flood in Nigeria

The southeastern and western part of Nigeria, particularly the coastal areas of the Delta States, often face vulnerability to floods in the raining season and during coastal floods which consequently impact the agroecosystem and food security in these communities. As a result, there is a need to examine the nature of the indigenous knowledge and the adaptation mechanisms used by the coastal communities to abate their vulnerabilities to flood.

The entire coastal line of Nigeria, which is about 853 kilometers, is vulnerable to flood from ocean surges and through the network of rivers and creeks. Most of the Nigerian coastal communities are rural except Lagos-Nigeria.[34] However, other communities like those in the Delta region of Nigeria are often challenged by coastal floods. These rural communities are confronted with two types of flooding that are referred to as river (warm) flooding and ocean (cold) flooding.[35]

The flooding ocean occurs when the rise in the sea level precipitates incessant ocean surges into coastal communities; on the other hand, the flooded rivers often inundate the communities when they flow into the sea through creeks in the coastal regions. It is instructive to note that some of the seasonal flooding are at times enabled by anthropogenic activities such as the dredging of canals for boat transport and oil exploration.[36]

The question of how these coastal communities are affected by flooding is pertinent for an understanding on how indigenous knowledge has been used to address seasonal flooding. These coastal communities, particularly those in and around Lagos are engaged primarily in fishing; except for those in the rural areas of the Delta region who are also engaged in farming. The positive aspect of flooding for the rural communities are improved fish catch.[37] These rural coastal communities have over time developed several indigenous spiritual approaches to appease the gods to alleviate the adverse effects of flooding on their farmlands. For instance, the gods are consulted to appease the water through sacrifices, and at times by building embarkment as a defense for flooding.[38]

The following are examples of some of the challenges that the rural coastal communities often encounter regarding flooding:

1. Destruction of farmlands when saltwater gets in contact with food crops.
2. When flooding occurs at night, these communities often account for human casualties especially children and old people and domestic animals.
3. At times, the flooding creates internal displaced persons (IDPs) because flooding leads to rural communities being washed out and consequently leading to re-location.
4. Rural coastal communities are also endangered by species such as crocodiles and snakes during flooding.
5. Rural communities' women are also restrained indoors to domestic chores because of flooding; as a result, they would have limited access to farmlands, education, and healthcare.

6. Rural coastal communities are challenged by high incidents of diarrhea, malaria, waterborne diseases, and typhoid during flooding periods.

To enhance the development of rural coastal communities, indigenes of these communities have used various coping mechanisms and indigenous technologies that mitigate against the adverse impact of flooding. Table 5.1 provides an illustration of these strategies and indigenous technologies

The indigenous coping mechanisms and technologies used by the rural coastal communities in Table 5.1 illustrate the participatory nature of coping strategies and the ingenuity of local communities to adapt local strategies to mitigate against flooding which invariably would enhance their quality of life.

It is important to note that the coping mechanism and indigenous technological strategies by the rural coastal communities are at times preceded or followed by other cultural beliefs and norms that often play a pivotal role in the development initiatives. For instance, the rural coastal often use various indigenous meteorological signs such as lunar observation and cloud study to prepare for flooding.

Lunar Observation, the advent of a full moon often signifies an emerging flood in the communities, although the sighting of the moon cannot be used to estimate the level of flooding. However, the indigenous communities believe that the tidal level is dictated by the approaching new moon.

Table 5.1. Coping Mechanism and Indigenous Technologies

Communities	Coping Mechanism	Indigenous Technologies and Local Adaptation Strategies
Abereke	Financial assistance from the community cooperative	Construction of wooden bridges, mud, and concrete embankments
Ori Oke	Mutual support in the community	Pathways for water
Araromi	Mutual support in the community	Culverts and gutters
Obefela	Mutual support in the community	Building on raised platforms or pile foundation
Awoye	Mutual support in the community	Sand filling
Ayetoro	Assistance from Church	Mud and concrete embankments
Ogulaba	Assistance from oil companies-Shell	Concrete embankments
Burutu	Assistance from oil companies and local governments area councils	Concrete embankments
Gbekebor	Mutual support in the community	Concrete embankments

Source: Fabiyi, O. O. and Oloukoi, J. (2013). Indigenous Knowledge system and local adaptation strategies to flooding in coastal rural communities of Nigeria. *Journal of Indigenous Social Development,* Vol. 2, Issue 1, p.15. Retrieved January 10, 2021 from https://scholarspace.manoa.hawaii.edu/bitstream/10125/29817/1/v2i1_05fabiyi.pdf.

Indigenous cloud study, the thick dark clouds often signify an approaching heavy rain and an indicator that the village will be subjected to heavy rain. It is important to note that at times there are variabilities in predictions among community members.[39]

Despite the challenges and unpredictability at times of lunar observation and cloud study, indigenous communities have been able to use these coping mechanisms and technologies in a sustainable manner for development initiatives which has consequently enhanced their agricultural development. The ability of the indigenous communities to address challenges such as floods using indigenous technologies along with cultural mores such as the offering of sacrifices to the gods must be contextualized as an integral and systemic way that rural people respond to change. Although modern technology is relevant, it is not often integrated into the social and cultural settings and values of rural communities. Thus, indigenous coping mechanisms and technologies used to address flooding in coastal communities are embedded with local relevance and are sustainable.[40] It is in this vein, that Iyam suggests

> The lack of locally relevant development formulas has left the concept of development open to many interpretations. For agencies such as the World Bank and the International Monetary Fund (IMF), Gross National Product (GNP) weighs profoundly in a concept of development that aims to shrink the national balance of payment. While such models have constituted the guiding principle for economic development in many less developed countries (LDC), they have had limited impact in much of Africa.[41]

INDIGENOUS KNOWLEDGE AND AGRO-ECO SYSTEMS IN GHANA.

Ghana has a population of thirty million, with a per annum growth rate of 2.19 percent. The population distribution is varied across the ten administrative regions and eco-zones of the country, with 68 percent living in the rural areas and 32 percent in the urban areas, respectively. About 52 percent of the labor force is engaged in agriculture, 29 percent in services and 19 percent in industry.[42]

Ghana is considered a lower middle-income country; rising GDP in oil production, gold and mining has contributed immensely to economic growth. However, wealth inequalities have remained pervasive mostly in the rural areas. The economic growth in Ghana has enabled the country to be the first African country to meet the millennium goal of halving hunger and poverty; malnutrition was reduced from seven million in the 1990s to less than one million in 2018. Nonetheless, hunger and poverty has remained a challenge particularly in Northern upper east and west regions where about one to two million have remained food insecure.[43] To abate the growing challenges from food insecurity in Ghana, the use of IK as an alternative development strategy is suggested for improving the agro-ecoysytem because it is environmentally friendly and sustainable. The following are examples of IK strategies for agri-development in Ghana:

Crop Rotation. Soil borne pathogens that infect plants are controlled through crop rotation. For instance, the loss of food crops such as tomato from pests can be controlled when cereals are planted after cultivation of tomato in a rotation. In other cases, rotation of sorghum with soybeans enhances the management of root-knot nematode population densities.[44]

Time of Planting. the traditional approach to planting crops also plays a vital role in enhancing food security. For example, the early sowing of groundnut reduces the incidence and severity of groundnut rosette virus infection. Similarly, maize and sorghum are likely to escape stem borer attack if sown early.[45]

Sanitation. Traditional pest management through sanitation practices such as the burning of sorghum stalks after grain harvest have been found to eliminate 95 percent of pests without damage to the stalks. IK sanitation practices are also used to reduce spoilage of harvests such as vegetables, fruits, and tubers.[46]

Tillage. Pest management through soil tillage have been found to be critical for eliminating weeds and other pests. The plough of soil after harvest has proven effective in destroying stubble, weeds, and species such as grasshoppers.[47]

Approximately 39 percent of Ghana's farm labor force are women. Agriculture contributes to 54 percent of Ghana's GDP, and accounts for over 40 percent of export earnings, while at the same time providing over 90 percent of the food needs of the country. Ghana's agriculture is smallholder, traditional and rain-fed. Ghana's farming systems vary with agro-ecological zones.[48] However, certain general features are profound throughout the country. For instance, droughts are common in Northern Ghana where it is not unusual to experience a dry spell of seven days once a year in June and once every four years in September during the raining season.[49] These features have invariably continued to impact food security in Northern Ghana. Accordingly, Agbadi, Urke, and Mittlemark, posits that 49 percent of children in Northern Ghana received minimum recommended meal frequency, and 31 percent received minimum dietary diversity; about 17 percent of the children received a minimum acceptable diet.[50]

The overall challenges of food insecurity in Ghana provide the context in which this section of the chapter examines how the sustenance and the application of indigenous agro-ecosystems and practices can enhance food insecurity against the background of climatic and other environmental challenges that can be mitigated with IK in some of the following areas: indigenous soil fertility practices, traditional pest management practices, and reducing vulnerability to drought.

Indigenous Soil Fertility Practices in Ghana.

Crop Rotation. Local farmers are of the knowledge that different crops feed from different depths and on different nutrients in the soil. For example, pigeon pea is usually grown as intercrop with other food crops such as maize, yam, and cassava in a relay form. In this practice, pigeon-pea is typically the last crop cultivated in this system. Thus, after harvesting the yam and maize and the pigeon-pea, the pigeon-pea is cut back to permit the cassava to grow to maturity. When the cassava is eventually harvested, the land is allowed to fallow under the pigeon pea for at least two years.[51]

Bush Fallow. In the event of a decline in soil fertility after cropping for three to five successive years, farmers tend to leave the land fallow for two to three years before going back to crop the land again. Fallowing for that period allows the land to regenerate its fertility. During this period, the growth of trees is allowed to protect the soil from direct sun and simultaneously sustaining soil moisture.

Construction of Ridges and Mounds. Traditional farmers dig ridges and mounds on less fertile plots on fallowed land to regenerate soil fertility. On grasslands, traditional farmers can plough the land or construct ridges or mounds to control weeds that evade the land and to enhance the productivity of the land.[52]

TRADITIONAL PEST MANAGEMENT PRACTICES

The efforts to reduce the loss of crops is a challenge for farmers in general because it impacts food security—particularly the loss of income and food availability. It is also profound in sub-Saharan countries like Ghana where prevailing pest management models that are dependent on synthetic agrochemical pesticides has had marginal outcomes on the productivity of poor small-holder farmers who constitute a major segment of the agricultural communities.[53] The following are some of the pest management practices that are also used by traditional farmers in Ghana.

Plant based pesticide; Indigenous farmers use plant species with pesticidal qualities to avert the destruction of crops by pests. These plant species such as Pyrethrum, Tanacetum, and Cinerariifolium have been found to be more effective than synthetic chemicals for pest management. The pest control using pesticidal species is also viable when grown by the farmers because it can be used in a manner which does not lead to adulteration along the supply chain.[54]

Weed Control, over time, *traditional* farmers in Ghana have also established the use of suppression crops to address the proliferation of weed on farmlands by cultivating cover crops. For example, in the Northern Ghana Savanna zone of Ghana, field studies have shown how weed suppression has been used in the northern region of Ghana to control drought once a year.[55] For instance, crops such as Mucuna and Canavalia were successfully used as cover crops on a maize farm to avert the vulnerability to weeds.[56]

The question remains—what steps are taken by small holders to mitigate against the impact of drought on rain fed agriculture? In the northeastern region of Ghana, consumption poverty is pervasive and manifested in hunger and malnutrition. The challenges of drought in this region have informed farmers to take the following indigenous steps to reduce vulnerability to drought:

1. the cultivation of drought resilient indigenous crops;
2. multiple farms combined with different rounds of seeding; and
3. indigenous soil and water conservation measure.[57]

Traditional farmers are purposeful in the selection of crops they cultivate during drought season. They typically select multiple resilient crop varieties for reducing vulnerability to drought and adapt rain agriculture to drought. These crops are Zea, Naara and Muu Kiliga.[58] The Naara plate and Zea are commonly intercropped on the Sammani. Naara seeds are also prepared for storage for the next planting season using IK. The bunch is hung in a dry place where smoke from burnt fuel wood used during cooking helps to protect the seeds from insects.[59] These crops are traditional staples that have been cultivated from one generation to another because of their adaptability of using rainfall agriculture to avoid drought.[60]

Multiple farms, and the application of different rounds of seedlings were also used by traditional farmers to reduce vulnerability to drought. Traditional farmers cultivate on different farms thus staggering plants of the same crops between different farms to mitigate against and reduce vulnerability to limited rainfall and drought.[61] The premise behind the staggering of the planting of food crops is that traditional farmers increase the probability of planting a least a cohort of crops which are likely to be more resilient to drought. In addition, traditional farmers are encouraged by the propensity to meet sustainable yields because this method has been used over time to address the challenges of drought.

Regarding indigenous soil and water conservation measures, soil conservation practices are used by traditional farmers in the northeastern region of Ghana to improve soil fertility. Traditional farmers in this region are cognizant that soil with high organic matter content has the propensity to improve soil fertility and water retention capacity.[62] In this regard, it is a widespread practice among traditional farmers in the northeastern region to apply organic matter content such as manure in the soil to improve fertility and sustain soil moisture to reduce vulnerability to drought.[63]

In addition, an agro-ecosystem is used to enhance indigenous methods of managing diversity of food varieties which enhances the cultivation of food such as vegetable legumes—sword bean, lima bean, cow pea and pigeon pea. The following provides examples of how food varieties are managed in Ghana:

Sword bean (*Canavalia ensiformis*), Different land varieties are used for the cultivation of sword bean. The sword bean is typically grown in food farms or home gardens using live trees as stakes. The locally cultivated varieties are long-season types that last for over nine months. Sword beans are consumed at the immature green stage or dried.[64]

Lima Bean (*Phaseolu lanatus*), The varieties are cultivated in pod and bean size. Their color ranges from white, brown, red, and white or purple. The lima beans are used in the same way as the sword bean and the leaves are used the same way as a sword bean.[65]

Cowpea (*Vigna Unguiculata*), The varieties of cowpeas encountered under forest conditions are climbers, albeit creeping and erect types are grown in Ghana. The common colors of this vegetables are black eye type and brown. They are cooked in soup and served with rice and other foods such as cassava.[66]

Pigeon Pea, the pigeon pea is cultivated in Ghana as a semi-perennial, mostly in home gardens or on the food farm. The mature or immature seeds are cooked in soups and stews. It is primarily used for food security crops.[67]

SUMMARY

The case for IK is profound in the attempt to address food security in sub-Saharan Africa and in other developing regions. The inability to achieve

sustainable agricultural development in sub-Saharan Africa with development strategies such as the Green Revolution in the 1970s and 1980s as
prescribed by development agencies such as the World Bank and the Food
and Agriculture Organization has drawn us to alternative methods such as
IK. Moreover, some of these development agencies such as the World Bank
have started to recognize the importance of development using Indigenous
Knowledge. According to the World Bank about 1.6 billion people around the
globe depend on forests for livelihoods and economic sustenance.[68]

The rich data on IK has shown that as a general framework, the use of
IK in Nigeria and Ghana is a viable approach for addressing food security.
This framework is closer to the social and economic realities of these communities. Moreover, the use of IK is dynamic and heterogenous to various
indigenous communities. For instance, various forms of IK have remained the
backbone for sustaining food security through practices such as soil fertility
management, pest control practices, and reducing drought vulnerability in
both Nigeria and Ghana. To accentuate the viability of IK for food security,
studies by Buabeng, Derbile, Lartey,[69] Singh and Singh show that IK covers
several areas of human activities, such as cultural, social, production organizations, land management and conservation.[70] Given the challenges of sustainable food production in the twenty-first century, particularly at a period
in which the world is confronted with major environmental challenges such
as land degradation, biodiversity loss and climate change that were not read-
ily addressed by agricultural strategies such as the Green Revolution, IK has
remained viable because it is also a "climate-smart" approach for sustainable
food production.[71]

The use of indigenous agro-ecology methods is critical for food security.
Examples of agro-ecology systems to abate the impact of drought in Northern
Ghana and floods in rural coastal communities in Nigeria reinforces the
importance of IK in developing coping strategies and mechanisms that are
integral for addressing food security in these communities.

NOTES

1. Lewis, Arthur (1954). Economic Development with Unlimited Supplies of
Labor. Manchester School of Economic Studies.

2. United Nations Development Program Report (2001). Making New Technologies Work for Human Development. pp. 1–278.

3. Biotechnology, http://www/encarta/html.

4. Keese, P., Omitogun, G. and Sonaiya, B. (2002). Seeds of promise: Developing a sustainable agricultural biotechnology industry in sub-Saharan Africa. *Natural
Resources*, Vol. 26(3): 234–244.

5. Ibid.

6. Ibid.

7. United Nations Development (July 2001). Making New Technologies Work for Human Development, pp. 1–278.

8. Ibid.

9. Brown, Kyle G. (April 16–22). Hunger and genetically modified crops in Africa. *West Africa*, pp. 16–34.

10. Harwood, Jonathan (2019). Was the Green Revolution intended to maximize food production? *International Journal of Agricultural Sustainability*, Vol. 17, (4): 312–325.

11. Pielke, Roger and Linnér, Bjorn-Ola (2019). From Green Revolution to Green Evolution: A critique of the political myth of averted famine. *Minerva*, Vol. 57: 265–291.

12. Mabogunje, Akin L. Framing the Fundamental Issues of Sustainable Development in sub-Saharan Africa, p.16–18. Also see, Tripp, Robert (2000). GMOs and NGOs, The policy process, and the presentation of evidence. *Natural resource Perspective*, no. 60: 1–6. www.odi.org.uk.nrp.

13. Rickard, Sean and Gorelick, Steven (2001). Can small farms feed the world? *Ecologist*, Vol. 3, No. 1: 20–25.

14. Ibid.

15. Tunji, Titilola (2000). Environment and sustainable agricultural development. *Journal of Sustainable Agricultural Development in Africa*, Vol. 2(1): 1–12.

16. Ibid.

17. Kimbrell, Andrew (1998). Why biotech and high-tech agriculture cannot feed the world. *Ecologist*, Vol. 28 (5): 294–298.

18. Powell, B., Haraksingh, S.T., Ickowitz, A., Termote, C., Sunderland, T. and Herforth, A. (2015). Improving diets with wild and cultivated biodiversity from across the landscape. *Food Security*, Vol. 7: 546.

19. Ibid., pp. 546–547.

20. Derbile, E.K. (2013). Reducing vulnerability of rain-fed agriculture to drought through indigenous knowledge systems north-eastern-Ghana. *International Journal of Climate Change Strategies and Management*, Vol. 5 (1): 75.

21. Adedipe, N.O., Okuneye, P.A. and Ayinde L.A. (March 16–19, 2004). The relevance of local and indigenous knowledge for Nigerian agriculture. Presented at International Conference on Bridging Scales and Epistemologies: Linking Local Knowledge with Global Science in Multi Scale Assessments. Alexandria Egypt, p. 1.

22. Ibid.

23. Olomola, Aderibigbe, S. (2017). Effective resource management for improved food and nutrition security in Nigeria. *Africa in Focus*, Accessed on February 3, 2021 from https://www.brookings.edu/topic/coronavirus-covid19/?__hstc=753710.b3642 95e278ebbd3a8213375a80bffc3.1612381323677.1612381323677.1612381323677.1 &__hssc=753710.1.1612381323677&__hsfp=797300925.

24. Ibid.

25. Adesoji, S.A. (2016). Eating today and tomorrow: Exploring indigenous farming systems of smallholder arable crop farmers in the age of climate change in Nigeria. *Agriculture and Forestry*, Vol. 62 (10): 350.

26. Adedipe, N.O., Okuneye, P.A. and Ayinde, L.A. (March 16–19, 2004). The relevance of local and indigenous knowledge for Nigerian agriculture. Presented at International Conference on Bridging Scales and Epistemologies: Linking Local Knowledge with Global Science in Multi Scale Assessments. Alexandria: Egypt, p. 3.

27. Qudus, M.A. (2000). Use of Indigenous Knowledge in the Sustainable Development of Bangladesh Farm Forestry. In Paul Sillitoe ed. Indigenous Knowledge Development in Bangladesh: Present and Future. London: Intermediate Technology Publications, p. 57.

28. Ibid., p. 59.

29. Raji, B.A., Malgwi, W.B., Berding, F.R. and Chude, V.O. (March 2011). Integrating indigenous knowledge and soil science approaches to detailed soil survey in Kaduna State Nigeria. *Journal of Soil Science and Environment Management*, Vol. 2 (3): 66–73.

30. Kolawole, O.D. (October17, 2017). Rural communities and indigenous knowledge systems in a changing world: soil fertility conservation practices amongst farmers. *The Anthropologist*, Vol. 6, 1ssue 4, pp. 283–288.

31. Alabi, O. O., Banwo, O.O. and S.O. Alabi (2006). Crop pest management and food security in Nigeria agriculture. *Archives of Phytopathology and Plant Protection*. Vol. 39, (6): 2.

32. Ibid., p. 3.

33. Ibid., p. 4.

34. Fabiyi, Oluseyi O. and Oloukoi, Joseph (2013). Indigenous knowledge system and local adaptation strategies to flooding in coastal rural communities of Nigeria. *Journal of Indigenous Social Development*, Vol 2, (1): 4.

35. Ibid.

36. Ibid.

37. Ibid.

38. Ibid.

39. Ibid., p. 15.

40. Iyam, David Uru (1995). The Broken Hoe: Cultural Reconfiguration in Biase Southeast Nigeria. Chicago; Illinois: University of Chicago Press, pp. 9–11.

41. Ibid.

42. Ghana at a Glance, FAO. Retrieved June 12, 2020, from http://www.fao.org/ghana/fao-in-ghana/ghana-at-a-glance/en/.

43.Assiedu, S.M., Dittoh, Saa, Newton, Kofi and Akota, Charity (WPF) (July 2017). World Food Program, Address Sustainable Development Goal 2: The Ghana zero hunger strategic review. p. xiii Accessed on February 3, 2021, from https://docs.wfp.org/api/documents/WFP-0000071730/download/?_ga=2.221088088 .1986724444.1612385369-2071872577.1612385369.

44. Ibid.

45. Ibid.

46. Ibid.

47. Ibid.

48. Ibid.

49. Derbile, E.K. (2013). Reducing vulnerability of rain-fed agriculture to drought through indigenous knowledge systems in north-eastern-Ghana. *International Journal of Climate Change Strategies and Management*, Vol. 5 (1): 76.

50. Agbadi, P. Urke, H.B. and Mittlemark, M.B. (2017). Household food security and adequacy of child diet in the food insecure region north in Ghana, pp. 1–16. https://doi.org/10.1371/journal .pone.0177377.

51. Nsiah, S.A. and Dawson, O.S. (2012). Promoting cassava as an industrial crop in Ghana: Effects on soil fertility and farming system sustainability. *Applied and Environmental Soil Science*, p. 3. Doci:10.1155/2012/9409954.

52. Ibid., p. 4.

53. Grzywacz, D., Stevenson, P.C., Mushhoboiz, W.L., Belmain, S. and Wilson, K. (2014). The use of indigenous ecological resources for pest control in Africa. *Food Security*, 6: 71. https:// DOI 10.1007/s12571-013-0313–5

54. Ibid., p. 74.

55. Agbadi, P., Urke, H.B. & Mittlemark, M.B. (2017). Household food security and adequacy of child diet in the food insecure region north in Ghana. *POLS* 1: 1–16. https://doi.org/10.1371/journal .pone.0177377.

56. Lawanson, I.Y., Dzomeku, I.K., Asempa, R. and Benson, S. (2006). Weed control in maize using Mucuna and Canavalia as intercrops in the Northern Guinea Savanna Zone of Ghana. *Journal of Agronomy*. Vol. 5 (4): 621–625.

57. Derbile, E.K. (2013). Reducing the vulnerability of rain-fed agriculture to drought through indigenous knowledge systems in north-eastern Ghana. *International Journal of Climate Change Strategies and Management.* Vol. 5(1): 75–78.

58. Ibid.

59. Ibid., p. 79.

60. Ibid.

61. Ibid., p. 81.

62. Ibid., p. 83.

63. Ibid.

64. Blay, Essie (2004). Vegetables: Traditional ways of managing their diversity food security in Southern Ghana. In Gyasi, E.A.; Berisalvljevic, G.K.; Blay, E.T. & Oduro, W. (ed). (2004). Managing Agrodiversity the Traditional Way. New York: United Nations University Press, p. 111.

65. Ibid.

66. Ibid.

67. Ibid.

68. World Bank Annual Report (2004). Vol 1. *Year in Review*, pp. 1–129.

69. Lartey, M.S. (2014). Harnessing indigenous knowledge for sustainable forest management in Ghana. *International Journal Food System Dynamics,* Vol. 5(4): 182–189.

70. Baubeng, S.N. (2004). Traditional methods of resource assessment relative to the scientific approach. In Gyasi, E.A., Berisalvljevic, G.K., Blay, E.T. & Oduro, W.

(ed). (2004). Managing Agrodiversity the Traditional Way. New York: United Nations University Press, p. 15.

71. Singh, R. and Singh, G.S. (2017). Traditional agriculture: A climate-smart approach for sustainable food production. Energy. *Ecology. Environment*. Vol. 2 (5): 296–316.

Chapter 6

Alternative Energy

THE CHALLENGES OF FOOD SECURITY IN AFRICA

The use of fossil fuels has been found to be environmentally less efficient in addressing energy problems in Africa. At the same time, the use of biofuels for energy development has also posed some challenges for sustainable agricultural development because food energy is likely to contribute to rising food prices and food insecurity.

Over the past one hundred years, the world has witnessed three major surges in food prices. The first occurred immediately after World War II, the second took place in the 1970s, and the third, began in 2007, and is still current.[1] In Africa there was a rise in food prices in the 1980s that resulted from civil war in several regions and countries such as Liberia, Rwanda, and the Democratic Republic of Congo (DRC); however, new systemic factors have led to the recent increase in food prices: (1) full liberalization of the agricultural markets, (2) rising income in some developing countries in Asia, and (3) the demand for biofuels. It should be noted that in the case of African economies, their integration into the global capitalist structures have further entrenched their vulnerability to rising food prices.[2]

The prices of agricultural commodities such as food crops reached astronomical levels in recent years, while world agricultural markets are developing rapidly.[3] The rise in food prices became noticeable in 2007 when wheat prices rose by 77 percent and rice by 16 percent. These increases in food prices were the sharpest ever.[4] Experts claimed that this trend will remain as such for the long run.[5] For instance, the Food and Agriculture Organization outlook for 2011–2020 projected that during the five years from 2015/2016 through 2019/20, world prices for rice, wheat, maize, and oilseeds would be higher in real terms by 40, 27, 48, and 36 percent respectively than in the five years from 1998 through 2003.[6] However, the recent global pandemic from

COVID-19 has also contributed to the recent hike in food prices. It is against the background of the demand for biofuels and the global pandemic that one should examine the surge in food prices between 2008 and 2020. The harsh impact of the current increases in the price of food is likely to be felt by those sub-Saharan African countries that are already facing declining food supplies. Figure 6.1 shows that the price of staple foods such as rice, maize, and wheat accelerated after January 2008.[7]

FOOD VERSUS OIL AND COMPETING INTERESTS

The relationship between food and biofuels has been inseparable since the rise in food prices in 2007.[8] One of the factors that has contributed to the recent rise in food prices is the full liberalization of the agricultural markets, which has consequently led to an increase in the prices of agricultural raw

Figure 6.1. Grain Prices 2007-2008. *Source: The Economist,* "The New Face of Hunger" April 19th, 2008, p.3. © The Economist Group Limited, London.

materials by 5.5 percent and for food prices by about 1.3 percent. The decline of the stocks of essential agricultural commodities in recent years has also contributed to the increase in global food prices. Consequently, this led to a supply deficit in agricultural commodities.[9]

The surge in food prices in 2007–2008 was also attributed to the rising demand for dairy, meat, and feed in China, India, and other parts of Asia. The impetus for this trend, according to the Director General of the International Food Policy Research Institute (IFPRI), stems from rising incomes in these developing regions.[10] For instance, ECA international salary trends surveys for 2007–2008 shows that salaries rose in China from the 7.3 percent average for Asia to 8 percent, and above the global average of 5.9 percent.[11]

Another factor that has led to the rise in global food prices is the high demand for fuel-crops such as wheat, maize, sugarcane, and oilseeds to produce biofuels, bioelectricity, and bio-heat in oil importing developed economies such as the United States. The ethanol industry statistics forecasts from 2008 through 2012 show that world ethanol production exceeded twenty billion gallons in 2012. The projections for world ethanol production underscore the increasing importance of biofuels as an alternative to fossil fuels.[12] However, the global ethanol and bio-fuel outlook shows that global ethanol production will surge to 36.9841 billion gallons by 2029, and the production of biodiesel is projected to reach 12.15 billion gallons much of which will depend on feed stock.[13]

The demand for alternative energy in sub-Saharan Africa stems from the need to reduce greenhouse gas emissions and the dependency on fossil fuels (petroleum) with its attendant unpredictable market-driven price. However, to promote the production of alternative energy, such as ethanol for transportation and other industrial activities, developed economies such as the United States embarked on public policies such as the Energy Policy Act of 2005 to promote the use of alternative energy such as Ethanol. The policy targeted the consumption of 28.4 billion liters of bioethanol by 2012. The Act also provided and extended the bio-diesel fuel excise tax credit through 2008 and provided a $0.03 per liter income tax credit to small bio-diesel producers in the United States.[14] Despite these measures and incentives to support biofuels, the price of fossil fuels continued to surge over $0.079 per liter in the spring of 2007 and generally remained constant during the summer of that year. It maintained this level of price into early 2008.[15]

The rising demand for fuel crops such as wheat, sugar cane, and maize has had mixed and profound effects on most sub-Saharan African countries. On the one hand, the use of biofuels as an alternative source of energy in sub-Saharan African countries is likely to reduce the dependency on petroleum. This could be the case given that thirty-nine countries in Africa are net importers of petroleum. In addition, about 39 percent of the total energy consumed in sub-Saharan Africa is imported against the world average of 19 percent.[16]

On the other hand, the reliance on biofuels in sub-Saharan Africa would reduce greenhouse effects and reduce the emissions of carbon monoxide (CO) and carbon dioxide (CO2). This is especially significant for sub-Saharan Africa economically and environmentally because it could reduce the cost of manufacturing and distribution, such as the cost of transportation and the generation of electricity with fossil fuels. Road transportation is the primary method of moving goods and services in the region. This commercial area accounts for about 85 percent of the total fossil fuel used in the transportation sector, while diesel fuel accounts for over 55 percent of the total fuel consumption in this sector.[17] However, the rising price and environmental implications of fossil fuels have attributed to the rising production of biofuels to an unimaginable volume over the last 15 years.[18]

The demand for biofuels also presents a major challenge for global food security. There are four main dimensions of food security that biofuel development is linked with: (1) availability, (2) access, (3) stability, and (4) utilization of food.[19] This demand will potentially lead to increased pressures to clear land for farming to increase the production of fuel crops such as sugarcane for ethanol, and palm oil plantations for biodiesel. The clearing of mass areas of land for farming presents major threats to animals and biodiversity.[20] Oil prices have dropped sharply since mid-2014 because of slow demand and record increases in supply, particularly shale oil from North America, as well as the policy decision by the Organization of Petroleum Exporting Countries (OPEC) to leave its production un-changed. However, the demand for biofuels has continued to be highly influenced by domestic policies in conjunction with sustained fuel demand globally.[21]

The demand for biofuels is also likely to have an adverse effect on food availability if food crops and staple foods are alternated to that of biofuels. Though the use of marginal and idle land is suggested to produce biofuel, land availability remains a challenge in most regions in sub-Saharan Africa.[22] However, investments in fuel crops production and the attendant competition for land is likely to lead to increased pressures on farm-based economies to produce alternative food crops. This has been the case in Latin America and sub-Saharan Africa, particularly in the horn of Africa when farmers switched from growing traditional food crops and coffee to coca and quat production in response to diminishing production in the food commodities sector.

The rising global population has also not abated the demand for food. Over the next forty years it is estimated that agricultural production will increase by 60 percent; at the same time, it is estimated that about a quarter of all agricultural land will suffer degradation.[23] Along the same lines, there is a potential loss of biodiversity with the unpredictability of climate change.

Thus, higher food feed and fiber demand is likely to place pressure on land and water resources demand.[24] Therefore, the changes in land use, particularly those linked with deforestation and expansion of agricultural production for food has contributed about 15 percent of the global emissions of greenhouse gases. Deforestation contributes to the loss of oxygen which reduces the percentage of greenhouse gases in the atmosphere. Currently, less than 3 percent of global agricultural land is used for cultivating biofuel crops, while land use for bioenergy represents 1 percent of the total emissions caused by land use. It is instructive to note that the proportion of land use for biofuels globally is about 2.5 percent or 40 million gross hectares (though there are differentiations from one region to another).[25]

The demand for fuel crops emerged at a time when the world food stocks were at their lowest in about 40 years. With seventy-six million more people to feed each year this presents enormous social and economic challenges for sub-Saharan Africa especially with the extensive food insecurity already existing in the region.[26] Thus, biofuel production may also impede access to food because it is one of the drivers of food commodity prices. Mitchell attributed the development of biofuels to the price surge which has had implications on food security.[27] The development of biofuels and its impact on food prices was estimated to be between 3 percent and 30 percent in some cases.[28]

The production of biofuels is also likely to impact food stability and consequently heighten food insecurity. The threat to food supply and security would occur because arable land is used for fuel crops. Consequently, food supply and stability are further threatened. One cannot ignore the potential viability of bio-energy to produce electricity and energy in sub-Saharan African countries such as Nigeria where power distribution is poor; 55 percent of the estimated 165 million population do not have access to grid electricity.[29] However, the production of biofuels crops may increase the use of nitrogen, pesticides, and herbicides which may invariably have an adverse effect on water resources in the event that irrigation is used for the cultivation of biofuel crops.[30] On the other hand, the use of bioethanol in other regions such as the United States and Brazil have contributed to positive results. For instance, Brazil has used maize and sugarcane as feedstocks for biofuel production. As a result, Brazil possesses an economic advantage in the production of biofuel because of the availability of land and suitable climatic conditions that are not always available in other regions, particularly in the global south. However, in other African countries there is a growing interest for biofuels primarily for energy purposes. For instance, the Botswana government embarked on biofuel production in 2012.[31] The interest of the Botswana government in biofuels is also driven by the need for alternative source of energy and the availability of idle land. The proportion of idle land in eastern Botswana was estimated at 72 percent in 2008, which shows that only 28 percent of the land is used for arable agriculture.[32]

BIOFUELS AND AGRI-DEVELOPMENT: THE CASE OF BOTSWANA

In 2007, the government of Botswana embarked on a feasibility study to guide and assess their national interests in the production of liquid biofuels for transportation in Botswana. The assessment indicated that Jatropha is a sound option for biodiesel and sweet sorghum could be used for ethanol production because of minimal production cost. In the case of Jatropha, it is a Latin American origin plant which is now cultivated in semiarid and tropical regions. It is a drought resistance perennial, and its seeds produce about 35 percent of non-edible oil.[33]

It was also decided that feedstocks for bioethanol should be grown in the *Chobe* district by large scale farmers and supported by small out-grower agricultural schemes. The projected production of bioethanol was twenty million liters per annum for processing the feedstocks. Along the same lines, it was recommended that the central district of the country would be dedicated to the production of biodiesel where contract farming was to be employed.[34]

To further develop biofuels policy in Botswana the government instituted national guidelines that have served as a framework for national policy. The guidelines cover the following: 1. Institutional framework for biofuel investment in Botswana; 2. Application and registration procedures; 3. Procedures for land acquisition and use; 4. Resettlement and contract farming; 5. Farming practice and seed management; 6. Efficient use of biofuel products; 7. Carbon markets and trading; 8. Community engagements; and 9. Blending ratios. The guidelines for biofuel production are profoundly important because it would ensure that idle land that could have been used for food production are not used to produce biofuel.[35] In this regard, scholars such as Ketlogetswe who have studied biodiesel development in Botswana have suggested that the increasing demand for petroleum-based fuels such as diesel fuels are likely to persist because of the use of draught power tractors in the agricultural sector unless the government remain committed to expansion of biofuels using waste such as from cooking oil to mitigate against the use of fossil fuels.[36]

SOUTH AFRICA BIOFUEL POLICY
AND AGRI-DEVELOPMENT

The South African (SA) Government initiated a policy in 2007 toward achieving biofuels development and agri-development. The specific requirement of the biofuels industry strategy was to create a link between developing and developed communities in SA. This requirement is linked to the creation of jobs in underdeveloped areas—such as in the former homelands, where agriculture development was undermined by the previous white led SA system of Apartheid.[37]

As a result, the SA government established a clear government policy and regulations that would serve as a pre-requisite for the development of the biofuels sector. This initiative was also driven by the nature of the volatile fossil fuel related product prices that biofuels had to compete with.[38] The foci of the SA national biofuels strategies are as follows:

1. Promotion of farming in areas previously neglected by the apartheid system that did not have access for their produce.
2. The strategy sought to stimulate rural development and to reduce poverty by creating sustainable income earning opportunities; thus, the SA government had envisioned biofuels investment that could serve as a catalyst for transforming rural economies and contribute to the country's growth and development.
3. The strategy, as envisioned, was greenhouse emissions expected to contribute towards the achievement of the renewable energy.[39]

Considering the initiatives embarked upon to develop biofuels by the SA government the initiatives are challenged in several areas. One is the concern that the SA government has about the potential for arable land for food to be used for biofuels development. The consequence of such an aggressive move towards biofuels development are poor agriculture output, hunger, and limited arable land.[40]

On the other hand, there are some perceptions that biofuels land may have social and economic benefits because the production of biofuels typically occurs on rural land which could also create opportunities for agriculture employment and the development of alternative energy.[41]

INDIGENOUS KNOWLEDGE AND
ALTERNATIVE ENERGY

As a result of the demand for alternative energy and some of the opportunities it presents, indigenous communities have continued to face the decline of human factor infrastructure such as the loss of land, water, and food.[42] The quest for biofuels has been a preoccupation of state governments and development agencies at the expense of the social, economic, and the development realities of the indigenous communities. For instance, Nigeria, during the peak of the oil boom in the 1970s, experienced a shift of population from the agriculture to other sectors such as the civil service.[43] This increased the country's inability to feed itself. Moreover, domestic food producers encountered an increase in food demand of well over ten percent per-annum while at the same time the country experienced a significant loss of labor.[44]

The consequences accompanying the development of alternative energy such as the loss of land and food, ecological degradation, and the loss of biodiversity, have been exemplified in the loss of farmlands to fossil fuel development in the Ogoni-land of Nigeria,[45] and the unsustainable proliferation of palm oil cultivation in Malaysia for biofuels. It is imperative that such developments must take place inconsonant with the vulnerable indigenous communities to be successful. In fact, the development knowledge of these communities is integral for sustainability. The use of IK in addressing the need for alternative energy can be better positioned for development if states and development agencies would integrate its use as exemplified in the following indigenous communities:

1. In Indonesia, the Dayak Pasar indigenous community developed a project to install clean energy electricity using micro-hydro to ensure sustainable and community-based development.[46]
2. Among the Igorot indigenous group in the Philippines, traditional practices such as rotational agriculture has remained in use to increase the overall health of the forests ecosystem and critical for abating global warm.[47]
3. In Nigeria indigenous coastal communities have developed barriers to abate flood on farmlands during seasonal floods. These communities often build embarkments using local materials to abate floods.[48]
4. Traditional agricultural methods called *dhap* or known as locally *asbaira* are used in Bangladesh districts of Gopalganji, Barisal and Pirojpur to mitigate climate change and to enhance agricultural sustainability. These are ancestral floating vegetables gardens—artificial islands that

rise and fall with swelling water. These are landscapes that use the of agricultural biodiversity, resilient ecosystems, and cultural heritage.[49]

SUMMARY

The surge in food prices has been driven by the combination of rising fuel costs, the demand for fuel-crops for biofuel production, and trade restrictions. In this regard, Popp et. al suggests in relation to Africa that even when forest conservation is accounted for, the food price index is likely to rise most prominently in sub-Saharan Africa by 82 percent, Latin America by 73 percent, and Pacific Asia by 52 percent until 2095.[50]

In addition, surging food prices is likely to lead to some households eating less in developing economies such as Ghana and Nigeria.[51] Thus, poor households have begun to switch from nutritious sources of food, such as fish, meat, and eggs, to less nutritious cereals. In a region where food security presents a challenge, the FAO reported in a recent study that malnutrition is profound in sub-Saharan Africa. Regional food and security and insecure population in the region increased by 11% from 18.2 million at the end of 2015 to 20.4 million people by February 2016.[52]

To address the opportunities and challenges that biofuels development presents in Africa, case studies of biofuels development in Botswana and South Africa shows that biofuels present some opportunities and challenges socially and economically. In the case of Botswana, biofuels development presents massive opportunities that will not involve the loss of land to biofuels food and crops because only 28 percent of arable land is used for agriculture. However, the use of tractors on drought land may further infuse the use of fossil fuels for operational use. On the other hand, the development of biofuels in South Africa highlights the economic opportunities that a national policy for biofuels development presents. It provides an opportunity to develop an alternative energy and employment in communities that had been marginalized during the apartheid period.

However, the challenge in the case of South Africa as in other parts of Africa is that the use of arable land for biofuels production could consequently contribute to food insecurity. Thus, the quest for alternative energy has also reinforced the grabbing of land and the marginalization of indigenous communities from major sources of their social and economic resources. According to Singh, Madhoo, Michel, Sagari, and Wakeford et. al. this reinforces the coloniality of power,[53] whereby the knowledge systems imposed by modern scientists for bio-fuel production found its origin in the colonial period.[54]

Given the nexus of food security and the search for alternative energy using biofuels, it is important to underscore that the environmental impacts and increasing prices of fossil fuels have led to increasing production volumes of biofuels over the last 15 years.[55] The implications of the search for alternative energy through biofuels and other sources of energy has begun to impact major oil companies like Exxon Mobil in terms of their profitability. For instance, Exxon Mobil reported $20 billion loss in the first quarter of 2021. This is Exxon-Mobil's highest loss in forty years.[56] At the same time, it is projected that with the COVID-19 global pandemic, the expansion of renewable energy is likely to contract by 13 percent during the 2020s because of the social and economic constraints that all nation states seem to be facing.[57]

NOTES

1. Braun, Joachim Von (2008). Responding to the World Food Crisis: Getting on the Right Track *International Food Policy Research Institute (IFPRI) Annual Report Essays* 2007–2008, 1–9.

2. Oritsejafor, E. and Cooper, A. (2021). Africa and the Global System of Capital Accumulation. London: Routledge, pp. 1–2.

3. Schmitz, P.M. and Kavallari, A. (2009). Crop plants versus energy plants-on the international food crisis. *Bio-organic and Medicinal Chemistry*, Vol. 17: 4020–4021.

4. *The Economist* (April 19, 2008). The New Face of Hunger, 32–34.

5. Schmitz and Kavllari, 4020–4201.

6. Food and Agriculture Organization of the United Nations (2011). The State of Food Insecurity in the World: How does international price volatility affect domestic economies and food security? pp. 4–50.

7. *The Economist* (April 19, 2008). The New Face of Hunger, 32–34.

8. Mofoluwake, M. Ishola, Brandberg, Tomas, Sikiru, A. Sanni and Taherzadeh, Muhammad, J. (2013). Biofuels in Nigeria: A critical and strategic evaluation. *Renewable Energy*, Vol. 55: 554–560.

9. Schmitz and Kavllar, p. 4020.

10. Braun, Joachim Von, 1–9.

11. ECA International Statistics: Policy and Salary Bench Marking (2009). Retrieved July 21, 2009, from http//www.eca-international.com/shop/benchmarking reports.

12. Renewable Fuel Association, Ethanol Industry Statistics. Retrieved June 15, 2009, from http://www.ethanolrefa.org/industry/statistics.

13. OECD - FAO Agriculture Outlook 2020–2029. Accessed from http://www.oecd-library.org/sites.

14. Bala, Mustafa and Bala, Havva (2009). Recent trends in global production and utilization of bioethanol fuel. *Applied Energy*. Vol 86: 2273–2282.

15. Ibid., p. 2274.

16. Mulugenta, Yacob (2009). Evaluating the economics of biodiesel in Africa. *Renewable and Sustainable Energy Reviews*. Vol. 13: 1592–1598.

17. Ibid., p. 1592.

18. Popp, J., Lakner, Z., Harangi-Rakos, M. and Frai, M. (2014). The effect of bioenergy expansion: food, energy, and environment. *Renewable and Sustainable Energy Reviews,* Vol. 32: 559.

19. Kgathi, D.L,. Mfundisi, K.B., Mmpolewa, G. and Mosepele, K. (2014). Potential impacts of biofuel development on food security in Botswana: A contribution to energy policy. *Energy Policy,* Vol. 43: 72.

20. Popp, J. Lakner, Z., Rakos, M.H. and Fari, M. (2014). The effect of bioenergy expansion: Food, energy, and the environment. *Renewable and Sustainable Energy Reviews*. Vol. 32: 560.

21. Food and Agriculture Organization of the UN OECD/FAO/2016. OECD-FAO Agricultural Outlook 2016–2025, OECD Publishing Paris. Retrieved June 19, 2020, from http://www.fao.org/3/a-i5778e.pdf.

22. Kgathi, D.L., Mfundisi, K.B., Mmpolewa, G. and Mosepele, K. (2014). Potential impacts of biofuel development on food security in Botswana: A contribution to energy policy. *Energy Policy.* Vol. 43: 72.

23. Popp, J. Lakner, Z., Rakos, M.H. and Fari, M. (2014). The effect of bioenergy expansion: Food, energy, and the environment. *Renewable and Sustainable Energy Reviews*. Vol. 32: 559–578.

24. Ibid.

25. Popp, J. Lakner, Z., Rakos, M.H. and Fari, M. (2014). The effect of bioenergy expansion: Food, energy, and the environment. *Renewable and Sustainable Energy Reviews*. Vol. 32: 562.

26. Mulugenta, Yacob (2009) Evaluating the economics of biodiesel in Africa. *Renewable and Sustainable Energy Reviews.* Vol. 13: 1592.

27. Mitchell, D. (2008). A note on rising food prices. Policy Research Working Paper 4682. The World Bank: Washington, DC.

28. Food and Agriculture Organization (2008). Biofuels: Prospects and Opportunities. FAO, Rome.

29. Oritsejafor, Emmanuel (2016). The deregulation of the Nigerian power sector: A case study of the Nigerian electric power authority. *Journal of Safety and Crisis Management*, 3(2):12–25.

30. Ravindranath, N.H., Lakshmi, C.S., Manuvie, R. and Balachandra, P. (2011). Biofuel production and implications for land use, food production, and environment in India. *Energy Policy*. Vol. 39: 5737–5745.

31. Kgathi, D.L., Mfundisi, K.B., Mmpoelwa, G. and Mosepele, K. (2012). Potential impacts of biofuels on food security in Botswana: A contribution to energy policy. *Energy Policy,* Vol. 43: 70.

32. Ibid., 77

33. World Bank IK Notes, No 47 (August 2002). Using the Indigenous Knowledge of Jatropha: The use of Jatropha curcas oil as a raw material and fuel. Retrieved August 27, 2021, from https://openknowledge.worldbank.org/bitsream/.handle/10986/10791/multi0page.pdf?sequence=1&isAllowed=y.

34. Ibid., p. 73.

35. Ibid., p. 74.

36. Ketlogetswe, C. (2011). Biodiesel development in Botswana—Opportunities and challenges. *Energy for Sustainable Development*, Vol. 15: 192–194.

37. Biofuels Industrial Strategy of the Republic of South Africa. Department of Minerals and Energy. (December 2007), p. 8.

38. Ibid., p. 8.

39. Ibid.

40. Pradhan, A. and Mbohwa, C. (2014). Development of biofuels in South Africa: Challenges and opportunities. *Renewable and Sustainable Energy* Reviews, Vol. 39: 1094.

41. Ibid., p. 1096.

42. United Nations Department of Economic and Social Affairs. *Challenges and Opportunities for Indigenous Peoples Sustainability.* Retrieved September 4, 2021, from https://www.un.org/development/desa/dspd/2021/04/indigenous-peoples -sustainability/.

43. Andrae, Gunnilla, and Beckman, Bjorn (1985). The wheat trap: Bread and underdevelopment in Nigeria. London: Zed Books, p. 5.

44. Ibid.

45. Fentiman, Alicia and Neinbarini, Zabbey (2015). Environmental degradation and cultural erosion in Ogoni-Land: A case study of the oil spills in Bodo. *The Extractive Industries and Society,* Vol. 12(4): 615–624.

46. McLean, K.G., Castillo, Ame R., and Barrett, B. (2012). Energy Innovation and Traditional Knowledge. Traditional Knowledge Bulletin, p. 4.

47. United Nations Department of Economic and Social Affairs. *Challenges and Opportunities for Indigenous Peoples Sustainability.* Retrieved September 4, 2021, from https://www.un.org/development/desa/dspd/2021/04/indigenous-peoples -sustainability/.

48. Fabiyi, Oluseyi O. and Oloukoi, Joseph, (2013). Indigenous Knowledge System and local adaptation strategies to flooding in coastal rural communities of Nigeria. *Journal of Indigenous Social Development*, Vol. 2 (1): 4.

49. Ibid.

50. Popp, J., Lakner, Z., Rakos, M.H. and Fari, M. (2014). The effect of bioenergy expansion: Food, energy, and the environment. *Renewable and Sustainable Energy Reviews*. Vol. 32: 563.

51. Food and Agriculture Organization of the United Nations. Acara, Ghana (2017). Africa Regional Overview of Food Security and Nutrition: The Challenges of Building Resilience to Shocks and Stresses, p. 2.

52. Food and Agriculture Organization of the United Nations (2016). "Peace and Food Security: Investing in resilience to sustain rural livelihoods around conflict, p. 11.

53. Singh, J., Madhoo, N., Michel, P., Sangari, R. and Wakeford, T (2016). Resisting biofuels: the coloniality of poer and indigenous knowledge systems decolonizing the land. *Dark matter,* Retrieved August 27, 2021, from http://www.darkmatter101 .org/site/2016/04/02/resisting-biofuels-the-%e2%80%98coloniality-of-power%e2

%80%99-and-indigenous-knowledge-systems-%e2%80%98decolonising%e2%80%99-the-land/.

54. Ibid.

55. Popp, J., Lakner, Z., Harangi-Rakos, M. and Fari, M. (2014). The effect of bio-energy expansion: Food energy and environment. *Renewable and Sustainable Energy Reviews*, Vol. 32: 559.

56. Blomberg News. Why Exxon-Mobil shares are up despite first annual loss in decades, Accessed on February 5, 2021 from https://www.bloomberg.com/news/videos/2021-02-02/why-exxon-shares-are-up-despite-first-annual-loss-in-decades-video.

57. International Energy Agency (IEA). The Impact of Covid-19 Crisis on Clean Energy Progress. Accessed on February 10, 2021, from https://www.iea.org/articles/the-impact-of-the-covid-19-crisis-on-clean-energy-progress.

Chapter 7

The COVID-19 Pandemic and Indigenous Knowledge—A Case Study

Amidst the recent global pandemic caused by the coronavirus, the global community is confronted with health and food security challenges. The food market has continued to encounter some uncertainties—for instance, the global rice production was set to recover by 1.6 percent in 2020 over the 2019 production level, global cereal production was projected to increase by 2.6 percent in 2020 over the 2019 production, while the production of sugar in 2020 declined by 2.9 percent over the 2019 production level.[1]

However, the spread of COVID-19 has further raised concerns regarding food insecurity in sub-Saharan Africa, a region that has faced food insecurity even before COVID-19 because of climate, environmental degradation, war, and other civil conflicts and recently the demand for food for oil production. With over 239 million people undernourished in the region as of 2018 and about 25 million undernourished in Nigeria the most populous country in the region, the emergence of the COVID-19 pandemic further heightened concerns for food security in the region.[2] Ghana and Nigeria in the West African sub-region experienced a surge in the price of staple food following the outbreak of COVID-19. In Ghana, the price of some basic commodities rose between 20 percent and 30 percent.[3] Similarly, in Nigeria, the closure of borders, ports, schools, and a national lockdown had some socio-economic challenges. Farmers had only limited access to credit, transportation services to move farm produce became limited, and border closures inhibited the importation of food.[4]

Measures to address the COVID-19 pandemic, such as limited credit facilities to farmers and limited transportation between rural and urban centers, also began to affect production, availability, and supply. As a result, the price of staple foods such as tubers, rice and wheat surged. For instance, the consumer price index shows that food increased by 1.18 percent from March to April 2020 caused by the increases in the prices of potatoes, yam and other tubers, bread, cereals, fish, oils, fats, meat, fruits, and vegetables. However, the annual rate of change between April 2019 and April 2020 was 14.22 percent.[5] Figure 7.1 reveals the consumer price index for food in Nigeria between April 2019 and April 2020.

Although there was a shortage of food in Nigeria before COVID-19, border closures in 2018 and 2019 respectively also contributed to the shortages. The border closures were implemented because of security threats by the terrorist group Boko Haram.[6] These threats led to increased smuggling of imported foods and the rise in food prices. The Nigerian Bureau of Statistics (NBS) reported that the rural inflation rate increased by 11.41 percent in December 2019 from 11.30 percent in November 2019. Along the same lines, the composite food index rose by 14.67 percent in December 2019 when compared to 14.48 percent in November 2019.[7]

Given the cost of staples and the challenges of food production and supply during the COVID-19 pandemic, Nigeria like most sub-Saharan countries is likely to face community health crises such as malnutrition, anemia, overweight and stunting. Accordingly, Obadofin, asserts that Nigeria:

. . . remains one of the worst-hit by malnutrition in the sub-Saharan region, with children and women in their reproductive age most affected. The 2018 NBS Demographic Health Survey revealed that 37% of children underage are stunted, 17% severely stunted and 7% wasted. 22% are underweight and 7% are severely underweight.[8]

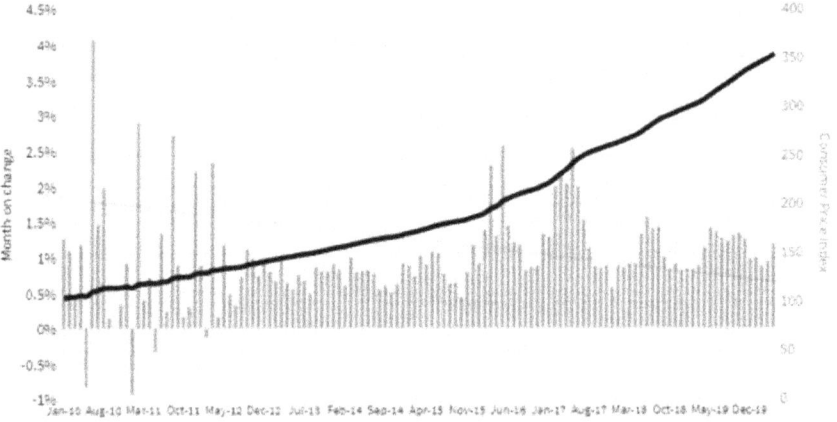

Figure 7.1. Consumer Price Index for Food. *Source:* Obadofin, Olufunmilayo, H. (May 28, 2020) Impact of COVID-19 on Nutrition and Food Shortages in Nigeria. Retrieved September 19, 2021, from *The Guardian* https://pulitzercenter.org/stories/impact -covid-19-nutrition-and-food-shortages-nigeria.

The consequences of COVID-19 on food production and supply are likely to be felt among poor households and small holders, several of which depend on food programs to feed their children. It is estimated that about 2 million Nigerian children already suffer from stunted growth, constituting one of the highest rates in the world.[9]

The COVID-19 pandemic has similarly had adverse effects in Ghana relative to food insecurity and the loss of lives. Regarding food security, it has been reported that the pandemic could create a situation that is comparable to the adverse situation created by Ebola in Liberia, Sierra Leone, Guinea, and the Democratic Republic of Congo (DRC). In the case of Ghana, as of March 26, 2020, 68 cases had been recorded and at least three deaths in a nation of thirty million.[10]

The global pandemic and the attendant closure of borders and transportation has had an impact on food production and supply, the price of staples, and nutrition in general. For instance, the panic buying of food and its limited supply led to the surge in the price of staples. It is reported that the price of food products rose between 20 and 30 percent. The pandemic also began to affect the price of some of Ghana's major agricultural exports such as cashew nuts. In this case, the price at which farmers sell a 100kg bag of cashews dropped between 40 and 50 percent, thus reducing farmers income.[11]

Moreover, the decline in the import of cashews from countries such as China, India and Vietnam also affected the employment of local farmers who depend on the global market for income.[12] The Ghana Food and Non-alcoholic Beverages Division recorded a year-on-year inflation rate of 14.4%. This is six percentage point higher than March 2020 (8.4%) and 6.5 percentage points higher than the average food inflation rate recorded in the previous eight months (7.9%). This translates to food being the predominant driver of year-on-year inflation.[13] Figure 7.2 shows the selected food price index of selected commodities in Ghana from February 2019 through April 2020 which was the global peak period of COVID-19. The price index shows the surge of the prices of selected commodities in 2020.

The challenges of COVID-19 are far reaching for rural farmers—men and women and their families and for those who must sell the end products of the farmlands in local markets. Moreover, the rapid and global spread of COVID-19 led to an economic crisis globally. Thus, we witnessed the economic implications of the pandemic relative to the surge in prices for consumers in Ghana and Nigeria. Recent data has shown that the numbers of people living on less than $5 a day may have increased by two hundred million to half a billion in 2020.[14] As a result, the poorest people in every country have seen their incomes fall due to the pandemic.[15] Along the same lines, the pandemic also contributed to the loss of employment for farmers who are plagued with high food inventories that did not make it to the marketplace.

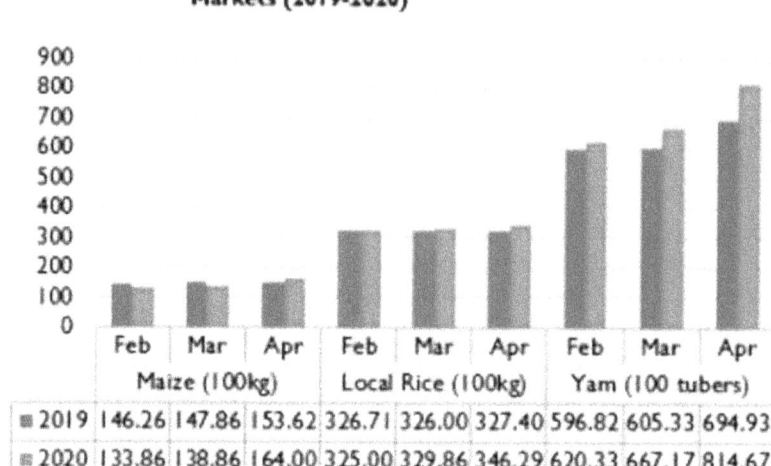

Figure 7.2 Ghana Price Index. *Source:* Obadofin, Olufunmilayo, H. (May 28, 2020) Impact of COVID-19 on Nutrition and Food Shortages in Nigeria. Retrieved September 19, 2021, from *The Guardian* https://pulitzercenter.org/stories/impact-covid-19 -nutrition-and-food-shortages-nigeria.

In addition to the economic challenges of the global pandemic, this chapter suggests that the COVID-19 pandemic also contributed to social challenges in global communities, where there are strong restrictive orders for social inter- actions. These restrictive orders would profoundly impact African countries differently because communal social interactions are important and unique to rural African settings. African rural communities are particularly driven by the pursuit of agricultural ventures and finding enough food for wellness and sustainability. Therefore, subjecting members of these communities to western-type lockdowns and isolation have proved to be a social challenge.[16]

However, considering the global prevalence of COVID-19 infections and death rates globally, African communities are challenged by the dearth of health care facilities, and they reside in high population density dwellings in urban centers such as Lagos (Nigeria) and Accra (Ghana). These dwellings are structured in a manner that makes social distancing challenging. It is important to note that about 56 percent of Africa's urban population lives in overcrowded dwellings.[17]

However, Table 7.1 shows the relative low fatality rates of COVID-19 in Ghana and Nigeria when compared to other developed economies, espe- cially considering the poor health care system, low health budgets, shortage of health practitioners, and poor health facilities. For instance, Ghana has only 200 ventilators for its approximated 30 million population. It appears

Table 7.1. COVID-19 Case Fatality Rates

Countries	Number of cases	Deaths
Brazil	8,444,577	217,037
Nigeria	130,557	1,578
Liberia	1,939	84
Benin Republic	3,782	48
Ghana	65,498	402
USA	25,217,690	420,267
France	3,116,295	73,635
Russia	3,698,246	68,841
South Africa	1,417,537	41, 117

Source: The Coronavirus Resource Center at John Hopkins University, January 29, 2021. Retrieved from https://coronavirus.jhu.edu/map.html.

that community-based and self-care strategies using indigenous methods are responsible for the low fatality rate of COVID-19 in most African communities. Moreover, African countries previous experiences with virus and pandemics such as Ebola and SARS may have been instructive to countries in the West African sub-region amidst the recent COVID-19 pandemic.[18] The next section will examine how indigenous methods were applied to abate the widespread contagion of COVID-19.

COVID-19—AND INDIGENOUS KNOWLEDGE IN GHANA

Ghana was not immune from the health crises that became pervasive in Africa and globally amidst the challenges of the COVID-19 pandemic. While the pandemic affected the social and economic well-being of most Ghanaians, the resilience of the people of Ghana (and other countries in the sub-region) was remarkable. The question to be addressed is how communities in Ghana were able to abate the rapid rate of COVID-19 infection in their communities especially in light of social and cultural norms such as the use of hands to greet, and embracing friends and family members within the communal nature of urban and rural dwellings?

The fact is that western medicines, such as the Pfizer and Moderna vaccines were new in the global market and not accessible to the African market. African countries also remained challenged by a lack of modern health facilities. As mentioned previously, in the case of Ghana, there are only two hundred ventilators to serve a country of thirty million people, thus drawing us closer to an examination of African ingenuity and innovation through indigenous knowledge as an alternative approach for abating COVID-19.[19]

There is a perennial precedence of the use of traditional or folk medicines in treating infectious diseases through human history.[20] African countries have consistently used indigenous medicine to treat diseases such as the Ebola and SARS. The following is a summary of African herbal plants with medicinal properties with a variety of chemical constituents that have been used to provide remedies by indigenous African communities in their struggle for wellness in countries such as Ghana and Nigeria:[21]

Strophanthus gratus is used for traditional herbal medicine in Ghana to manage inflammation.[22] Although, little scientific literature exists to validate its use. However, Ofori, Bah and Borquaye in their clinical studies provides validation that in Ghana *Strophantus gratus* is effectively used for managing inflammation resulting from wounds and snake bites[23] and the leaf extracts have been shown to possess anti-inflammatory and antioxidant activities.[24]

Azadirachta Indica (neem). This traditional medicine has been employed as an antiviral and the leaf extract has been found to be active against several viruses such as polio virus, and Dengue.[25] In the case of COVID-SARS where there is no specific treatment, herbal exploration as ensued as a precautionary method to boost immunity against SARS-COV2. One of such measures is the use of *Neem terpenoids* as an inhibitor of membrane and envelop.[26] It is important to note that *Azardirachta indica* is an indigenous plant commonly grown in India and its subcontinent and its leaf extract has been reported by the scientific community to be effective in inhibiting tumors such as colon cancer and skin carcinogenesis.[27]

Allium sativum (Garlic). There has been ongoing research regarding Garlic antiviral effects to inhibit Herpes, Influenza B, Rhinovirus, and Cytomegalovirus.[28] However, the scientific community in a recent study in Nigeria have also illustrated the inhibitory effect of Allium sativum to renal dysfunction associated with kidney disease.[29]

Phyllanthus amarus. The aqueous extract shows strong antiviral activity for this plant. The anti-viral activity of this plant has been studied over time. Thus, substantial progress on chemical and pharmacological properties and as well as clinical studies have been facilitated. *Phyllantus amarus* plants are used to treat diabetes patients who are considered susceptible to infection diseases.[30]

Hibiscus Tea (Sabdariffa). Clinical evidence has shown that sour tea such as *Hisbiscus Sabdariffa* may be beneficial to improve blood pressure levels and fasting plasma glucose (FPG). Sour tea is a safe natural herbal product with therapeutic effect.[31]

COVID-19 AND INDIGENOUS
KNOWLEDGE IN NIGERIA

The outbreak of Coronavirus in Nigeria overwhelmed Nigerians socially and economically. Nigeria, with a population of 170 million and with significant urban dwellings such as Lagos and Ibadan, faced extraordinary challenges abating the spread of the Coronavirus. By January 2021, there were 130,557 cases of COVID-19 in Nigeria and 1,578 reported dead from the pandemic.[32] Nigeria, as in the case of Ghana, was confronted with several social challenges that could not be entirely addressed with modern medicine. For instance, the lack of antiviral drugs and vaccines in an environment with a poor health system created an adverse social environment that became a challenge for Nigerian communities. Given these challenges, it appears that many Nigerians took advantage of more accessible indigenous anti-viral medicines. Besides, developing economies like Ghana and Nigeria did not obtain the Coronavirus vaccines before the ten largest economies including the United States.[33] The following are among the common indigenous anti-viral plants used in Southwest Nigeria to manage wellness:

1. Mimosaceae, *Mimosa pudica L.* Known locally among the Yoruba people as *patanmo,* it is used to manage fevers, piles, jaundice, leprosy, and dysentery.[34]
2. Boraginaceae, *Hellotropium indicum L.* Locally in the Southwest Nigeria it is known as *Apari-igun* is used to manage wounds, flatulence, inflammation, skin ulcers and conjunctivitis.[35]
3. Euphorbiaceae, *Croton gratissimus.* It is locally known as *Ajekobale,* and used to manage coughs, bleeding gums, eye disorders, influenza, fever, malaria, and skin infections.[36]
4. Verbenaceae, *Lippia multiflora Moldenke.* The plant, locally known as *Eforomoba,* is used to manage fever, constipation, ear infection, eye troubles, and diabetes.[37]

To buttress the importance of IK in social development, the World Health Organization recognized the amalgamation of IK and modern health as a pathway to development.[38] In this vein, Isola suggest that African traditional medicine could serve as an alternative to healthcare delivery system in Nigeria.[39] He posits as follows:

1. African traditional medicine predated orthodox medicine in Nigeria.
2. Traditional medical care is strong in some areas where the orthodox medicine is not effective.

3. There are problems associated with the administration of traditional care such as issues related with the measurability of drugs, dosage, documentation, preservation, potency, and determination of the side effect.
4. However, if the limitations of traditional medicines are addressed their benefits are far reaching and save the lives of African citizens.[40]

The view that at times IK is a viable social development option when it is amalgamated with modern medicine in most developing regions prompted my need to interview a western trained medical practitioner in Lagos, in January 2021.

Dr. CUC reemphasized the importance of IK and how it is used along with modern medicine. Dr. CUC, as denoted by his pseudo name, is an obstetrician and a neonatologist. He has been a medical practitioner since 1984 in urban and semi-rural areas such as Lagos and Ile Ife. Dr. CUC was selected for this study because of his thirty-seven years of experience in urban and semi-rural patient care in Lagos and Ile Ife. He was also selected for this study because he encourages the use of modern medicine along with IK when applicable in his medical practices.

According to Dr. CUC, IK has been an integral part of human development in Nigeria and, because of colonial education it has lost some of its essence and value for contributions to development. This IK includes indigenous food such as vegetables that all have health benefits. For instance, there are medicinal values in the use of Kola nuts and Alligator pepper. Such indigenous crops are used as antibacterial agents to enhance human growth and development.

Dr. CUC acknowledged that IK is at its infancy in this area but boiling and bathing with herbal leaves such as *dongoyaro* and steaming with these leaves are potent for anti-malaria treatment which could otherwise complicate the symptoms of COVID-19. In addition to local diets, and exposure to sunlight for vitamin D, Nigerians, (and most Africans that live in urban and rural dwellings) are frequently exposed to pathogens which weakens the immune system; herbs such as *dongoyaro* has proved useful for these communities.

In his practice, Dr. CUC, often provides health and nutritional information to patients with emphasis on locally produced foods and fruits for pre- and post-natal care. He re-emphasized the use of Kola-nuts and alligator pepper in the morning to abate the spread of infectious diseases. These food crops are often in the offering to guests as an extension of good will and health in traditional and modern homes across the country.

SUMMARY

The effects of COVID-19 in Nigeria as in the case of Ghana, was likely to affect the health and nutrition of the most vulnerable members of the community. For example, about 45 million people were acutely food insecure globally since February 2020, the majority of whom reside in South and Southeast Asia (estimated at 33 million people) and the remainder are in sub-Saharan Africa.[41] There are growing concerns that food insecurity in the present climate in Ghana would cause chronic malnutrition and stunting growth of adolescent children. However, the government of Ghana, along with civic organizations, has embarked on efforts to provide access for food palliatives.[42]

The high food and fuel prices created pressures on poor households to withdraw their children from schools. Women and young girls in sub-Saharan Africa appeared to be profoundly affected by these social crises. Albeit women are responsible for 60 to 80 percent of the agricultural labor supplied in the marketplace and form most of the labor in the commercial sectors in many African cities and towns. They have remained inhibited by the lack of formal economic support and education opportunities. Thus, their recognized economic role in most African countries has remained challenged by the direct and indirect social cost of the limited access to resources such as land, affordable health care, and educational opportunities.[43]

The COVID-19 global pandemic also exacerbated the prices of food in most sub-Saharan African countries. Recent cases of the surge in food prices in Nigeria and Ghana suggests that the closure of borders and seaports have adversely affected the supply and production of food. Invariably, the surge in food prices and the limited access to food will further contribute to nutritional challenges such as stunted growth for vulnerable groups such as adolescent children.

The rise of COVID-19 in most African countries has also brought about other social challenges such as healthcare in developing communities that are confronted with the dearth of healthcare systems and infrastructures. However, the challenges of COVID-19 in Ghana and Nigeria also brought about the need to further examine the value of IK as an alternative approach to wellness amidst the global pandemic and challenges.

The COVID-19 pandemic drew attention to the use of IK for addressing wellness in both rural and urban communities. The ability to meet the demand for food in an environment mired by the lack of healthcare infrastructure depends upon community wellness. The use of IK provides an alternative intervention for wellness in communities where there is a dearth of social infrastructures. The interview with Dr. CUC, a western trained medical practitioner, advances the argument that IK is a viable option for wellness in developing communities.

NOTES

1. Food Agriculture Organization. Bi-Annual Report on Global Food Markets 2020-COVID 19, pp. 1–6.

2. Ehui, Simeon (May 14, 2020). Protecting food security in Africa during COVID-19. Brookings Institute. Retrieved June 19, 2020, from https://www .brookings.edu/blog/africa-in-focus/2020/05/14/protecting-food-security-in-africa -during-covid-19/.

3. Ibid.

4. Obadofin, Olufunmilayo Hbibat (May 28, 2020). Impact of COVID-19 on nutrition and food shortages in Nigeria. Putltzer Center. Retrieved June 19, 2020, from *The Guardian Nigeria*. https://pultzercenter.org/publication/guardian-nigeria.

5. Ibid., p. 2.

6. Iseghe, Ajayi (Sunday, June 24, 2018). Food Shortages in Nigeria. *Independent Newspaper*.

7. Olusegun, Abisoye (January 2019). Nigeria's inflation rises to 11.98%, Highest rate since June 2018. *Independent Newspaper*. Retrieved June 19, 2020, from independent.ng/nigeria's-risesto11.98-highest. rate-since-june-2018/.

8. Obadofin, Olufunmilayo Habibat (May 28, 2020). Impact of COVID-19 on nutrition and food shortages in Nigeria. Pulitzer Center. Retrieved June 19, 2020, from *The Guardian Nigeria*. https://pultzercenter.org/publication/guardian-nigeria.

9. Ibid.

10. Gakpo, Joseph Opoku (March 26, 2020). COVID-19 virus spreads prompt food insecurity fears in Africa. Alliance for Science. p. 2. Retrieved June 22, 2020 from: http://allianceforscience.cornell.edu/blog/2020/o3/covid-19-virus-spread-prompts -food-insecurity-fears-in-africa/.

11. Ibid., p. 4.

12. Ibid.

13. Ghana Statistics Consumer Price Index. April 2020. Retrieved June 22, 2020, from: https://statsghana.gov.gh/gssmain/fileUpload/Price%20Indices/Newsletter _CPI_April_2020.pdf.

14. Oxfam (2020). The Inequality Virus: Bringing together a world torn apart by coronavirus through a fair, just, and sustainable economy. p. 24. Retrieved from www .oxfam.org January 27, 2021.

15. Ibid.

16. Kassa, M.D. and Grace, J.M. (2020). Race against the death or starvation? COVID-19 and its impact on African populations. *Health Reviews*, Vol. 41(30): 2.

17. Oppong, R. Joseph (2020). The African COVID-19 anomaly. *African Geographical Review*, Vol. 39(3): 283.

18. Ibid., p. 284.

19. Ibid., pp. 282–288.

20. Lifongo, Lydia L., Simboen, Conrad V., Ntie-Kang, Fidele, Babiaka, Smith B. and Judson, Philip N. (2014). A bioactivity versus ethnobotanical survey of medicinal plants from Nigeria West Africa. *Journal of National Product Bioprospect,* Vol. 4: 1.

21. Ibid., p. 1.

22. Offori-Baah, Sam & Borquaye, Lawrence Sheringham (2019). Ethanolic leaf from Strophnatus gratus (Hook) Franch. (Apocynaceae) exhibits anti-inflamatory and antioxidant activities. *Cogent-Biology*, Vol. 5: p. 1-2. Accessed December 9, 2021, from https://doi.org/10.1080/23312025.2019.1710431.

23. Ibid., p. 11.

24. Ibid.

25. Singh, Namita, Kumar, Pradeep & Kumar, Naresh (2020). Spices and herbs: Potential antiviral preventives and immunity boosters during COVID-19. *Phytotherapy Research*, Issue 2021 (35): 2747.

26. Ibid., pp. 2747–2749.

27. Perumal, Elumalai; Dharmalingam, Nanadagopal Gunadharini; Kalimuthu, Senthilkumar; Sivanantham, Banudevi; Ramachandran, Arunkumar; Chelakkan, Selvansean-Benson; Govindaraj, Sharmila and Jagadeesan, Arunakara (2012). Ethanolic neem (Azaidrachta indica A. juss) leaf extract inducies apoptosis and inhibits the IGF signaling pathway in breast cancer cell lines. *Biomedicine & Preventive Nutrition,* Vol. 2: 59.

28. Namita Singh; Pradeep Kumar & Naresh Kumar (2020). Spices and herbs: Potential antiviral preventives and immunity boosters during COVID-19. *Phytotherapy Research*, Issue 2021 (35): 2747–2749.

29. Ganiyu Oboh, Ayodele, J. Akinyemi, Adedayo, O. Ademiluyi, (2013). Inhibitory effects of Phenolic Extract from Garlic on Angiotesin-1 Converting Enzyme and Cisplatin induced Lipid Peroxidation—*In Vitro.* (2013). *International Journal of Biomedical Science,* Vol. 9 (2): 98–105.

30. Hasenah Ali; P.J. Houghton; & Amala Soumyanath, (2006). *Journal of Ethnopharmacology*, Vol. 107: p. 454.

31. Said N. Bousheri; Razieh, Karimbeiki; Sara Ghasempour; Samira-Sadat, Ghalishourani; Makan Pourmasoumi; Ami, Hadi; Munirah, Mbabazi; Ziyaaddin, Keshavarpou, Pour; Mostafa, Assarroudi; Marzieh, Mahmoodi; Abdolrasool, Khosravi; Fariborz, Mansour-Ghanael & Farahnazz, Joukar; (2020). The efficacy of sour tea (Hsibiscus Sabdariffa L.) on selecxted cardiovascular disease risk factors: A systematic review and meta-analysis of randomized clinical trials. *Phytotheraphy Research*, Vol. 34: 337.

32. John Hopkins University Coronavirus Resource Center. Global Report (2021). Accessed on January 29, 2021, from https://coronavirus.jhu.edu/map.html.

33. Nancy Brenan (Sunday, January 31, 2021: 10:30am). Facing Challenges, CBS *Face The Nation.*

34. Omonike, O. Ogbole; Toluwanmi, E. Akinleye; Peter, A. Segun; Temitope, C. Faleye; & Adekunle, J. Adeniji; (2018). In vitro antiviral activity of twenty-seven medicinal plant extracts from southwest Nigeria against three serotypes of echoviruses. *Virology Journal*, Vol. 15(10): 3. Accessed from https://doi.org/10.1186/s12985 -018-1022-7.

35. Ibid.

36. Ibid.

37. Ibid.

38. Oritsejafor, E and Jones, E. (2004). Folk and modern medicine in Africa: A case study of mental health care in Liberia. *Liberian Studies Journal*, Vol. XXIX (2): 1.

39. Isola, O.I. (2013). The relevance of the African traditional medicine (Alternative Medicine) To health care delivery system in Nigeria. *The Journal of Developing Areas,* Vol. 47(1): 319–338.

40. Ibid., p. 319.

41. United Nations Policy Brief, (June 2020). The impact of COVID-19 on food security and nutrition.

42. Apiah-Tokuh, Rachel (April 21, 2020). COVID-19 Pandemic could cause widespread stunting in Ghana. Retrieved June 22, 2020, from hhtps://www.globalcitizen.org/en/content/ghana-food-insceurity-covid-19/.

43. Gappah Petina, (2011, August-September) Women are our best hope for the continent. *The African Report,* pp. 24–25.

Chapter 8

Land Tenure and the Role of Women in Economic Development in Africa

The internationalization of the food system regimes and capital accumulation as discussed was accompanied by the process of deregulation and denationalization, particularly in the global south. This pattern of accumulation exposed the global south to food dumping, and price surges in the cost of food, especially imported food which the domestic producers and consumers have to contend with.[1] The corporatist nature of the political economy of the agriculture development in the new food regime after the 1980s also fermented the growth of niche markets, contract farming, and semi-manufacturing food processing markets that have further marginalized indigenous farmers.[2] To understand the conditions of primitive accumulation, which is predatory at best, it is instructive to examine how the growth of the liberal market forces have reinforced this form of accumulation through land tenure systems and the subjugation of women as one of the primary productive forces in indigenous agriculture development.

LAND TENURE

In indigenous communities of sub-Saharan West Africa, agricultural land is guided by indigenous regulations which determines the extent of agricultural productivity. In some indigenous communities land is owned communally by extended families. This is the case in Ghana. In the Gyamfiase-Adenya community, land is owned exclusively by the extended families on the principles of matrilineal or patrilineal kingship principles.[3] Through this arrangement, land is granted permanently or temporarily to others for farming or any other form of agriculture projects. Meanwhile in other indigenous communities

such as the *Krobo* in Ghana, land is acquired for farming through an arrangement that allows for individuals to pool their financial resources.[4]

However, the challenges of land tenure and its predatory nature in the colonial and post-colonial state appears to be quite glaring compared to the challenges of land tenure in Zimbabwe which was established as a settler colony.

LAND TENURE IN ZIMBABWE COLONIAL
AND POST-COLONIAL DIMENSIONS

The evolution of the land tenure system in modern day Zimbabwe began
prior to the arrival of the colonialists in the 19th century. Though the political
structures among the indigenous groups were hierarchical, land was communally owned. For instance, among the Shona ethnic groups, the indigenous
chiefs controlled resources as the guardian of the land. The founding lineages
established communal right on the land for the collective whole and future
generations of their own kin and any others within the *niyika* or chiefdom.[5]
The ancestral history of the Shona tribe is also known for the powerful
agnatic ancestors of the founding lineage referred to as the *mhondoro,* which
were responsible for ensuring rain and the authority to confer the authority
over land possession on the living representatives of the chiefs.[6]

It is important to note that the relationship between land guardianship and
the political dominance between the various lineages regarding land ownership is at times far more complex in two ways. Firstly, the term ownership
of land does not describe all forms of control over land in the pre-colonial
period. Secondly, the belief in land guardianship did not necessarily enable
political dominance in a direct and mechanistic way among lineages. Instead,
since ownership of resources was not contested, the ability of dominant lineages to employ the sacredness of a particular resource to reinforce authority
varied from one region to another in pre-colonial Zimbabwe.[7]

COLONIAL LAND TENURE DIMENSIONS

Zimbabwe was a settler colony for 90 years and until independence in 1980,
had a sizable portion of its customary fertile land taken through physical and
exogenous land tenure regulations.[8] In the case of Zimbabwe, the predatory
acquisition of land began under the British South African Company in 1890.
The company led an expedition for the colonization of Zimbabwe as a settler
colony between 1890 and 1893. The expedition led to the defeat of the Shona
and the Ndebele states. Given the successful outcome of the expedition, the

British South African Company was given a Royal Charter and the members of the expedition were subsequently recruited with the promise of free farmlands that was approximated at 1500 morgen which is an equivalent of 3175 acres and 15 reefs of gold.[9]

The predatory nature of the colonial accumulation was reinforced by the British South African Company through regulatory processes such as survey regulations. In this regard, the Company issued survey regulations which converted land occupation permits into land deeds. Invariably, section 27 of the regulations promulgated that the company administrator is the owner of all designated lands and possesses the right as the owner of all vacated or un-allotted land regarding native reserves or customary lands. As a result, native reserves and or customary lands were taken away from original indigenous owners.[10]

POST-COLONIAL DIMENSIONS

The issue of land tenure played a primary role in the nationalist agitation for independence in Zimbabwe. The primary issues in the quest for independence was the issue of customary land tenure. The political framework at independence was socialist and it was believed at that juncture to be consistent with the customary approach to land tenure. Thus, Robert Mugabe, the Prime Minister and President of Zimbabwe at Independence, suggested:

> In respect of agriculture, we have no difficulty because our own traditional system is identical with the Marxist-Leninist approach: at least in so far as ownership of land is concerned. Land has never belonged to individuals. . . . [11]

Invariably, Prime Minister Robert Mugabe equated customary ownership with common ownership and the state by arguing that the state will serve as the custodian of the people and dictate the means of production rather than market interests. As a result, the Communal Land Act of 1982 gave the president the power to authorize land occupation.[12] The rural district councils were also given the power to grant consent to whosoever would like to use land for agricultural and residential activities. Consequently, under the administration of President Mugabe there appears to be a competing interest between the traditional leaders and the state regarding where power lies when it comes to land allocation. The traditional chiefs maintained their influence regarding land tenure but not without state intervention in several cases.[13]

Therefore, what emerged in the post-colonial state is a reinforcement of social and class differentiation which was an extension of the colonial state machinations that alienated traditional rulers from their primary mode of production. As a result, the social relations between the state and traditional rulers were equally exploitative.[14] A challenging issue that emerged during the return of indigenous lands to Black Zimbabweans by the Mugabe administration was the capital flight that accompanied the changes in the tenure system. Several white farmers either moved out of Zimbabwe and/or lost employment and revenue. At the same time, the economic conditions of the new black owners did not necessarily improve because of the dire economic conditions in Zimbabwe in the early 2000s. As a result, some of the new black owners forged partnerships with white farmers for mutual economic opportunities.[15]

GENDER DIMENSION OF CAPITAL ACCUMULATION: THE CASE OF ZIMBABWE AND NIGERIA

Women and indigenous agricultural development in Zimbabwe

African women, and in particular, women in rural communities have historically been the backbone of rural agricultural development. Women farmers globally are responsible for about half of world food production and about 80 percent of food production in sub-Saharan Africa.[16] However, rural women in Zimbabwe, like other parts of Africa, are linked to the land they live and work on as well as the environment and its natural resources.[17]

Thus, as in other parts of Africa there is an inseparable linkage between rural communities and their mode of production. Therefore, Zimbabwean rural women are active participants in indigenous agricultural development. For instance, indigenous women in the eastern region of Zimbabwe use wild fruits and animals to predict the weather in the same manner as the Swazis in South Africa. In this case, the women delay the fruiting of trees such as tsambatsi (lannea *edulis*), maroro, (*annona senegalenis*) and hute (syszygium *cordatum*), and along with the delayed growth regrowth of grasses from the months of August to September are used to determine that drought has ensued. Along the same lines, rural women in the southern part of Zimbabwe depend on wild fruit trees Umtshwankela (vitex *Mombasa*), Umkhuna (*parinari curatellifolia*), and Umthunduluka (*xmenia caffra*) as an indicator of coming rainy season; abundance availability of these wild fruits towards the rainy season shows that below normal rainfall should be expected.[18] The use of these wild fruits are profound examples of the role women play in the agricultural production system in Zimbabwe.

Land Tenure and Gender Challenges in Zimbabwe

Traditionally, African women from a production perspective have focused on the production of household food production while men have focused on the production of cash crops and often migrate.[19] Women play several roles as producers, mothers, nurturers and to a larger extent, provide a social safety next against the background of social and economic inequities. In this regard, Akello and Sarr[20] suggest that to understand the context in which rural women experience poverty, provide labor for agriculture, and provide livelihoods to their families, one must understand the social and gender differentiations created by development policies. Therefore, development policies such as economic liberalization processes have not necessarily improved the lot of women in agriculture in Africa as a productive force and as a class of beneficiaries.[21] In fact, policies such as liberalization and privatization have further contributed to the marginalization of women because these policies have promoted the reduction of state resources such as credit and educational facilities that have subsequently entrenched women and their families in poverty.[22] Accordingly, Butt, Hassan, Mehmood, and Muhammad suggest that rural women have continued to be confronted with social and economic problems compared to men:

> Rural women face more problems and difficulties than that of men in gaining access to credit and extension education services related to agriculture and livestock management and food security.[23]

Therefore, it is important to examine African rural communities in the context of the social differentiation that has remained pervasive. It is even more apparent for women who are engaged in agriculture. For instance, in the case of Zimbabwe, indigenous communities tend to marginalize women through the process of labor recruitment practices which often depends on social networks or a network of alliances. The family plays an integral part in the recruitment and the mobilization of labor processes. Quite often the labor of women is acquired through marriage. Thus, men acquire lands through marriage and consequently the labor of women are sustained through the marital arrangement.[24] While women in some societies can own property, the nature of social-cultural values that have persisted over time has continued to inhibit the overall well-being of women in the colonial and post-colonial state.

Land Tenure in Nigeria

Land tenure is the process through which land is owned and possessed. It is a framework that embodies legal and or customary structure whereby individual groups or organizations gain access to the economic and social opportunities through the possession of land.[25] Most land systems irrespective of culture are interwoven into property rights that are linked to the property rights which are linked to the propriety land units. The propriety land units are the decision-making unit which is important to all decision-making process about land use. Land uses comprise of two elements:

1. the run of property rights
2. the area of physical property[26]

Any land system may portray categories of estates or rights in land. These rights are absolute or derivative. An absolute interest are those rights in land that confers upon their holder's ownership. The absolute interests tend to confer absolute ownership and as such allow for the highest scope of propriety decisions as to the use of land and management of land.[27]

However, the land ownership structure in Nigeria is based on the absolute and derivative interests. The ownership of land has evolved over three epochs:

1. **Land Ownership in the Pre-Colonial Period,** the land tenure system in Nigeria during the pre-colonial period was the customary land tenancy, where land is owned by villages, towns, communities, and families in trust of all family members. During the pre-colonial period land belonged to the community or a family.

   Therefore, individuals are not preoccupied with monetary compensations or fees since the land would be in the actual ownership or absolute ownership of the community. The absolute ownership is often vested in the community interests or the rights of individuals which are derivative.[28]

Thus, customary land was held as follows:

a. Communal Land
b. Stool or Chieftaincy
c. Family Land
d. Individual or separate property[29]

Land during the pre-colonial period was held under customary tenure and could not be sold or alienated.

1. *Land Ownership in the Colonial Period,* Land ownership structure in Nigeria during the colonial period was primarily influenced by the British colonialists. British colonial rule was predicated by economic and governance in the colonies. Central to the British interests in

colonies such as Nigeria was land. Thus, land was a major factor of production that was central to the colonialist's economic, social, and political interests. British conglomerates, such as the National African Company and, subsequently, the Royal Niger Company dominated this process.[30] However, two major Land Acts were promulgated to advance land ownership, occupancy, alienation, and management in Nigeria.

2. *The Land Tenure Decree of 1962,* the 1962 land tenure decree was promulgated to replace the Land and Native Rights Act of 1916 which indicated that all lands in each of the states in Northern Nigeria were under the authority of the Minister responsible for land matters who administers the use of the land on the behalf of the natives. Consequently, all other persons that are not indigenous Northerners are not in consideration as natives. However, the natives are granted land occupancy titles for a few years.[31]

3. *The Land Use Act of 1978,* this Land Act was enacted on March 29, 1978, as the primary policy that governed land ownership, alienation, acquisition, administration, and management within the Federal Republic of Nigeria. Section 1 and 2 of the 1978 Land Act vests all land comprised in the territory of each state in the Governor of each state in the Federal Republic of Nigeria. The Governor of each states has the right of maximum holding period for ninety-nine years and subject to payment of a fixed ground rent to the Governor.[32]

WOMEN AND INDIGENOUS AGRICULTURAL DEVELOPMENT IN NIGERIA

Nigeria is the most populous country in Africa with a population of 180 million people with an annual growth rate of 3.8 percent from 2009–2014. Fifty-nine percent or 105 million Nigerians are under the age of 35 years old. Nigeria is also Africa's biggest economy. 53 percent of the population lives in the rural areas.[33]

It is among the rural communities that the issues related to poverty and hunger are more profound. At the same time, over 90 percent of food produced in the country is cultivated by small holder farmers in rural communities. About 80 percent of these small holders live below poverty level and their communities have limited modern health infrastructures. Poverty in Nigeria is acutely severe in the rural areas at a rate of 44. 9 percent.[34] In the rural settings, poor rural women and men depend on agriculture and about 70 percent are subsistence small holders who produce about 90 percent of Nigeria's food on un-irrigated plots that primarily depend on rainfall.[35]

However, the contributions of the indigenous population and particularly women are undoubtedly important for agricultural development in Nigeria

THE GENDER ROLE

In Nigeria men constitute about 50.4 percent and women 49.6 percent of the population.[36] Both men and women are responsible for producing the country's food.[37] However, the role of both men and women have often been misconstrued due to a lack of the understanding of how socio-economic factors shape gender roles.

To better understand the challenges of land tenure in Nigeria, one must assess these challenges in the context of the changing political, social, economic, and cultural landscape of Nigeria. Yet, it is important to acknowledge that gender inequality is also an attributive factor in the limited access to land for women. For instance, men and women are invariably affected differently in their operational abilities like markets.[38] Women are more constrained than their male counterparts in terms of access to information technology, inputs, credit facilities and land. To accentuate the gender inequalities, some crops are even labeled man's crops and other crops are regarded as women's crops.[39]

A closer look at the production sector of the Nigerian agriculture sector shows that Nigerian rural women farmers have continued to play pivotal roles in the sector. They are responsible for 70 percent of agricultural labor, 50 percent of work in animal husbandry, and 60 percent of food processing activities.[40] Nevertheless, men are often presumed to be primarily the main participants of production units. However, it can be argued that efforts by men and women in the agriculture production sector can be complimentary. Nonetheless, unlike men, women's roles in rural agriculture is often relegated and undervalued because of social, cultural, and economic factors such as the male dominated culture in Nigeria that often places women in an inferior position; customs that forbid women from owning land; and beliefs that keep women in subordinated positions relative to men; and unpaid labor such as child and elder care within their communities.[41]

Nigerian rural women have played an integral role in agricultural development using indigenous knowledge for food production and medicinal purposes. For instance, rural women in Tonkere village in Ife, the southwestern part of Nigeria, who are herb sellers (about 80 percent) have been able to determine the viability of soaked seeds for agricultural production.[42] Similarly, in Ogun State, Nigerian women have used indigenous knowledge for numerous purposes including the drying of vegetables and the smoking of fish and meat used for food preservation. The soaking of seeds is also employed by women in Ogun State to determine appropriate seed selection for food production. Indigenous Knowledge is also used for medicinal purposes by rural women. In this case, coconut oil is used to treat rashes; Bitter leaf, a vegetable, when combined with local gin is used to treat measles; and Unripe pawpaw is used to treat young children with jaundice.[43]

The essence of indigenous rural agricultural development in Nigeria is inherent in the role women play in the agriculture sector. Nigerian rural women provide most of the labor and are involved in important agriculture activities such as the production of cash crops and the farming of livestock.[44] In indigenous communities in Nigeria, the men prepare the land for farming by clearing and burning the bushes while the women perform the planting, weeding, harvesting, and processing of the crops.[45]

However, despite the integral role that women play in the production activities of most farming communities, rural women have remained the neglected majority in development programs that directly impact rural communities. For instance, women's work in the non-wage sector of the production of agriculture is often neglected; and women's work and contributions in the agriculture sector in general are often misrepresented by development officers. Conversely, men's work in the agriculture sector is reflected in the development analysis.

LAND TENURE AND GENDER CHALLENGES IN NIGERIA

When it comes to land tenure the extent of social differentiation between male and female farmers is profound. In Nigeria, gender roles are shaped by social rights and entitlements and must be examined in the context in which women are denied economic and political empowerment. As a result, women in Nigerian communities are vulnerable to poverty, poor healthcare, and education.

In Nigeria, just like other African societies, gender discrimination has been a profound challenge in the colonial and post-colonial period. Historically, social differentiation has found its roots in the family where gender norms are first reflected and later became expansive in the larger society as part of the traditional values. However, post-colonial communities in Africa and Nigeria in this case are not better off in terms of wealth distribution.[46]

Thus, land as capital has remained a scarce resource for women because of discriminatory regimes that tend to contribute to social inequalities. These inequalities are evident in post-colonial Nigeria when considering land reforms, such as the Nigerian Land Use Reform Act of 1978. Access to rural land for women has remained elusive for the most part and the possession of rural lands are primarily in the hands of men.

As discussed, in Nigeria, gender roles are linked to social rights. These rights quite often deny women the political and economic power to own land. Therefore, the consequence of such gender inequity is the alienation and dis-empowerment of rural women from the right to own agriculture land which is a primary source of wealth. The economic implications of such economic dis-empowerment are far reaching; rural women are at times the head of house-holds and are often care givers, therefore, the social and economic conditions of rural women are likely to be further entrenched in poverty and hunger.[47]

The relationship between gender issues and the ownership of land pre-dated the colonial period. Gender roles in most African cultures as we have discussed earlier precludes women from owning property such as land. However, in the case of Nigeria, post-colonial land reforms such as the Nigerian Land Use Act of 1978 has not gone far enough in addressing the problem of gender inequity when it comes to land ownership. Although the Act was established primarily to address the challenges of land redistribution among all Nigerians equally, instead it has further enabled landlessness and the vulnerability of women to poverty since they could not own rural land for agriculture production.[48]

The Nigerian Land Use Act of 1978, by extension, removed original farm owners under customary laws to titles of their land in the interest of all citizens. However, the mother deed of the land is sometimes changed, and the land is re-sold time over time to prospective buyers. The mere fact that women cannot own most customary land excludes them from the economic benefits of land ownership.[49]

In this regard, the 2019 National Bureau of Statistics report on poverty and inequality shows that 40 percent of the total population of Nigeria, or 80 mil-lion, live below the country poverty level of N137, 430 ($381.75) per year.[50] Forty-nine percent of those living below the poverty line are women and only about 7.2 percent of the Nigerian women own agricultural land.[51]

Although, some Nigerian women own personal land, it is important to note that most of these women have limited access to farmland. Studies have shown that even in the case where women acquired land through inheritance, or through loans, these women are likely to lose the land if they are divorced from their husbands or in the case of death to their partner. Thus, the chal-lenge for women in some rural communities in Nigeria is not only access to land but their ability to control land ownership.[52] Rural women in Nigeria also face other forms of social differentiation particularly in the areas of agricul-ture extension services and education. It has been noted by some scholars that women face challenges in obtaining extension services because of limited involvement in agriculture development policies and the general bias towards women.[53] Although women and young girls are engaged in education, this has not translated into greater rates of educational participation for women when compared to men.[54] Therefore, women have remained the neglected members of indigenous communities despite their profound contributions to agriculture activities in these communities.

SUMMARY

Lessons from Zimbabwe and Nigeria illustrate the arguments that colonial and post-colonial social and economic structures have contributed to the peasantization of indigenous communities. In the process of creating this class structure, indigenous rural women are disproportionately neglected and marginalized in the development process.

However, liberal policies such as Structural Adjustment Programs (SAP) and some of the nationalist approaches towards land tenure have further accentuated social inequalities, such as gender marginalization in the agricultural sector of most sub-Saharan African countries. In this regard, the modernist development model which accompanied the SAP had served as a veil for gender bias. The policy seems to have favored capitalists' interests in the production and export of cash crops with investible funds. This support was advantageous to a sector dominated by men. While at the same time, the policy marginalized women by given extraordinarily little financial attention to the food crops production sector which is dominated by women.[55] An area often dominated by women but also pivotal for agricultural development in sub-Saharan Africa.

NOTES

1. McMichael, P. (1992). Tensions between national and international control of the world food order: Contours of a new food regime. *Sociological Perspectives*, Vol. 35(2): 353.

2. Ibid., pp. 346–347.

3. Gyasi, Edwin A. and William, S.A. (2004). Aspects off resources tenure that conserve biodiversity: The case of southern and northern Ghana. in Gyasi, Edwin A. & Kranjac-Berisalvlejevic, G. (2004). Managing Agro-diversity the Traditional Way: Lessons from West Africa in Sustainable of Biodiversity and Related Natural Resources. New York: United Nations University Press, p. 217.

4. Ibid., p. 218.

5. O'Flaherty, M. (1998). Communal tenure in Zimbabwe: Divergent models of collective land holding in the communal areas. *Journal of the International African Institute*, Vol. 68(4): 541.

6. Ibid.

7. Ibid., pp. 541–542.

8. Tshuma, L. (1998). Colonial and post-colonial reconstructions of customary land tenure in Zimbabwe. *Social and Legal Studies*, Vol.7(1): 77.

9. Ibid., p. 78.

10. Ibid.

11. Ibid., p. 85.

12. Ibid., p. 86.

13. Ibid., p. 87.

14. Ibid., p. 90.

15. Sieff, Kevin (September 14, 2015). Zimbabwe seized white farmers land. Now some are being invited back. *Washington Post*, Retrieved on December 10, 2020 from https://www.washingtonpost.com/world/africa/zimbabwe-seized-white-farmers-land-now-some-are-being-invited-back/2015/09/14/456f66d6-45d2-11e5-9f53-d1e3ddfd0cda_story.html

16. CPAR Report, Winter 2009. Empowering female farmers in rural Africa, p. 1.

17. Maunganidze, L. (2016). A moral compass that slipped: Indigenous knowledge systems and rural development in Zimbabwe. *Cogent Social Sciences,* p. 2. Accessed on January 3, 2021, from http://dx.doi.org/10.1080/2331886.2016.1266749.

18. Sithole, A. and Lekorwe, M. (2019). Women's use of indigenous knowledge systems to cope with climate change. *Advances in Social Sciences Research Journal*, Vol. 6, No. 6: 115. Accessed on January 3, 2012, from DoI: 10.14738/ASSRJ.66.6470.

19. Ibid.

20. Akello, S. and Sarr, F. (1999). The economic role of women in agricultural and rural development: The promotion of income-generating activities. CTA Annual Report, p. 5.

21. Doss, C.R. (2018). Women and agricultural productivity: Reframing the issues. *Development Policy Review*, Vol. 36: 36.

22. Akello, S. and Sarr, F. (1999). The economic role of women in agricultural and rural development: The promotion of income-generating activities. CTA Annual Report, p. 5.

23. Butt, T.M, Hassan, Z.Y., Mehmood, K.K. and Muhammad, S. (2010). Role of rural women in agricultural development and their constraints. *Journal of Agriculture & Social Sciences*, Vol. 6(3): 54.

24. Tshuma, L. (1998). Colonial and post-colonial reconstructions of customary land tenure in Zimbabwe. *Social and Legal Studies*, Vol. 7(1): 84.

25. Udoekanem, N.B., Adoga, D.O., and Onwumere, V.O. (2014). Land ownership in Nigeria: Historical development, current issues, and future expectations. *Journal of Environment and Earth Science*, Vol. 4 (21): 182.

26. Ibid.

27. Ibid.

28. Ibid.

29. Ibid.

30. Ibid., p. 184.

31. Ibid., p. 185.

32. Ibid., p. 185.

33. Gbossa, N., Odoemena, B. and Kamara, M. (April 03, 2012). Nigeria-Country Case International Fund for Agricultural Development. Accessed February 15, 2021, from https://www.ifad.org/en/web/operations/country/id/nigeria.

34. Ibid.

35. Ibid.

36. Mohammed, B.T. and Abbdulquadri, A.F. (2012). Comparative analysis of gender involvement in agricultural production. *Journal of Development and Agricultural Economics*, Vol. 4(8): 241.

37. Ibid.

38. Ibid.

39. Ibid.

40. Ibid.

41. Ibid., p. 242.

42. Olatokun, W. and Ayanbode, O.F. (2009). Use of indigenous knowledge by women in a Nigerian rural community. *Indian Journal Traditional Knowledge*, Vol. 8(2): 288.

43. Ibid., p. 291.

44. Chikwendu, D.O. and Arokoyo, J.O. (1997). Women and sustainable agricultural development in Nigeria. *Journal of Sustainable Agriculture*, Vol. 11 (1): 55.

45. Ibid.

46. Ajala, T. (2017). Gender discrimination in land ownership and the alleviation of women's poverty in Nigeria: A call for new equities. *International Journal of Discrimination and the Law*, Vol. 17, No. (1): 51–53.

47. Ibid., p. 51.

48. Ibid., p. 58.

49. Ibid., p. 59.

50. The World Bank Brief. May 28, 2020. Nigeria releases new report on poverty and inequalities in the country. Accessed December 19, 2020, from https://www.worldbank.org/en/programs/lsms/brief/nigeria-releases-new-report-on-poverty-and-inequality-in-country.

51. Ajala, T. Gender discrimination in land ownership and the alleviation of women's poverty in Nigeria: A call for new equities. *International Journal of Discrimination and the Law*, Vol. 17, (1): 57.

52. Chikwendu, D.O. and Arokoyo, J.O. (1997). Women and Sustainable Agricultural Development in Nigeria. *Journal of Sustainable Agriculture*, Vol.11(1): 55.

53. Ogunlela, Y.I. and Mukhtar, A.A. (2009). Gender issues in Agriculture and rural development in Nigeria: The role of women. *Humanity and Social Sciences Journal*, Vol.4(1): 26.

54. Ibid., p. 54.

55. Dibbua, J.I. (2006). Modernization and the Crisis of Development in Africa: The Nigerian Experience. London: Ashgate Publisher, p. 273.

Chapter 9

The Way Forward

The vulnerability of developing economies to food insecurity has remained undoubtedly a global challenge. In this regard, the World Bank issued an agenda to end poverty and hunger by 2030. The Bank suggested that to end poverty and hunger by 2030, the world will need a food system that provides food for every person, every day and everywhere. It requires an approach that will raise the income of the poorest people and provide safe food and adequate nutrition.[1] The World Bank Group suggests that the agenda for ending poverty and hunger will lean on multi-facet strategies and partnerships to achieve these goals. The strategies are targeted to increasing income gains of at least 60 percent in sub-Saharan Africa by increasing farming yields and reducing waste. The World Bank projected that a co-relation between poverty reduction with higher yields will lead to poverty reduction.[2]

Similarly, the Food and Agriculture Organization of the United Nations has embarked upon initiatives to advance agricultural development with the adoption of the Sustainable Development Goals (SDGs). The SDGs were adopted by 195 member countries of the United Nations in 2015. The SDGs replaced the Millennial Development Goals (MDGs). Central to the SDGs is the goal to eradicate hunger and poverty by 2030.[3] Table 9.1 illustrates the seventeen SDGs.

The FAO proposed plan to scale and transform food and agricultural systems was directed towards the SDGs. The FAO envisioned multiple partnerships to eradicate hunger through an integrated framework that entails agroecology. Agroecology, as envisioned by the FAO, will advance the eradication of poverty and hunger by ensuring that agricultural development for developing economies is pursued through scientific and local experiences. This approach is intended to be people-centered and would engage communities from diverse settings to achieve the goal to eradicate hunger and poverty. Through this approach, the FAO also propose to contribute to multiple SDGs.[4]

Table 9.1. United Nations Sustainable Development Goals-2030

Sustainable Development Goals Number	*Description of SDG-Goals*
1.	Eradicate Poverty
2.	Zero Hunger
3.	Good Health
4.	Quality Education
5.	Gender Equality
6.	Clean Water
7.	Affordable and Clean Energy
8.	Decent Work and Economic Growth
9.	Industry, and Innovation
10.	Reduced Inequalities
11.	Sustainable Cities and Communities
12.	Responsible Consumption and Production
13.	Climate Action
14.	Life Below Water
15.	Life on Land
16.	Peace, Justice and Strong Institutions
17.	Partnerships for goals

Source: From "The United Nations Sustainable Development Goals" by the United Nations, © 2021 United Nations. Reprinted with the permission of the United Nations. https://sdgs.un.org/goals.

The accelerated development approaches prescribed by multilateral institutions such as the FAO and the World Bank would only become viable and sustainable if indigenous development cultures are central to the strategies for attaining the SDGs. However, the FAO report did not include substantive discussion of traditional diets. The report lacked the cultural consideration and priorities that is committed to promoting culture and traditional management as a major part of agroecology.[5]

The failure to infuse indigenous strategies in agricultural development projects has historically contributed to the decline of indigenous and traditional foods crops in agricultural production in the Global South. This decline, which begun in the 1960s, was reinforced by agricultural development projects such as the Green Revolution. These projects primarily promoted conventional cereal and horticultural food crops which consequently replaced locally produced crops, thus leaving indigenous food crops undervalued.[6] It is along these lines that Dibua suggests as follows:

the pervasive influence of modernization on the agricultural transformation policies is fundamentally responsible for the poor performance of agriculture. By completely discountenancing the cultural, social, material, and scientific bases of indigenous agriculture, as well as its complexity, the transplanted modern agriculture practices were destined to fail.[7]

Therefore, agricultural development initiatives that are projected to halve hunger and poverty must be examined in the context of the anthropological and cultural context of indigenous communities. The social realities of indigenous societies must be sustained against the background of Western ethnocentric development outlooks that tend to provide development projects with the notion that indigenous development models are adjunct to Western development models. In this regard, Iyam suggests that international development prescriptions must be provided within the context of local relevancy, and they must be germane to indigenous realties.[8] He asserts:

> Despite the "liberal" stance of some funding agencies, target communities as well as anthropologists must conform with donor agencies criteria for implementing specific programs. Anthropologists working in development inevitably have to walk within the familiar but narrow path of satisfying the stipulations of funding agencies and also to make their recommendations locally relevant and culturally acceptable.[9]

Given the global challenges of food security and the failure of accelerated growth models, the strategies that have been used to address global hunger and malnutrition in developing economies have simply taken place in an environment in which traditional and indigenous food systems have been neglected thus contributing to erosion of cheap staple foods and cereal. What has emerged in developing economies globally is massive food insecurity which is not likely to be sustained primarily by technology driven yield improvements nor by an amalgamation of technology and indigenous methods without consideration for the cultural context in which food systems can be further improved.[10] Instead, indigenous agricultural development approaches should be sustained because it is vital to reducing the vulnerability of food-insecure households because indigenous agricultural development approaches are positioned to mitigate in situations where there is high food prices and threats to ecological diversity and biodiversity.[11]

However, Africa seems to still be living with the legacy of colonialism and primitive accumulation. Therefore, the challenge for African countries is to harness the Indigenous Knowledge (IK) transferred from generations to generations because they remain invaluable for sustainable development. Some African leaders and particularly scientists trained in Western models and technologies fail to recognize that western development models have become an obstacle to "development," and they overlook the benefits of IK. The socio, cultural and economic dominance of Western development models have not led to sustainable agricultural development.

Therefore, it would bode well for African leaders, development scholars and policy makers to integrate IK as a primary framework for addressing food security. The global challenge to halve poverty and hunger by 2030 will only become a reality if efforts to use indigenous and technological agricultural development approaches are contextualized with the following considerations:

1. The amalgamation of indigenous and modern technologies must be used only if the indigenous food systems and approaches are not adjunct to western models of agricultural development.[12]
2. Indigenous agricultural practices are holistic and responsive to climate changes as demonstrated by farmers in Northern Ghana that have been able to use traditional framing practices to mitigate against drought.[13]
3. Gender sensitive development programs that would factor in challenges that women face in the global south such as land tenure, and comprehensive education that would alleviate the present social and economic impact of high food prices.[14]
4. Eating less and switching from expensive sources of protein such as fish, meat, and eggs to cheaper cereal will invariably have long health consequences for poor households. Younger children and pregnant women are more susceptible to weight loss and malnutrition. Therefore, national governments and multilateral institutions must collaboratively intervene to address food and healthcare shortages during crisis periods to the poor households.[15]

It is imperative in the efforts to address global hunger and poverty to have a better understanding and appreciation for the technical and scientific contributions of indigenous communities to agriculture and community wellness through their various coping strategies. In this regard, Hendry suggests that indigenous peoples are ingenious with their technologies which are locally adopted but they are sustainable and transferable.

> Indigenous peoples around the world have worked out efficient and sustainable ways of growing or simply gathering their food . . . but it is interesting to point out first that a common feature of all them is that they include mechanisms of sustaining the resources, a crucial feature that we "moderns" seem to have forgotten in the use of machinery, chemicals, and even genetic modifications. . . . [16]

It is the failure of what we "moderns" consider technologies that has also prompted the FAO and other multilaterals to now begin to consider the integration of IK in agriculture development. The idea that these modern technologies can address global hunger and poverty, particularly in rural agriculture communities, has just not produced the anticipated outcomes for sustainable development. It is in this vein that Iyam in the case of Nigeria suggests that focusing on modern technologies as the only variable for development do not go far enough in addressing the development challenges of rural communities because they are not comprehensive.[17] Moreover, their use is often not accessible to members of the communities that are supposed to be directly impacted by these technologies.

Given the need to address global food security, I am urging that the international community to accept the premise that development goals such as agriculture wellness, and ecological and environmental sustainability are achievable with the "old replacing the new" and with the adoption of IK. The following are proffered considerations for the "way forward":

1. *Bi-Cultural Perspective.* The adoption of IK must be advanced with consideration for the cultural context in which such technologies are adopted. To this end, it is important that development initiatives must be examined from what Hendry alluded to as "bi-cultural" lenses. This is a situation whereby the local relevance of development is maintained, and indigenous perspectives are pre-eminent in development initiatives along with what is considered the modern.[18] The approach must be relevant and participatory. It must also be congruent with the cultural realties of indigenous communities. In this vein, Paul Sillitoe in the case of Bangladesh suggests that the recognition and embracement of indigenous technologies and cultures through various agriculture extension program is an important pathway for sustainable development.[19]

2. *Management and Organization of Agro-Diversity.* To address the challenges of halving global hunger and poverty, it is important that states and developers continue to look closer and deeper into the diverse methods used by traditional communities to enhance biodiversity. For instance, native Indian tribes in the California area in North America have used various land management systems that have improved the quality of land.[20] Similarly, the Aboriginal people in Australia have taken advantage of the controlled burning of land, *Mosaic Burning,* to improve ecological challenges in the Northern region of Australia.[21] This manuscript also provided substantive examples of land management in Africa (especially in Ghana and Nigeria) where the management of drought in Northern Ghana and other coastal rural communities have been able to manage and cope with floods in the Southwest of Nigeria.

3. *Polyculture and development.* I have also highlighted the polyculture of indigenous knowledge which should be considered for development initiatives particularly in the context of addressing agriculture development initiatives in Africa and other developing regions. The nature of polyculture development processes such as pest management and food regimes management was discussed in detail in several case studies in

this book. For instance, in the case of Ghana we found that land management in southern Ghana is different from similar management in
the Northeastern part of Ghana because of weather conditions. Along
the same lines, land management in Ghana is different from that of
Nigeria. What remains important, is the recognition by agriculturalists
and policy makers to pay attention to the diversity of cultures in the
African context. That is, the various peoples, regardless of technologies, are not homogenous. Moreover, cultures are not static, and they
are dynamic over time. Thus, this book shows the parallel connection of
these various cultures to nature—be it African, South-Asian, or Native
Americans. Therefore, development initiatives must be applied with
consideration for the social and economic realities of indigenous communities. In this regard, Senanayake encouraged policy makers to pay
greater attention in the development process at a policy level because
rural farmers represent a diverse group that are not homogenous.[22]

4. *Indigenous Knowledge and Wellness.* The use of indigenous knowledge is not limited to agriculture development. In fact, the wellness of
   rural agriculture communities which is the backbone of most African
   countries economic development is of immense importance and
   pre-eminence in the development aspirations of these communities.
   Therefore, the wellness of indigenous communities is inextricable from
   agricultural development. The advantage of indigenous food regimes
   for community wellness is also illustrated in this book and was supported by evidence from primary data from Western medical practitioners in developing countries such as CUC who has from time to time
   encouraged his patients to use indigenous medicine to remedy various
   illnesses. In addition, this book highlighted how botanical plants in
   Ghana and Nigeria are used to enhance wellness in rural communities.

5. *Indigenous Knowledge and Modern World.* Indigenous Knowledge in
   its applicability and use for development should be further examined in
   the context of how it enhances the modern world through various principles such as food regimes management, land management, and ecological management. The way the wisdom of Indigenous Knowledge
   has continued to contribute to modern life was highlighted in this book,
   and reinforced by extant literature such as Anderson[23] who proffers that
   indigenous knowledge would *tend* the world if the following IK principles were adhered to:

   a. *Understanding the Ecological History of the Land.* Indigenous link-
      ages with nature are a pivotal part of the land's ecological history.
      Thus, the interruption of indigenous management in this area is
      responsible for decreased biodiversity. Therefore, departure from
      indigenous practices that protect the land and wildlife is detrimental

to nature and subsequently development. However, the accommodation of indigenous management practices will bode well for restoring natural landscapes and biodiversity.

b. *Sustaining natural resources to meet developmental needs.* In the case of Native Americans, Anderson suggests that lessons from indigenous communities have shown us how they have been able to use available natural resources to meet human needs without compromising the ecological essence for their renewal. This is the case in global indigenous communities where botanical plants are used for food and community wellness. For instance, the Northern Hill Yokuts use endangered species such as *Trifolium barbigerum*-leaf for food. In Nigeria, *Bitter leaf* is used for food as a vegetable and for treating diabetes.

c. Achieving sustainable use of the earth's resources will involve cultural changes as much as advances in knowledge and transformation of economies. lessons from indigenous native communities have also taught us about the co-existence of plants and animals. In this vein, ecological knowledge must be accompanied by changes in culture and values.

The effort to change the landscape of global development, whereby poverty and hunger can be better addressed, would require a plan to harness indigenous knowledge. As discussed earlier, quite often IK is ignored by policy makers and other stakeholders. Globally, IK can no longer be ignored or relegated to the back burner of development strategies. To enable its continuous use, it must be harnessed so that the wealth of knowledge is not lost. In this regard, Margaret Sraku Lartey[24] suggests that IK can be better harnessed in developing regions through the following methods for sustainability of knowledge:

a. *Use of Information technologies to manage IK.* Lartey had called for the use of information and communication technology (ICT) to harness IK because the storage and generation of knowledge is easily lost without a data base and a process for harnessing and preserving information systematically.

b. *IK and intellectual property rights.* The data base that is created for IK must also be protected for local communities so that indigenous communities can benefit socially and economically from the wealth of this knowledge.

Indigenous knowledge for climate and weather change's mitigation, it has been illustrated in this book that indigenous knowledge can be used for abating climatic conditions such as drought and floods. In the case of coastal rural communities in Nigeria, I have offered various coping strategies and medicine used by these communities to abate destruction to farmlands and other rural lives. Therefore, indigenous knowledge is pivotal for addressing climatic and weather challenges. Along these lines, Singh and Singh suggest that IK is gaining the attention it deserves because it is a climate smart approach for sustainable food production.[25] Similarly, in Australia, ethnometeorologists have provided a wealth of information on how the diverse cultures among the Australian aboriginal tribes are pursuing efforts to capture climate and weather information that can be useful for hunting, agriculture, and abating fire in the Northern region.[26]

The use of IK for weather predictions in other parts of Africa, particularly in Southwestern Free State of South Africa, is also important for mitigating against adverse weather conditions. Rural farmers in the Southwestern Free State are dependent on their understanding of the natural environment to fulfill weather predictions. Their abilities to predict weather in connection with the natural environment range from studying the constellation of stars, understanding animal behavior, cloud cover and type, the blossoming of certain indigenous trees, appearance and disappearance of reptiles, and the migration of bird species and other animals.[27]

Indigenous Knowledge and disaster management. The use of IK to manage disasters in rural farming communities such as floods, fire, erosion, and drought is an important consideration for development. The book has captured the use of IK to address floods in coastal rural areas of Nigeria, drought in the Northeastern region of Ghana, and pest management in Nigeria and Ghana. The book also captured how indigenous knowledge has been used to mitigate the effect of global pandemics such as COVID-19 in African communities. IK provides African states some clues on how to deal with risk management through practices that are sustainable over several millennia. In this regard, Iloka suggests that indigenous knowledge is imperative for weather hazards in Asia where communities are often vulnerable to natural disasters.[28] The use of IK in farming communities is evident in practices such as when pastoral farmers store away fodder as part of their coping strategies, so that they can protect farm animals during adverse weather. For instance, in Africa, during droughts, local farms rely on cattle for meat because of limited grazing, while they rear goats and sheep for other products by feeding them fodder. As a result of this type of farming system local farming communities can adapt to drought periods.[29]

In South Asia, and especially India, the Red Cross and Red Crescent have adopted early warning indigenous strategies that assisted in the evacuation of one million people when *Cyclone Phailian* struck India.[30]

Indigenous Knowledge and Education. The challenges of sustaining the essence of indigenous knowledge can be nurtured through a commitment by modern African states in ensuring that indigenous agriculture methods are woven into the pedagogical approach for teaching agriculture, science, and wellness. This point was elucidated by Shukla et al. in their seminal work in Krishnagiri, District in Tamil Nadu, India. Their study suggests that such intentional educational processes will enhance indigenous knowledge not only in rural farming communities but will contribute to the overall development aspirations of the state.[31] It is in the same vein that one must encourage the same development approach for other developing regions. Also, the integration of IK knowledge from early school age all through tertiary education will bode well for sustaining IK knowledge over time. This will also protect against the potential loss of viable development information.

Overall, the importance of indigenous knowledge has been emphasized in this book to serve as the way forward as policy makers and development agencies embark on models for halving poverty and hunger by 2030. Consideration for IK must be an imperative action for sustainable development.

The consideration of IK as one of the central models for addressing food security in Africa is important given the development challenges African states have continued to encounter despite the integration of accelerated methods of development such as fertilizers and biotechnologies such as genetically modified crops. I have asserted that the use of innovative technologies for agriculture production must be appropriate to the social and cultural environment in which they are planted if they are going to be successful.

Therefore, a rapid move to modernize the agriculture sector using advanced technologies could prove inappropriate unless, from the outset, plans are put into place to ensure that all strata of society have reasonable opportunities of benefitting from these agriculture inputs. The nature and characteristics of agricultural modernization is monocropping, mechanization, hybridization, fertilizers, pesticides, and large-scale capital-intensive farms.[32] These methods are encouraged by development agencies under the guise of agricultural standardization and universalism to promote accelerated growth.[33]

The implications for the use of modern technologies and other accelerated methods for agriculture development in most developing regions such as Africa are quite complex, and their implications are far reaching. The use of modern technologies portends several problems. They are as follows:

1. aggravation of the prosperity gap between the global north and south through the possible substitution of tropical agricultural exports

with genetic-engineered products which exploit indigenous genetic resources.

2. it may also lead to increased inequalities in the distribution of income and wealth among farm holdings. That is, the privileged class, with their large holdings, are likely to benefit from the introduction of technologies when compared to the smaller indigenous holdings that are socially disadvantaged.

3. the economic risks of using modern technologies such as biotechnology in developing countries are also contingent on international trade. As a result of modern technologies, it has become possible to produce crops that are usually produced tropically in the laboratory, or in temperate zones. This production process often raises concerns that the resultant competitive edge that could push tropical crops off the market.

4. The use of modern technologies such as genetically modified crops and fertilizers also draws attention to the appropriateness of such modern inputs for farming because genetically modified seeds must be meticulously adapted to specific farming environments in which they are planted before they can become agriculturally viable. However, farmers in most developing countries are hindered by limited access to research and the development of new seeds which are capital intensive.

Considering the inability of modern technology to halve hunger and poverty, it is important for policy makers and development agencies to continue to place Indigenous Knowledge management as a central focus on how to address poverty and hunger in Africa. The centrality of approaches that have concentrated primarily on modern technologies has not been able to sustain food security and consequently the wellness of rural communities that are the nucleus of agriculture development in Africa.

To this end, I suggest that to abate poverty and hunger in Africa and globally, an alternative paradigm that is rooted in indigenous knowledge (IK) is well positioned to address what Quan calls the *materiality of savage developmentalist:*

> Over half of the world or more than three billion people, live on less than $21.50 a day. The poorest 40 percent of the world's people accounts for 5 percent of global income whereas the richest 20 percent controls 75 percent of the income . . . During the first nine years of the 21ST century some 88 million children died, mainly killed by poverty, hunger, preventable diseases, and related causes.[34]

Thus, traditional knowledge offers a positive way forward because it takes into consideration the specificities of local conditions and relies on the knowledge, environment and lived experiences of these communities that are the focus of the global development agenda.[35]

NOTES

1. World Bank Group Report (May 2015). Ending poverty and hunger by 2030: An agenda for the global system. p. 4. http://documents1.worldbank.org/curated/en/700061468334490682/pdf/95768-REVISED-WP-PUBLIC-Box391467B-Ending-Poverty-and-Hunger-by-2030-FINAL.pdf

2. Ibid., p. 5.

3. The United Nations Sustainable Development Goals 2030. Accessed on December 21, 2020, from https://sdgs.un.org/goals.

4. FAO and Agriculture Organization of the United Nations (April 3–5, 2018). Scaling up agroecology initiative: Transforming food and agricultural systems in support of the SDGs. A proposal prepared for the international symposium on agroecology. Accessed on December 21, 2020, from http://www.fao.org/3/i9049en/i9049en.pdf.

5. Morgan, C.B. and Trubek, A.B. (2020). Not yet the table: The absence of food and tradition in agroecology literature. *Elementa Science of the Anthropocene,* p. 4. Accessed December 21, 2020, from https://www.semanticscholar.org/paper/Not-yet-at-the-table%3A-The-absence-of-food-culture-Morgan-Trubek/53707cf251ce53e8a bc8be69a9342ddbbd34b0a8?p2df.

6. Akinola, R., Pereira, L.M., Mabhaudhi, T., de Bruin, F.-M. and Rusch, L. (2020). A review of indigenous food crops in Africa and the implications for more sustainable and healthy food systems. *Sustainability,* Vol. 12, No. 8: 1. Accessed on December 22, 2020, from https://www.mdpi.com/2071-1050/12/8/3493.

7. Dibua, Jeremiah I. (2006). Modernization and the Crisis of Development in Africa: The Nigerian Experience, p. 177.

8. Iyam, David Uru (1995). The Broken Hoe: Cultural Reconfiguration in Biase Southeast Nigeria. Chicago: University of Chicago Press.

9. Ibid., p. 205.

10. Cloete, P.C. and Idsardi, E.F. (2013). Consumption of indigenous and traditional food crops: Perceptions and realties from South Africa, *Agroecology and Sustainable Food System*, Vol. 37, p.902–903. Accessed on December 28, 2020, from https://www.tandfonline.com/doi/abs/10.1080/21683565.2013.805179.

11. Van der Merwe, J.D., Cloete, P.C. and Van der Hoeven, M. (2016). Promoting food security through indigenous and traditional food crops. *Agroecology and Sustainable Food Systems,* Vol. 40, No. 8: 831.

12. Gyasi, E. A. (2004). Lessons learnt and future research directions. in Gyasi, Edwin A. & Kranjac-Berisalvlejevic, G. (2004). Managing Agro-diversity the Traditional Way: Lessons from West Africa in Sustainable of Biodiversity and Related Natural Resources. New York: United Nations University Press, pp. 253–254.

13. Singh, R. and Singh, G.S. (2017). Traditional agriculture: A climate smart approach for sustainable food production. *Energy, Ecology and Environment*, Vol. 2, No. 5, p.296–316. Also see, Derbile, E.K. (2013). Reducing vulnerability of rain-fed

agriculture to drought through indigenous knowledge systems in north-eastern Ghana. *International Journal of Climate Change Strategies and Management,* Vol. 5(1): 71–94.

14. World Bank (October 12, 2008). Rising food and fuel prices: Addressing the risks to future generations, p. 8. Accessed on December 28, 2020 from https://www.semanticscholar.org/paper/RISING-FOOD-AND-FUEL-PRICES-%3A-ADDRESSING-THE-RISKS-FOOD/507318c27d82382686fa303acb3e0e379f190a 62

15. Ibid.

16. Hendry, Joy (2014). Science and Sustainability: Learning from Indigenous Wisdom. New York: Palgrave Macmillan, p. 40.

17. Iyam, D.U. (1995). The Broken Hoe: Cultural Reconfiguration in Biase Southeast Nigeria, p. 10.

18. Hendry, Joy (2014). Science and Sustainability: Learning from Indigenous Wisdom. New York: Palgrave Macmillan, pp. 153–168.

19. Sillitoe, Paul (2000). The state of indigenous knowledge in Bangladesh. in Sillitoe, P. Indigenous Knowledge Development in Bangladesh: Present and Future, pp. 3–20.

20. Hendry, Joy (2014). Science and Sustainability: Learning from Indigenous Wisdom. New York Palgrave Macmillan, p. 359.

21. Hendry, Joy (2014). Science and Sustainability: Learning from Indigenous Wisdom. New York Palgrave Macmillan, p. 22–23.

22. Senanayake, S.G.J.N (2006). Indigenous Knowledge as a key to sustainable development. *The Journal of Agricultural Science*, Vol. 2 (1): 91.

23. Anderson, M.K. (2005). Tending the Wild: Native American Knowledge and the Management of California's Natural Resources. University of California Press, pp. 358–361.

24. Lartey-Sraku, M. (2014). Harnessing indigenous knowledge for sustainable forest management in Ghana. *International Journal of Food System* Dynamics, Vol. 5(4): 186–187.

25. Singh, R. and Singh, G.S. (2017). Traditional agriculture: A climate-smart approach for sustainable food production. *Energy, Ecology, Environment*, Vol. 2(5): 296.

26. Green, Donna, Billy, Jack and Tapim, Alo (2010). Indigenous Australians' Knowledge of Weather and Climate. 100:337–354. DOI 10.1007/s10584-010-9803-xz.

27. Netshiukhwi-Zuma, G., Stiger, K. and Walker, S. (2013). Use of traditional weather/climate knowledge by farmers in the South-Western free state of South Africa: Agrometeorological learning by scientists. *Atmosphere*, 4: p.1. Accessed from www.mdpi.com/journal/atmosphere, doi: 10.3390/atmos4040383.

28. Iloka, G. Nnamdi (2016). Indigenous knowledge for disaster risk reduction: An African perspective. *Journal of Disaster Risk Studies.* Accessed from http://www.jamba.org.za.

29. Ibid., p. 4.

30. Ibid.

31. Shukla, S., Barkman, J. and Patel, K. (2017). Weaving *indigenous Pedas* agricultural knowledge with formal education to enhance community food security: School competition as a pedagogical space in rural Anchetty, India. *Pedagogy, Culture, & Society*, Vol. 25, No. 1: 87–103.

32. Jeremiah, I. Dibua (2006). Modernization and the Crisis of Development in Africa: The Nigerian Experience. London: Ashgate Publishing Limited, p. 178.

33. Ibid.

34. Quan, H.L.T (2012). Growth Against Democracy: Savage Developmentalist in the Modern World. Lanham, MD: Lexington Books, p. 2.

35. Briggs, J. and Sharp, J. (2004). Indigenous Knowledges and Development: A Postcolonial Caution. *Third World Quarterly*, Vol. 25(4): 661.

Bibliography

Abdulquadri, A. F. & Mohammed, B. T. (2012). Comparative Analysis of Gender Involvement in Agricultural Production. *Journal of Development and Agriculture Economics*, Vol. 4(8): 240–244.

Abegunrin, O. (2014). Africa in the New World Order: Peace and Security Challenges in the Twenty-First Century. Maryland: Lexington Books.

Acemoglu, D. & Robinson, J. (2012). Why Nations Fail. New York: Currency Books.

Adedayo, O. A.; Ayodele, J. A. & Oboh, G. (2013). Inhibitory Effects of Phenolic Extract from Garlic on Angiotesin-1 Converting Enzyme and Cisplatin Induced Lipid Peroxidation—*In Vitro. International Journal of Biomedical Science,* Vol. 9 (2): 98–106.

Adedipe, N.O.; Okuneye, P.; & Ayinde, L.A. (March 16–19, 2004). The relevance of local and indigenous knowledge for Nigerian agriculture. Presented at International Conference on Bridging Scales and Epistemologies: Linking Local Knowledge with Global Science in Multi Scale Assessments. Alexandria, Egypt, 1–20. Accessed from https://www.millenniumassessment.org/documents/bridging/papers /adedipe.nimbe.pdfm.

Adeniji, A.; Akinleye, T. E.; Faleye, T. C.; Ogbole, O. O. & Segun, P. A. (2018). In Vitro Antiviral Activity of Twenty-Seven Medicinal Plant Extracts from Southwest Nigeria against Three Serotypes of Echoviruses. *Virology Journal,* Vol. 15(10): 3–8. Accessed from https://doi.org/10.1186/s12985-018-1022-7.

Adesoji, S. A. (2016). Eating today and tomorrow: Exploring indigenous farming systems of smallholder arable crop farmers in the age of climate change in Nigeria. *Agriculture and Forestry*, Vol. 62(1): 349–358.

Adeyeye, S. A. O. (2017). The Role of Food Processing and Appropriate Storage Technologies in Ensuring Food Security and Food Availability in Africa. *Nutrition and Food Sciences,* Vol. 47(1): 122–139.

Agbadi, P.; Mittlemark, M. B.; & Urke, H. B. (2017). Household food security and adequacy of child diet in the food insecure region north in Ghana. *POLS One*: 1–16. https://doi.org/10.1371/journal.pone.0177377.

Aigbe, J. O.; Okoli, R. I.; Obodo-Ohaju, J. O.; & Mensah, J. K. (2007). Medicinal herbs used for managing some common ailments among Esan people of Edo State Nigeria. *Pakistan Journal of Nutrition,* Vol. 6(5): 490–496.

Ajala, T. (2017). Gender discrimination in land ownership and the alleviation of women's poverty in Nigeria: A call for new equities. *International Journal of Discrimination and the Law*, Vol. 17(1): 51–66.

Ajibade, I. T. & Shokemi, O. O. (2003). Indigenous approach to weather forecasting in ASA local government, Kwara State Nigeria. *Indilinga: African Journal of Indigenous Knowledge System*s, Vol. 2: 37–46.

Akello, S. & Sarr, F. (1999). The economic role of women in agricultural and rural development: the promotion of income-generating activities. CTA Annual Report.

Akinola, R.; Pereira, L. M.; Mabhaudhi, T.; de Bruin, F.-M. & Rusch, L. (2020). A review of indigenous food crops in Africa and the implications for more sustainable and healthy food systems. *Sustainability*, Vol. 12(8) 3493: 1–30. Accessed on December 22, 2020, from https://www.mdpi.com/2071-1050/12/8/3493.

Alabi, O. O. B. & Alabi, S. O. (2006). Crop pest management and food security in Nigeria agriculture. *Archives of Phytopathology and Plant Protection*, Vol. 39(6): 1–8.

Alase, A. (2017). The interpretative phenomenological analysis: A guide to good qualitative research approach. *International Journal of Education and Literacy Studies*, Vol. 5(2): 9–19.

Ali, H.; Houghton, P. J. & Soumyanath, A. (2006). α-Amylase inhibitory activity of some Malaysian plants used to treat diabetes; with particular reference to *Phyllanthus amarus*. *Journal of Ethnopharmacology*, Vol. 107(3): 449–455.

Anderson, M. K. (2005). Tending in the Wild: Native American Knowledge and the Management of California's Natural Resources. California: University of California Press.

Andrae, G. & Beckman, Bjorn (1985). The Wheat Trap: Bread and Underdevelopment in Nigeria. London: Zed Books.

Apiah-Tokuh, R. (April 21, 2020). COVID-19 Pandemic could cause widespread stunting in Ghana. Retrieved June 22, 2020, 1–8. from: hhttps://www.globalcitizen.org/en/content/ghana-food-insceurity-covid-19/.

Arokoyo, J. O. & Chikwendu, D. O. (1997). Women and Sustainable Agricultural Development in Nigeria. *Journal of Sustainable Agriculture*, Vol. 1(1): 53–69.

Arunkumar, R.; Arunakaran, J.; Banudevi, S.; Benson Selvansean, C.; Elumalai, P.; Sharmila, G.; Gunadharini, D. N. & Govindaraj, S. (2012). Ethanolic neem (Azaidrachta indica A. juss) leaf extract induces apoptosis and inhibits the IGF signaling pathway in breast cancer cell lines. *Biomedicine & Preventive Nutrition*, Vol. 2: 59–68.

Asase, A. & Yeboah, A. A. O. (2012). Plants used in Wechiau community hippopotamus sanctuary in Northwest Ghana. *Ethnobotany Journal and Applications*, Vol. 10(1): 605–618. Accessed on December 3, 2020, from http://www.ethnobotanyjournal.org/index.php/era.

Asempa, R.; Lawanson, I. Y.; Dzomeku, I. K. & Benson, S. (2006). Weed Control in maize using Mucuna and Canavalia as intercrops in the Northern Guinea Savanna Zone of Ghana. *Journal of Agronomy*, Vol. 5(4): 621–625.

Auffray, C.; Biao-Zhou, G.; Brahmachari, S. K.; Chen, Z.; Lemonnier, N.; Mukerji, M.; Prasher, B. & Sagner, M. (2017). Traditional Knowledge -based medicine. A review of history, principles, and relevance in the present context of p4 systems medicine. *Progress in Preventive Medicine*, Vol. 2(7): 1–14.

Ayanbode, O. F. & Olatokun, W. (2009). Use of indigenous knowledge by women in Nigeria rural community. *Indian Journal of Traditional Knowledge*, Vol. 8(2): 287–295.

Baah-Ofori, S. & Borquaye, L. S. (2019). Ethanolic leaf from Strophnatus gratus (Hook) Franch. (Apocynaceae) exhibits anti-inflamatory and antioxidant activities. *Cogent-Biology*, Vol. 5: 1–11. Accessed December 9, 2021, from: https://doi.org/10 .1080/23312025.2019.1710431.

Babiaka, Smith B.; Judson, N. Phillip; Lifongo, Lydia L.; Nite-Kang, Fidele & Simboen, Conrad V. (2014). A bioactivity versus ethnobotanical survey of medicinal plants from Nigeria West Africa. *Journal of National Product Bioprospect,* Vol. 4: 10–19.

Bala, Mustafa & Bala, Havva (2009). Recent trends in global production and utilization of bioethanol fuel. *Applied Energy*, Vol. 86: 2273–2282.

Bales, K. (2012). Disposable People: New Slavery in the Global Economy. California: University of California Press.

Bamikole, M. A. & Ikhatua, U. J. (2009). Compilation and adoption of ethnoveterinary medicine, traditional and other management practices by small ruminant farmers in Edo State Nigeria. *Tropical Animal Health Production*, Vol. 41: 1549–1561. DOI 10.1077/s11250-009-9346-3.

Barkman, J.; Patel, K. & Shukla, S. (2017). Weaving *indigenous Pedas* agricultural knowledge with formal education to enhance community food security: School competition as a pedagogical space in rural Anchetty, India. *Pedagogy, Culture, & Society*, Vol. 25(1): 87–103.

Barrett, B.; Castillo, R. & McLean, K. G. (2012). Energy Innovation and Traditional Knowledge. *Traditional Knowledge Bulletin,* 1–8. Retrieved from https://www .researchgate.net/profile/Kirsty-Galloway-Mclean/publication/267868067_Energy _Innovation_and_Traditional_Knowledge/links/545bf7510cf249070a7a8507/ Energy-Innovation-and-Traditional-Knowledge.pdf?origin=publication_detail.

Baubeng, S. N. (2004). Traditional methods of resource assessment relative to the scientific approach. In Gyasi, E. A.; Berisalvljevic, G. K.; Blay, E.T. & Oduro, W. (ed). (2004). Managing Agrodiversity the Traditional Way: Lessons from West Africa in Sustainable Use of Biodiversity and Related Natural Resources. New York: United Nations University Press.

Beckert, S. & Rockman, S. (2018). Slavery Capitalism: A New History of American Economic Development. Philadelphia: University of Pennsylvania.

Begum, N., Haq, M. F. & Naher, K. (2000). Medicinal plants for the survival of rural people. In Sillitoe, P. (ed); Indigenous Knowledge Development in Bangladesh: Present and Future. London: Intermediate Technology Publications.

Belinga S. E. & Guyer, J. (1995). Wealth in people as wealth in knowledge accumulation and composition in equatorial Africa. *Journal of African History*, Vol. 36: 91–120.

Blay, E. (2004). Vegetables: Traditional ways of managing their diversity food security food security in Southern Ghana. In Gyasi, E. A.; Berisalvljevic, G. K.; Blay, E.

T. & Oduro, W. (ed). Managing Agrodiversity the Traditional Way: Lessons from West Africa in Sustainable Use of Biodiversity and Related Natural Resources. New York: United Nations University Press.

Bodanrenko, D. M. & Roese, P. M. (1999). Benin prehistory: The origin and settling down of the Edos. *Anthropos*, Vol. 4(6): 542–552.

Boeke, J. H. (1953). Economic and Economic Policy of Dual Societies as Exemplified by Indonesia. New York: Institute of Pacific Relations.

Bousheri, S. N.; Ghasempour, S.; Ghanel, F. M.; Ghalishourani, S. S.; Hadi, A.; Joukar, F.; Karimbeiki, R.; Khosravi, A.; Pourmasoumi, M.; Mbabazi, M.; Mostafa, A.; Marzieh, M. & Pour, Z. K. (2020). The efficacy of sour tea (*Hsibiscus Sabdariffa L.*) on selected cardiovascular disease risk factors: A systematic review and meta-analysis of randomized clinical trials. *Phytotherapy Research*, Vol. 34: 329–339. Accessed from https://DOI:10.1002/ptr.65451.

Brass, T. (2013). Labor Regime Change World in the Twenty-First Century: Unfreedom Capitalism and Primitive Accumulation. Chicago: Haymarket Books.

Braun, J. V. (2008). Responding to the world food crisis: Getting on the right track. *International Food Policy Research Institute (IFPRI) Annual Report Essays* 2007–2008, 1–9.

Brenan, N. (January 31, 2021, 10:30am) Facing Challenges. CBS Face the Nation.

Brett, E. A. (1973). Colonialism and Underdevelopment in East Africa: The Politics of Economic Change 1919–1939. New York: Nook Publishers.

Briggs, J. & Sharo, J. (2004). Indigenous knowledge and development: A postcolonial caution. *Third World Quarterly*, Vol. 25(4): 661–676.

Brocki, J. & Wearden, A. J. (2006). A critical evaluation of the use of Interpretative Phenomenological Analysis (1PA). *Health Psychology*, Vol. 21(1): 87–108.

Brown, H. Cecil. (2000). Folk classification. In Paul Minnis (ed). Ethnobotany: Reader. Norman: University of Oklahoma Press.

Brown, K. G. (April 16–22,) Hunger and genetically modified crops in Africa. *West Africa*, 16–34.

Buntze, I. R. (February 2015). Impact of Ebola on food security in West Africa. *Rural 21- International Journal of for Rural Development*, 43. Retrieved on March 18, 2019, from https://info.brot-fuer-die-welt.de/sites/default/files/blog-downloads/rural2015_ebola_impact.pdf.

Burns, A.; Cliff, J.; Cavagnaro, T. & Gleadow, R. (2010). Cassava: The drought, war, and famine crop in a changing war. *Sustainability*, Vol. 2: 3572–3607.

Butt, T. M.; Hassan, Z. Y.; Mehmood, K. K. & Muhammad, S. (2010). Role of rural women in agricultural development and their constraints. *Journal of Agriculture & Social Sciences*, Vol. 6: 53–56.

Calvert, C. C.; Grivett, L. E. & Lockett, C. T. (2000). Energy and micronutrient composition of dietary and medicinal wild plants consumed during drought. Study of rural, Northeastern Nigeria. *International Journal of Food Sciences and Nutrition*, Vol. 51: 195–208.

Cassell, D. L., Jr. (2013). Agricultural policy in Liberia: A vision of the future. *Liberian Studies Journal*, Vol. 38(1): 72–82.

Cloete, P. C. & Idsardi, E. F. (2013). Consumption of indigenous and traditional food crops: Perceptions and realties from South Africa, *Agroecology and Sustainable Food System*, Vol. 37(8): 902–914. Retrieved on December 28, 2020, from https://www.tandfonline.com/doi/abs/10.1080/21683565.2013.805179.

Cook, M. (2013). Medicine Generations: Natural Native American Medicines Traditional to the Stockbridge-Munsee Band of Mohicans Tribe. Middletown, DE: M. Cook, 10–138.

CPAR Report, (Winter 2009). Empowering female farmers in rural Africa. 1–7.

Crawford, S. S. & Vargeghese, J. (2021). A cultural framework for indigenous, local and science knowledge systems in ecology and natural resource management. *Ecological Monographs*, Vol. 9(1): 1–23.

Currie, J. T. & Meeuwig, J. (2003). Bushmeat and food security in the Congo Basin: Linkages between wildlife and the people's future. *Environmental Conservation*, Vol. 30(1): 71–78.

Daidone, S.; Daris, B.; Handa, S. & Winters, P. (2017). The household and individual level economic impacts of cash transfer programmes in sub-Saharan Africa. *American Journal of Agriculture Economics,* Vol. 10(5): 1401–1431.

Davis, B.; Di Giuseppe, S. & Zezza, A. (2017). Are African households (not) leaving agriculture? Patterns of households' income sources in rural sub-Saharan Africa. *Food Policy*, Vol. 67: 153–174.

Derbile, E. K. (2013). Reducing vulnerability of rain-fed agriculture to drought through indigenous knowledge systems in north-eastern Ghana. *International Journal of Climate Change Strategies and Management,* Vol. 5(1): 71–799.

Dibua, J. I. (2006). Modernization and the Crisis of Development in Africa: The Nigerian Experience. London: Ashgate Publishing Limited.

Djebou, D. C. S.; Price, E.; Kibriya, S. & Ahn, J. (2017). Comparative Analysis of Agricultural Assets, Incomes, and food Security of Rural Households in Ghana, Senegal, and Liberia. *Agriculture,* Vol. 7(38): 1–13. Doi:10.3390/agriculture7050038.

Doss, C. R. (2018). Women and agricultural productivity: Reframing the issues. *Development Policy Review*, Vol. 36: 35–50.

Dr. CUC Interview on the of IK and Modern Medicine in Nigeria. January 30, 2021, 5:39am Eastern Time.

Dr./Prince Interview on Plants and Use for Wellness Among the Bini's. February 13, 2021, 9:00am Eastern Time.

ECA International Statistics: Policy and Salary Bench Marking. (2009). Retrieved July 21, 2009, from http//www.eca-international.com/shop/benchmarking reports.

The Economist. (April 19, 2008). The New Face of Hunger, 32–34.

Edelman, M. (2013) Food Sovereignty: Forgotten Genealogies and Future Regulatory Challenges of Food Security: A Critical Dialogue, International Conference, Yale University, September 14–15. Accessed December 6, 2020, from https://academicworks.cuny.edu/gc_pubs/104/.

Ehinmore, O. M. & Ogunode, S. A. (2013). Fish in indigenous healing practices among the Ilaje of coastal Yoruba land of Nigeria: A historical perspective. *European Scientific Journal*, Vol. 9(14): 196–206.

Ehui, S. (May 14, 2020). Protecting food security in Africa during COVID-19. Brookings Institute. Retrieved June 19, 2020, from https://www.brookings.edu/blog/africa-in-focus/2020/05/14/protecting-food-security-in-africa-during-covid-19/.

European Center for Disease Prevention and Control (February 15, 2021). Outbreak of Ebola Virus Disease in North Kivu Democratic Republic of the Congo 2021. Accessed from https://www.ecdc.europa.eu/en/news-events/outbreak-ebola-virus-disease-north-kivu-democratic-republic-congo-2021.

Fabiyi, O. O. & Oloukoi, J. (2013). Indigenous knowledge system and local adaptation strategies to flooding in coastal rural communities of Nigeria. *Journal of Indigenous Social Development*, Vol. 2(1): 1–19. Retrieved January 10, 2021, from https://scholarspace.manoa.hawaii.edu/bitstream/10125/29817/1/v2i1_05fabiyi.pdf.

Famine Early Warning Systems Network (FEWS NET) Assessment of Chronic Food Insecurity in Liberia, June 2017. Retrieved from https://reliefweb.int/report/liberia/assessment-chronic-food-insecurity-liberia-june-2017.

Fentiman, A. & Neinbarini, Z. (2015). Environmental degradation and cultural erosion in Ogoni-Land: A case study of the oil spills in Bodo. *The Extractive Industries and Society,* Vol. 12(4): 615–624.

Ferguson, J. (2007). Global Shadows: Africa in The Neoliberal World Order. Durham, NC: Duke University Press.

Food and Agriculture Organization of the United Nations. Acara, Ghana. (2017). Africa Regional Overview of Food Security and Nutrition: The Challenges of Building Resilience to Shocks and Stresses, 2.

Food and Agriculture Organization of the United Nations. Bi-Annual Report on Global Food Markets 2020. COVID-19 Special Edition, 1–6.

Food and Agriculture Organization of the United Nations. (2008). Biofuels: Prospects and Opportunities. FAO, Rome.

Food and Agriculture Organization of the United Nations. (April 3–5, 2018). Scaling up agroecology initiative: Transforming food and agricultural systems in support of the SDGs. A proposal prepared for the international symposium on agroecology. Retrieved on December 21, 2020, from http://www.fao.org/3/i9049en/i9049en.pdf.

Food and Agriculture Organization of the United Nations. Peace and food security: Investing in resilience to sustain rural livelihood and amid conflict. Retrieved on March 11, 2020, from http://www.fao.org/resilience/resources/resources-detail/en/c/405395/.

Food and Agriculture Organization of the United Nations. (2011). The state of food insecurity in the world: How does international price volatility affect domestic economies and food security? 4–50.

Foster, G. M. (1967). Tzintunzan: Mexican Peasants in a Changing World. Boston: Little Brown.

Friedman, K. E. & Friedman, J. (2007). Modernities, Class, and the Contradictions of Globalization: The Anthropology of Global Systems. Lanham, MD: Rowman & Littlefield.

Friedmann, H. (1994). The international relations of food: The unfolding crisis of national regulation. In Harris-White, B. & Hoffenberg, R. (ed). Food Multidisciplinary Perspectives. Oxford: Blackwell.

Fugar, S. (2020) Esoko Food Prices in Ghana 2019–2020. Retrieved February 2021 from https://esoko.com/category/food-prices/.

Gakpo, J. O. (March 26, 2020). COVID-19 virus spreads prompt food insecurity fears in Africa. Alliance for Science. 2. Retrieved June 22, 2020, from: http://allianceforscience.cornell.edu/blog/2020/o3/covid-19-virus-spread-prompts-food-insecurity-fears-in-africa/Gana, F.S. (2003). The usage of indigenous plant materials among small-scale farmers in Niger State agricultural development. *Indilinga: African Journal of Indigenous Knowledge Systems,* Vol. 2: 53–64.

Gappah, P. (August-September 2011). Women are our best hope for the continent. *The African Report,* 24–25.

Gbossa, N.; Kamara, M. & Odoemena, B. (2012). Nigeria-Country Case International Fund for Agricultural Development. Retrieved February 15, 2021, from https://www.ifad.oreg/en/weboperations/country/id/nigeria.

Ghana at a Glance, FAO. Retrieved June 12, 2020, from http://www.fao.org/ghana/fao-in-ghana/ghana-at-a-glance/en/.

Ghana Statistics Consumer Price Index. April 2020. Retrieved June 22, 2020, from https://statsghana.gov.gh/gssmain/fileUpload/Price%20Indices/Newsletter_CPI_April_2020.pdf.

Giustozzi, A. (2001). The Art of Coercion: The Primitive Accumulation and Management of Coercive Power. New York: Columbia University Press.

Global Food Biotechnology Market Size by Type. Industry Analysis and Report, Regional Outlook Growth Potential, Price Trends, Competitive Market Share and Forecast, 2019–2025.

Goldstein, S. T.; Logan, A. L.; Orjemie, E. A.; Stump, D. & Schoeman, M. H. (2019). Critically engaging African food security and usable pasts through archaeology. *African Archaeological Review*, Vol. 36: 419–438.

Goodman, D. (1991). Some recent tendencies in the industrial organization of agri-food system. In Friedland, W.; Busch, L.; Buttel, F. & Rudy, A. (ed). Towards a New Political Economy of Agriculture. Boulder: Westview Press.

Gramsci, A. (1973). The Prison Notebooks. London: Lawrence Wishart Books.

Grzywacz, D.; Stevenson, P. C.; Mushhoboiz, W. L.; Belmain, S. & Wilson, K. (2014). The use of indigenous ecological resources for pest control in Africa. *Food Security,* Vol. 6: 71–86. https:// DOI 10.1007/s12571-013-0313-5.

Gunder, F. A. (1977). On so-called primitive accumulation. *Dialectical Anthropology*, Vol. 2(2): 87–106.

Gyasi, Edwin A. & Kranjac-Berisalvlejevic, G. (2004). Managing Agrodiversity the Traditional Way: Lessons from West Africa in Sustainable Use of Biodiversity and Related Natural Resources. New York: United Nations University Press.

Gyasi, Edwin A. (2014). Demonstration sites and expert farmers in conservation of biodiversity. In Gyasi, E. A.; Berisalvljevic, G. K.; Blay, E. T. & Oduro, W. (ed). (2004). Managing Agrodiversity the Traditional Way: Lessons from West Africa in

Sustainable Use of Biodiversity and Related Natural Resources. New York: United Nations University Press.

Gyasi, E. A., and William, S. A. (2004). Aspects of resources tenure that conserve biodiversity: The case of southern and northern Ghana. In Gyasi, E. A.; Berisalvljevic, G. K.; Blay, E. T. & Oduro, W. (ed). (2004). Managing Agrodiversity the Traditional Way: Lessons from West Africa in Sustainable Use of Biodiversity and Related Natural Resources. New York: United Nations University Press.

Haraksingh, S. T.; Herforth, A.; Ickowitz, A.; Powell, B.; Sunderland, T. & Termote, C. (2015). Improving diets with wild and cultivated biodiversity from across the landscape. *Food Security*, Vol. 7: 535–554.

Harwood, Jonathan. (2019). Was the Green Revolution intended to maximize food production? *International Journal of Agricultural Sustainability,* Vol. 17(4): 312–325.

Hayami, U. & Ruttan, V. W. (1976). Agricultural Development: An International Perspective. Baltimore: Johns Hopkins University Press.

Hendry, Joy. (2014). Science and Sustainability: Learning from Indigenous Wisdom. New York: Palgrave-Macmillan Publisher.

Higgins, B. (1954). The "Dualistic Theory" of underdeveloped areas. *Economic Development and Cultural Change*, Vol. 4(2): 99–115.

Hill, P. (1970). Studies in Rural Capitalism in West Africa. London: Cambridge University Press.

Iloka, G. N. (2016). Indigenous knowledge for disaster risk reduction: An African perspective. *Journal of Disaster Risk Studies*, 1–7. Accessed from http://www.Jamba.org.za.

Iseghe, A. (June 24, 2018). Food shortages in Nigeria. *Independent Newspaper*.

Ishola, Mofoluwake M.; Brandberg, Tomas; Sanni, Sikiru A. & Taherzadeh, Muhammad J. (2013). Biofuels in Nigeria: A critical and strategic evaluation. *Renewable Energy*, Vol. 55: 554–560.

Isola, O. I. (2013). The relevance of the African traditional medicine (alternative medicine) to health care delivery system in Nigeria. *The Journal of Developing Areas,* Vol. 47(1): 319–338.

Iyam, D. U. (1995). The Broken Hoe: Cultural Reconfiguration in Biase Southeast Nigeria. Chicago: University of Chicago Press.

Johns Hopkins University Coronavirus Resource Center. Global Report 2021. Retrieved on January 29, 2021, from https://coronavirus.jhu.edu/map.html.

Johnson, W. S., Jr.; (2010). Post-conflict food security and peace building. *Liberian Studies Journal*, Vol. 35(2): 28–54.

Joko, T.; Angorro, S.; Sunsko, H. R. & Rachmawati, S. (2017). Pesticide's usage in the soil quality degradation potential in Wanasari subdistrict Berbes Indonesia. *Applied and Environmental Soil Sciences*, Vol. 2017: 1–2. Retrieved from https://doi.org/10.1155/2017/5896191.

Kassa, M. D. & Grace, J. M. (2020). Race against the death of starvation? COVID-19 and its impact on African populations. *Health Reviews*, Vol. 41(30): 1–17.

Keese, P.; Omitogun, G.; and Sonaiya, B. (2002). Seeds of promise: Developing a sustainable agricultural biotechnology industry in sub-Saharan Africa. *Natural Resources*, Vol. 26(3): 234–244.

Kgathi, D. L.; Mfundisi, K. B.; Mmpolewa, G. & Mosepele, K. (2014). Potential impacts of biofuel development on food security in Botswana: A contribution to energy policy. *Energy Policy*, Vol. 43: 70–79.

Kolawole, O. D. (October 17, 2017). Rural communities and indigenous knowledge systems in a changing world: Soil fertility conservation practices amongst farmers. *The Anthropologist*, Vol. 6(4): 283–288.

Koren, Ore & Begozzi, Benjamin E. (2017). Living of the land: The connection between cropland, food security and violence against civilians. *Journal of Peace Research*, Vol. 45(3): 351–364.

Kumar, Pradeep; Kumar, Naresh & Singh, Namita. (2020). Spices and herbs: Potential antiviral preventives and immunity boosters during COVID-19. *Phytotherapy Research*, Issue 2021; (35): 2745–2757. Accessed from https://DOI:10.1002/ptr .7019.

Kumaraswamy, S. (2012). Sustainability issues in agroecology: Socio-ecological perspective. *Agricultural Sciences*, Vol. 3(2): 153–169.

Lartey, M. S. (2014). Harnessing indigenous knowledge for sustainable forest management in Ghana. *International Journal Food System Dynamics*, Vol. 5(4): 182–189.

Lecoutere, E.; Raeymaekers, T. & Vlassenroot, K. (2009). Conflict, institutional changes and food insecurity in eastern D.R. Congo. *Africa Focus*, Vol. 22(2): 41–63.

Lekorwe, M. & Sithole, A. (2019). Women's use of indigenous knowledge systems to cope with climate change. *Advances in Social Sciences Research Journal*, Vol. 6(6): 111–119. Retrieved on January 3, 2012, from DoI: 10.14738/ASSRJ.66.6470.

Lewis, Arthur. (1954). Economic development with unlimited supplies of labor. *Manchester School of Economics and Social Studies*, 139–191.

Liberia Ministry of Agriculture. (November 14, 2015). World Food Day. Theme: Social Protection and Agriculture: Breaking the Cycle of Rural Poverty. Retrieved March 17, 2019, from http://moa.gov.lr/doc/MOA%20_%20WFD%20SPECIAL %20EDITION.pdf.

Logan, Amanda. (2020). The Scarcity Slot: Excavating Histories of Food Security in Africa. California: University of California Press,.

Lovendall, T. (2007). Mechanization and Post-Harvest Study. (ed) Institutional Capacities and Renewal Strategies for Rural Development in Liberia. International Food Policy and Research institute (IFPRI) Consultancy White Paper.

Luxembourg, R. (1951). The Accumulation of Capital. New Haven: Yale University Press.

Mamdani, M. (2018). Citizen and Subject: Contemporary Africa and the Legacy of Late Colonialism. Princeton: Princeton University Press.

Marx, K. (1977). Capital. Vol 1. New York: Vintage Books.

Mbohwa, C. & Pradhan, A. (2014). Development of biofuels in South Africa: Challenges and opportunities. *Renewable and Sustainable Energy Reviews*, Vol. 39: 1089–1100.

McMichael, P. (2014). Historicizing food sovereignty. *Journal of Peasant Studies*, Vol. 41(6): 933–957. Retrieved December 6, 2020, from https://doi.org/10.1080 /03066150.2013.876999.

McMichael, P. (1992). Tensions between national and international control of the world food order: Contours of a new food regime. *Sociological Perspectives*, Vol. 35(2): 343–365.

McMichael, P. (2009). A food regime analysis of the world food crisis. *Agriculture and Human Values*, Vol. 26: 290. DOI 10.1007/S10460-009-9218-5.

McMichael, P. (2010). Agrofuels in the food regime. *The Journal of Peasant Studies*, Vol. 37(4): 609–629.

McMichael, P. (2005). Global development and the corporate food regime. *Rural Sociology and Development,* Vol. 11: 269–303.

Milburn, Richard. (2014). The roots to peace in the Democratic Republic of Congo: Conservation as a platform for green development. *Royal Institute of International Affairs*, Vol. 90(4): 871–887.

Miles, R. (1987). Capitalism and Unfree Labor: Anomaly or Necessity? London: Tavistock Publisher.

Minnis, Paul. (2000). Ethnobotany: A Reader. Norman: University of Oklahoma Press.

Mitchell, D. (2008). A note on rising food prices. Policy Research Working Paper 4682. The World Bank, Washington, DC.

Morgan, C. B. & Trubek, A. B. (2020). Not yet the table: The absence of food and tradition in agroecology literature. *Elementa Science of the Anthropocene,* 4. Retrieved December 21, 2020 fromhttps://www.semanticscholar.org/paper/Not-yet -at-the-table%3A-The-absence-of-food-culture-Morgan-Trubek/53707cf251ce53e 8abc8be69a9342ddbbd34b0a8?p2df.

Moss, T. J. (2011). African Development: Making Sense of the Issues and Actors. Boulder: Lynne Rienner Publisher.

Mouzeli, Nicolas. (1980). Modernization, underdevelopment, uneven development: Prospects for theory of Third World formations. *Journal of Peasant Studies*, Vol. 1: 13–15.

Mukhtar, A. A. & Ogunlela, Y. I. (2009). Gender issues in agriculture and rural development in Nigeria: The role of women. *Humanity and Social Sciences Journal*, Vol. 4(1): 19–30.

Mulugetta, Y. (2009). Evaluating the economics of biodiesel in Africa. *Renewable and Sustainable Energy Reviews*, Vol. 13: 1592–1598.

Netshiukhwi-Zuma, G.; Stiger, K. & Walker, S. (2013). Use of traditional weather/ climate knowledge by farmers in the South-Western State of South Africa: Agrometeorological learning by scientists. *Atmosphere*, Vol. 4: 383–410. Accessed from www.mdpi.com/journal/atmosphere, doi:10.3390/atmos4040383.

Newell, P. (2012). Globalization and the Environment: Capitalism, Ecology and Power. Cambridge: Polly Press.

Nils, G. (2007). Mandarins of the Future: Modernization Theory in Cold War America. Baltimore: Johns Hopkins University.

Nkansa B. S. (2004). Traditional methods of resource assessment relative to scientific approach. In Gyasi, E. A.; Berisavljevic, G. K; Blay, E. T. & Oduro, W. Managing Agrodiversity the Traditional Way: Lessons from West Africa in Sustainable Use of Biodiversity and Related Natural Resources. New York: United Nations University Press.

Nsiah, S. A. & Dawson, O.S. (2012). Promoting cassava as an industrial crop in Ghana: Effects on soil fertility and farming system sustainability. *Applied and Environmental Soil Science*: 1–8. DOI:10.1155/2012/9409954.

Nwosu, M. A. (2002). Ethnobotanical studies on some Pteridophytes of Southern Nigeria. *Economic Botany,* Vol. 56(3): 255–259.

Obadofin, O. H. (May 28, 2020). Impact of COVID-19 on nutrition and food shortages in Nigeria. Retrieved September 19, 2021, from *The Guardian,* 1–6 https://pulitzercenter.org/stories/impact-covid-19-nutrition-and-food-shortages-nigeria.

Odum, F. (August 6, 2001). Between ignorant farmers and fertilizer quality. *The Guardian*, 21.

OECD-FAO, Agricultural Outlook, 2016–2025, 60. Accessed on January 16, 2021, from https://www.oecd-ilibrary.org/sites/agr_outlook-2016-en/index.html?itemId=/content/publication/agr_outlook-2016-en#wrapper.

O'Flaherty, M. (1998). Communal tenure in Zimbabwe: Divergent models of collective land holding in the communal areas. *Journal of the International African Institute*, Vol. 68(4): 537–557.

Olatokun, W. & Ayanbode, O. F. (2009). Use of indigenous knowledge by women in a Nigerian rural community. *Indian Journal Traditional Knowledge*, Vol. 8(2): 287–295.

Olomola, A. S. (2017). Effective resource management for improved food and nutrition security in Nigeria. *Africa in Focus.* Accessed on February 5, 2021, from https://www.brookings/topiccorona-virus19/?.

Olusegun A. (January 2019). Nigeria's inflation rises to 11.98%, highest rate since June 2018. *Independent Newspaper.* Retrieved June 19, 2020, from independent.ng/nigeria's-risesto11.98-highest.rate-since-june-2018/.

Oppong, R. J. (2020). The African COVID-19 anomaly. *African Geographical Review,* Vol. 39(3): 282–288.

Oritsejafor, E. (2004). Food security in Africa: The case of biotechnology and environmental conservation in Nigeria. *Journal of African Policy Studies,* Vol. 10(2): 1–22.

Oritsejafor, E. (2016). The deregulation of the Nigerian power sector: A case study of the Nigerian Electric Power Authority. *Journal of Safety and Crisis Management*, Vol. 3(2): 12–25.

Oritsejafor, E. (2018). The nexus of food security and biofuels in sub-Saharan Africa. In Kieh, G. K., Jr. (2018). The Elusive African Renaissance: Essays on Today's Critical Development Issues. Jefferson, North Carolina: McFarland.

Oritsejafor, E. & Cooper, A. D. (2021). Africa and the Global System of Capital Accumulation. Abingdon, UK: Routledge.

Oritsejafor, E. & Jones, E. (2004). Folk and modern medicine in Africa: A case study of mental health care in Liberia. *Liberian Studies Journal*, Vol. 29(2): 1–15.

Osadolor, O. B. & Otodie, E. L. (2008). The Benin kingdom in British imperial historography. *History in Africa,* Vol. 35: 401–418.

Oyedijo, O. (2020). Use Herbs to Combat COVID-19 Infection. Accessed on January 27, 2021, from https;//oyedijooluwasegun.wordpress.com/2020/04/15/use-herbs-tocombat-covid-19-infection/.

Oyetayo, V. O. (2011). Medicinal uses of mushrooms in Nigeria: Towards full and sustainable exploitation. *African Journal of Traditional Complement Alternative Medicine*, Vol. 8(3): 267–274.

Patnaik, U. & Moyo, S. (2011), The Agrarian Question in the Neoliberal Era: Primitive Accumulation and the Peasantry. Cape Town: Pambazuka Press.

Perelman, M. (2000). The Invention of Capitalism: Classical Political Economy and Secret History of Capital Accumulation. Durham: Duke University Press.

Pfizer. What Is wellness? Retrieved August 21, 2021, from https://www.pfizer.com/health-wellness/wellness/what-is-wellness.

Pielke, R. & Linnér, B.-O. (2019). From green revolution to green evolution: A critique of the political myth of averted famine. *Minerva*, Vol. 57: 265–291.

Pierre, J. (August 1, 2020). COVID-19 death surge: Can traditional medicine and herbs help? In Opinion. 1–12. Retrieved January 27, 2021, from https://coronavirus.com.gh/covid-19-deatrh-surge-can-traditional-medicine-and-herbs-help/.

Pietkrewicz, I. & Smith, J. A. (2012). A practical guide to using interpretative phenomenological analysis in qualitative research. *Psychological Journal,* Vol. 182(2): 361–369.

Polshivok, P. (1981). Capital Accumulation and Economic Growth in Developing Africa. Moscow: Progress Publishers.

Popp, J., Lakner, Z.; Rakos, M. H. & Fari, M. (2014). The effect of bioenergy expansion: Food, energy, and the environment. *Renewable and Sustainable Energy Reviews*, Vol. 32: 559–578.

Puwanto, B. (February 2002). Peasant economy and institutional changes in late colonial Indonesia. International Conference on Economic Growth and Institutional Chang in Indonesia in the 19th and 20th Centuries. Amsterdam 25–28, 1–23.

Quan, H. L. T. (2012). Growth Against Democracy: Savage Developmentalist in the Modern World. Lanham, MD: Lexington Books.

Qudus, M. A. (2000). Use of Indigenous Knowledge in the Sustainable Development of Bangladesh Farm Forestry. In Sillitoe, Paul (ed). Indigenous Knowledge Development in Bangladesh: Present and Future. London: Intermediate Technology Publications, 57–64.

Raji, B. A.; Malgwi, W. B.; Berding, F. R. & Chude, V. O. (March 2011). Integrating indigenous knowledge and soil science approaches to detailed soil survey in Kaduna State Nigeria. *Journal of Soil Science and Environment Management,* Vol. 2(3): 66–73.

Rani, G. (September 2003). Is dualism worth revisiting? Yale University Economic Growth Center. Center, Paper No. 870, 1–19/ Retrieved August 20, 2021, https://egc.yale.edu/.

Ravindranath, N. H.; Lakshmi, C. S.; Manuvie, R. & Balachandra, P. (2011). Biofuel production and implications for land use, food production, and environment in India. *Energy Policy,* Vol. 39: 5737–5745.

Redvers, Nicole & Blondin, Be'sha. (2020). Traditional Indigenous medicine in North America: A scoping review. *PLOS ONE*, 2–3. Retrieved from https://doi.org/10 .1371/journal.pone.0237531.

Renewable Fuel Association, Ethanol Industry Statistics. Retrieved June 15, 2009, from http://www.ethanolrefa.org/industry/statistics.

Ricardo, D. (2004). The Principles of Political Economy and Taxation. London: Dover Press.

Rickard, S. & Gorelick, S. (2001). Can small farms feed the world? *Ecologist*, Vol. 3(1): 20–25.

Risk Communication and Community Engagement Preparedness and Readiness Framework: Ebola Response in the Democratic Republic of Congo in North Kivu https://apps.who.int/iris/bitstream/handle/10665/275389/9789241514828-eng.pdf ?ua=1.

Rodney, W. (1974). How Europe Underdeveloped Africa. Washington, DC: Howard University Press.

Roediger, D. (2017). Class, Race, and Marxism. London: Verso Press.

Samir, A. (1976). Unequal Development: An Essay on the Social Formations of Peripheral Capitalism. New York: Monthly Press Review Press.

Sangari, R.; Singh, J.; Madhoo, N.; Michel, P. & Wakeford, T. (2016). Resisting bio-fuels: The coloniality of power and indigenous knowledge systems decolonizing the land. *Dark Matter.* Retrieved August 27, 2021, from http://www.darkmatter101 .org/site/2016/04/02/resisting-biofuels-the-%e2%80%98coloniality-of-power%e2 %80%99-and-indigenous-knowledge-systems-%e2%80%98decolonising%e2%80 %99-the-land/.

Sanyal, K. (2013). Rethinking Capitalism, Development, Primitive Accumulation, Governmentality, and Post-colonial Capitalism. New Delhi: Routledge.

Schmitz, P. M. & Kavallari, A. (2009). Crop plants versus energy plants: On the inter-national food crisis. *Bio-organic and Medicinal Chemistry*, Vol. 17: 4020–4021.

Senanayake, S. G. J. N. (2006). Indigenous knowledge as a key to sustainable devel-opment. *Journal of Agricultural Sciences*, Vol. 2(1): 87–94.

Sheeran, J. (2008). High global food: The challenges and opportunities. International Food Policy Research Institute (IFPRI), Annual Report Essays.

Sieff, K. (September 14, 2015). Zimbabwe seized white farmers' land: Now some are being invited back. *Washington Post*. Retrieved on December 10, 2020 from https://www.washingtonpost.com/world/africa/zimbabwe-seized-white-farmers -land-now-some-are-being-invited-back/2015/09/14/456f66d6-45d2-11e5-9f53 -d1e3ddfd0cda_story.html.

Singh, R. & Singh, G. S. (2017). Traditional agriculture: a climate smart approach for sustainable food production. *Energy, Ecology and Environment*, Vol. 2(5): 296–316.

Smith, A. (1976). An Inquiry into the Nature and Causes of the Wealth of Nations. Campbell, R. H. & Skinner, A.S. (ed.). Vol. 2. New York: Oxford Press.

Stanziani, A. (2014). Bondage: Labor and Rights in Eurasia from the Sixteenth to the Early Twentieth Centuries. Oxford: Clarendon Publisher.

Steuart, J. (2019). An Inquiry into the Principles of Political Economy: Being an Essay on the Science of Domestic Policy in Free Nations, in which Are Particularly Considered Population, Agriculture, Trade Industry, Money. FL: Hard Press.

Sustainable Development Solutions Network (2013). Transformative Changes of Agriculture and Food Systems. 3–4. Retrieved from https://sustainabledevelopment .un.org/content/documents/6484106-Transformative%20changes%20of %20agriculture%20and%20food%20systems.pdf.

Tamba, G. T. (2018). New farm technologies will make Liberia food-secure. *Liberian Observer.* Retrieved March 17, 2019, from https://www.liberianobserver.com/news /new-farming-technologies-will-make-liberia-food-secure/.

Termote, C.; Van Damme, P. & Djailo, Benoit D. (2011). Eating from the wild: Turumbu, Mbole, and Bali traditional knowledge on no-cultivated edible plants, District Tshopo, DRC Congo. *Genetic Resource Crop Evol.*, Vol. 58: 585–618. https://DOI 10.1007/s10722-010–9602–4.

Thomas, N. W. (1910). The Edo-speaking people of Nigeria. *Journal of the Royal Africa Society*, Vol. 10(37): 1–15.

Thomasson, G. L. (1991). Liberia's seeds of knowledge. *Cultural Survival Quarterly Magazine.* Retrieved March 15, 2019, from https://www.liberianobserver.com/ news/new-farming-technologies-will-make-liberia-food-secure/.

Tripp, R. (2000). GMOs and NGOs: The policy process, and the presentation of evidence. *Natural Resource Perspective*, no. 60: 1–6. www.odi.org.uk.nrp.

Tshuma, L. (1998). Colonial and post-colonial reconstructions of customary land tenure in Zimbabwe. *Social and Legal Studies*, Vol. 7(1): 77–95.

Udoekanem, N. B.; Adoga, D. O. & Onwumere, V. O. (2014). Land ownership in Nigeria: Historical development, current issues and future expectations. *Journal of Environment and Earth Science,* Vol. 4(21): 182–188.

United Nations Department of Economic and Social Affairs. Challenges and Opportunities for Indigenous Peoples Sustainability. Retrieved September 4, 2021, from https://www.un.org/development/desa/dspd/2021/04/indigenous-peoples -sustainability/.

United Nations Development. (July 2001). Making New Technologies Work for Human Development, 1–278.

United Nations Policy Brief. (June 2020). The impact of COVID-19 on food security and nutrition.

United Nations Sustainable Development Goals 2030. Retrieved on December 21, 2020, from https://sdgs.un.org/goals.

Van der Merwe, J. D.; Cloete, P. C. & Van der Hoeven, M. (2016). Promoting food security through indigenous and traditional food crops. *Agroecology and Sustainable Food Systems,* Vol. 40(8): 830–847.

Wallerstein, I. (1974). The Modern World System. New York: Academic Press.

Watts, M. (1983). Silent Violence: Food, Famine and Peasantry in Northern Nigeria. California: University of California Press.

What Is Bushfire? Australian Government: Applying Geoscience to Australia's Important Challenges. Retrieved March 10, 2020, from https://www.ga.gov.au/scintific-topics/community-safety/bushfire.

Wiggins, S. Poor Diet. *BBC Focus*, 19, no. 10 (July–September 2008), 11.

Winger, H. W. (1976). The distribution of gains between investing and borrowing countries. In Agricultural Development: An International Perspective, Hayami and Ruttan (ed). Baltimore: Johns Hopkins University Press.

Wood, E. M. (2017). The Origins of Capitalism: A Longer View. London: Verso Publisher.

World Bank. (October 12, 2008). Rising Food and Fuel Prices: Addressing the Risks to Future Generations, 8. Accessed on December 28, 2020 from https://www.semanticscholar.org/paper/RISING-FOOD-AND-FUEL-PRICES-%3A-ADDRESSING-THE-RISKS-FOOD/507318c27d82382686fa303acb3e0e379f190a62.

World Bank. (October 12, 2008). Rising Food and Fuel Prices: Addressing the Risks to Future Generations. Retrieved March 17, 2019, from http://documents.worldbank.org/curated/en/701151468339092400/pdf/457890BR0Box3310ONLY10SecM200810423.pdfWorld Bank Group Report. (May 2015). Ending poverty and hunger by 2030: An agenda for the global system. http://documents1.worldbank.org/curated/en/700061468334490682/pdf/95768-REVISED-WP-PUBLIC-Box391467B-Ending-Poverty-and-Hunger-by-2030-FINAL.pdf.

World Bank IK Notes, No. 47. (August 2002). Using the Indigenous Knowledge of Jatropha: The use of Jatropha curcas oil as a raw material and fuel. Retrieved August 27, 2021, from https://openknowledge.worldbank.org/bitstream/handle/10986/10791/multi0page.pdf?sequence=1&isAllowed=y.

World Data Atlas Democratic Republic of Congo, Agriculture Production Quantity (Tons). Retrieved from: https://knoema.com/atlas/Democratic-Republic-of-the-Congo/topics/Agriculture/Crops-Production-Quantity-tonnes/Sugar-cane-production.

World Health Organization Food Security. Accessed June 18, 2008, from http://wwww.who.intl/trade/glossary.

Worzie, P. T. (2016). Reducing rice importation in Liberia. *NEPAD Transforming Africa- Policy Brief,* 1–2.

Zaman, H. (2000). Indigenous knowledge and sustainability: On the brink of disaster or revolution? In Sillitoe, P. (ed.) Indigenous Knowledge Development in Bangladesh: Present and Future. London: Intermediate Technology Press.

Z. S. Interview on Traditional Food Management Regimes. Interpreter. Mr. Thomas Tweh. Mama - Point Monrovia, Liberia. May 24, 2018. 5:30pm GMT-West Africa.

Index

About the Author

Emmanuel O. Oritsejafor is a professor of political science at North Carolina Central University. He has published extensively on thematic issues related to food security, indigenous knowledge (IK), economic development and the political economy of developing states with a focus on sub-Saharan Africa. He is the co-author of *Africa and the Global System of Capital Accumulation* and the co-author of the African Studies and Research Forum best book award-2021, entitled *Governance and Democracy in Africa: Regional and Continental Perspectives.*

African Studies | Sociology

"Finally, we have 'the' book that explains why more than sixty years of projects from the World Bank, the IMF, and USAID have failed to overcome global hunger and malnutrition. Emmanuel Oritsejafor doesn't just show where modern science has failed Africa, he offers a solution by showing how Indigenous Knowledge actually provides many scientific principles that can complement Western technologies that address food security and wellness. Oritsejafor also shows the shortcomings of corporate food management regimes and land tenure systems, as well as how integrating women more fully into the wellness sectors of African economies can help overcome food insecurities. His analysis of Indigenous Knowledge borrows from African sources as well as South Asian, Native American, and the Aboriginals of Australia."

—Allan D. Cooper, North Carolina Central University

"Food insecurity is one of Africa's major paradoxes. This is because the African continent is endowed with fertile land for agricultural production that could ensure food self-sufficiency for the constituent states. Oritsejafor has done a masterful job in deciphering the various external models of food production that are currently being used in Africa and concluded that they are not adequate frameworks. Alternatively, he proposes the use of indigenous African models of food production as the pathways to food security on the African continent. Thus, this is a major contribution to the debate on food security in Africa."

—George Klay Kieh, Texas Southern University

"Oritsejafor demonstrates how the international agrotechnology industry has weakened the food production capacity of sub-Saharan Africa, making the continent food insecure and dependent on food import. Drawing expertly on the various indigenous food production systems among farming communities, he illuminates how African Indigenous Knowledge can be useful in addressing the continent's food insecurity challenge."

—Samuel Wai Johnson, Delaware State University

"This book debunks the ethnocentric views of agricultural development and advocates for the utilization of sustainable Indigenous Knowledge as an alternative approach for food security in Africa. It is a must-read for all development scholars and policymakers with keen interest in finding sustainable solutions to global food insecurity."

—Andrew I. E. Ewoh, Texas Southern University

In this book, Emmanuel O. Oritsejafor argues that Indigenous Knowledge (IK) needs to play a central role in addressing food insecurity because IK methods result in sustainable agricultural practices which improve wellness.

Emmanuel O. Oritsejafor is professor of political science at North Carolina Central University.

LEXINGTON BOOKS
An imprint of
Rowman & Littlefield
800-462-6420 • www.rowman.com

Cover art by Tayo Fatunla

ISBN 978-1-7936-1510-7

90000

9 781793 615107

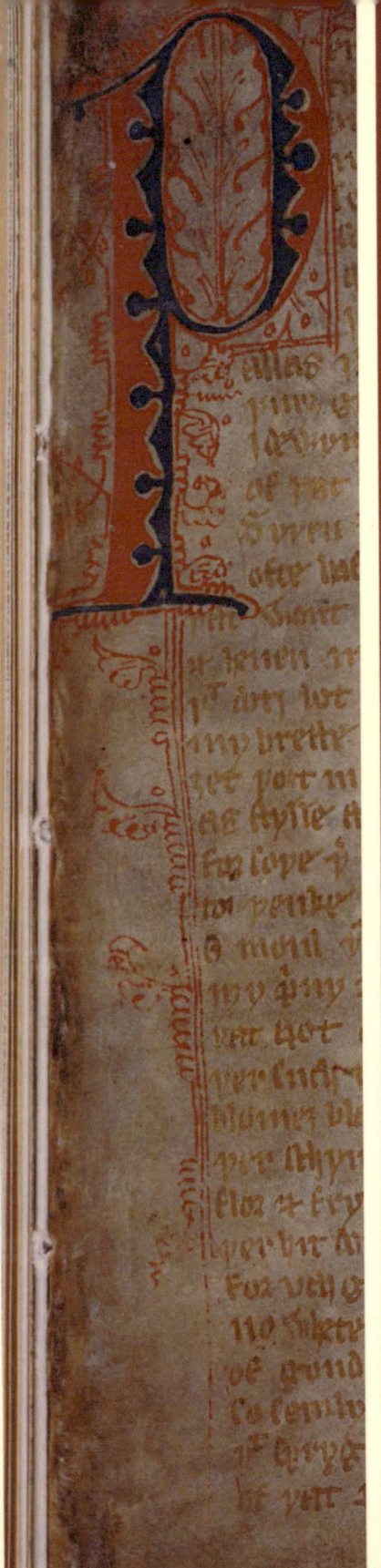

Becoming the *Pearl-Poet*

Perceptions, Connections, Receptions

Edited by
Jane Beal